Library in a Book

Library in a Book

compiled by

Jennifer Hall and Rachel Greenblatt

of the Telshestone English Library

TARGUM/FELDHEIM

First published 2004

All proceeds from this book will be donated to the Telshestone English Library.
ISBN 1-56871-336-3

Published by:
TARGUM PRESS, INC.
22700 W. Eleven Mile Rd.
Southfield, MI 48034
E-mail: targum@netvision.net.il
Fax: 888-298-9992
www.targum.com

Distributed by:
FELDHEIM PUBLISHERS
208 Airport Executive Park
Nanuet, NY 10954

Printing plates: "Frank," Jerusalem

Printed in Israel

לזכר ולעילוי נשמות

חיים יהודה בן דוב אריה ז״ל

ואשתו

עטא בת שלמה הלוי ע״ה

יהודה בן נח ז״ל

ואשתו

יענטלא בת יהודה ע״ה
ואת בתם לאה ע״ה

תנצב״ה

לזכרון עולם בהיכל ה׳

ונח מצא חן בעיני ה׳

אלה תולדת נח נח איש צדיק תמים היה בדרתיו

את האלקים התהלך נח.

לע״נ

הר״ר נח בן שמעון ז״ל

HaRav Noach miLissa Haltrecht, *zt"l*

Author of *Toldos Noach*, published in Warsaw, 1830

And his descendants from Przedecz, Plock, Warsaw, Zgierz, Lodz, France, Germany, Spain, Argentina, America, Canada, England, Israel.

"Keep the *derech*."

Acknowledgments

This book is dedicated to all of the writers who have given freely of their time and talent to create this inspiring collection.

We would also like to acknowledge the generous assistance of those who worked behind the scenes to bring this book to publication.

Our gratitude goes to our copyeditor, Ita Olesker, and to our publisher, Targum Press, and especially Rabbi Moshe Dombey and Miriam Zakon, who had the foresight to encourage this project when it was just a great idea.

Our deepest feelings of appreciation go to our spouses and family members, and, finally, to the "Great Supporter in the Sky" without Whom this book could not have been written.

The Readers and Organizers
of the Telshestone English Library

Contents

TRAVEL

THE JEWISH FAMILY

HISTORY AND BIOGRAPHY

RACHEL GREENBLATT

Preface

Kiryat Ye'arim Telshestone nestles in the Judean Hills fourteen kilometers from Jerusalem. The Kiryah is named after Telshe Yeshiva, which it housed for a short time, and after Irving Stone who financed it.

In order to raise money to finance the purchase of new books for the Telshestone English Library, it was decided to put together a book. This is the book that you are holding.

When the Jewish people stood on the shores of the Reed Sea, the murderous Egyptians at their backs, and Moshe beseeched Hashem for mercy, God answered, "Why are you crying out to Me? Tell the Children of Israel to go" (*Shemos* 14:15).

In his book *Trust Me*, Rabbi Eliezer Parkoff explains this incredible exhortation. At this moment prayer would not have worked. The prosecuting angels in *Shamayim* were claiming that the Children of Israel, as idol worshipers, were not worthy of being saved. The only path open to them was to strengthen Hashem's *rachamim* (mercy). They had to rely on their *emunah* and *bitachon* (faith and trust) and enter the sea before it split. If they could have faith in every fiber of their being, then in the merit of that unyielding faith Hashem would perform miracles for them that would match their willingness to jump into the unknown.

We jumped into the unknown.

One of our first telephone calls to the widely published and never before published authors from around the world was to Miriam Zakon. We explained that the Telshestone English Library was collecting articles as a fundraising project to raise money to buy books. With typical friendliness and encouragement she replied, "Targum may be interested in publishing the book."

Armed with this encouragement, fired by a greater ambition, and enthused beyond measure, we continued our task of approaching the vast talent in our worldwide community.

We were astounded by the response. From New York to Cleveland, from Har Nof to Rehovot, from London to Manchester, the articles flooded in. Beyond all our expectations, almost every single individual we approached not only acquiesced, but also responded with alacrity. Within seven short and frenetic weeks, we were contacting Targum once more.

Rabbi Zev Leff, in his book *Outlooks and Insights*, asks, "Who's carrying whom?" We are told that the "staves shall remain in the rings of the ark, they may not be removed from it" (*Shemos* 25:15). The ark did not need the staves because it would lift up those who were carrying it. This book, too, seemed to "lift us up," carrying us with an incredible *siyata d'Shmaya*.

Rabbi Leff tells the story of Rabbi Eliezer Gordon, *zt"l*, who, for the first years of his marriage, was supported by his father-in-law, Rabbi Avraham Yitzchak Neviezer. Thus he was able to devote himself to learning.

Rabbi Avraham Yitzchak refused, despite difficult financial times, to allow Rabbi Gordon to accept a rabbinic position. Rabbi Avraham Yitzchak's wife asked her husband for how long he intended to support their daughter and son-in-law. He replied, "My dear wife, who is supporting whom?" Finally Rabbi Avraham Yitzchak felt compelled to allow Rabbi Gordon to accept the position of the Rabbinate of Eisheshok.

The day after the Gordon family left for Eisheshok, Rabbi Avraham Yitzchak passed away. It then became clear who had been supporting whom.

As Rabbi Parkoff says in his book, "Prayer only relates to the world of nature. In the world above nature the concept of prayer is irrelevant. This is the meaning of Hashem's response to Moshe Rabbeinu. Hashem was revealing to Moshe the secret of the Jewish people. They exist in a realm above nature."

"Why are you crying out to Me? Tell the Children of Israel to go."

We did.

RABBI BORUCH SMITH
Rabbi Emeritus of Telshestone English Library

Introduction

To commit a thought to paper is to coalesce that which is abstract, to shape that which is pliable, and to give form to energy. The consequence of this action can never truly be evaluated, since once that thought is on paper it may affect the lives of many people. Sometimes, the influence will be readily perceived; sometimes it can take generations.

The story is told of a young cheder boy who in a moment of enthusiasm managed to squeeze a goat into the *aron hakodesh.* When the cheder was about to begin davening, a loud bleating was heard from the ark. One of the teachers investigated the cause of the strange noise. To the shock of the rebbes and the joy of the children, the goat was finally freed. The young culprit was apprehended and in due course was brought before the principal, obviously to be immediately expelled from the cheder. The principal, a fair man, asked the young offender if there was anything he wanted to say. The young man composed himself and declared, "If I am to be suspended from cheder, not only will this action be detrimental for my future but for the future of my descendants."

This short, eloquent speech pierced the heart of the principal, and the child was allowed to stay. And indeed, this move on the part of the principal proved to be to the benefit of the child's Torah-centered descendants, who are today a credit to the Jewish people.

Any action we take not only affects the present but also the future. One should never give up trying to positively influence others to come closer to Hashem. We cannot abandon any Jewish soul.

With this idea in mind I would like to raise another issue.

Over the years the religious world has placed great emphasis on glatt kosher. For some, Judaism has become synonymous with "*issur v'heter.*" However, Torah is not just a book of permitted and forbidden, but a set of instructions for the life of a Jew. Frequently, what exists in the Camp of Yaakov may not transgress the letter of the law but it can be the antithesis of a Torah home. These institutions may take the form of music, tours, trips, cruises, games, sport, or any arena of entertainment.

It is my belief that books are one of the most prevalent tools of Eisav in the Camp of Yaakov.

When Yaakov and Eisav sit in the same camp, reading the same books, magazines, and papers, then Eisav is free to prosecute. When we separate the camps, then Eisav will dwell in Har Seir and Yaakov will dwell safely in Sukkos.

Rav Shimshon Pincus, *zt"l*, writes that "Yom Kippur clarifies to whom each camp belongs — to Hashem or, *chas v'shalom*, to Azazel. There are two goats and each — Yaakov and Eisav — do with their goat that which interests them. Our goat is sacrificed to Hashem. Eisav receives his portion and is allowed to enjoy the violence of the goat being torn limb by limb as it falls down the cliff of Azazel.

The Camp of Yaakov has its own books, magazines, and papers filled with Torah. We owe it to the future of ourselves and our children and our grandchildren to the end of time, to keep separate the Camp of Yaakov. No Jewish soul is *hefker*.

It is our *zechus* to provide this compilation of inspiring Torah literature. These articles should serve as a stimulus for continued Torah reading, of these and other Jewish authors, and as a preview or reminder of the great writing talent that the Torah world has to offer.

Philosophy and Judaica

RABBI BEREL WEIN

"What's Your Family Business?"

Someone asked me on the plane, coming over to Israel, "What do you do?" I said, "I'm in my family business." "What's your family business?" I replied, "My family business is the same as your family business." He said, "You mean you are in textiles, too?" I said, "No, I'm not in textiles." He said, "What do you mean, that your family business is the same as my family business?"

I said, "The family business of the Jewish people is Torah." That's our family business. How we make a living, what titles we have, what professions we have, how Hashem chooses to give us *parnasah*, those things all differ. Some people are lawyers, some are doctors, some are accountants, some are in the textile business, but one should never think for a moment that that is the family business. You should never think, that is what you are.

What you are is something else completely. We are *b'nei* Avraham, Yitzchak, and Yaakov. A Chosen People at the end of a long and painful story. We are special and the only people in the world in that business, the business of justice, morality and honesty, greatness and eternity. There is no one else in our business.

We have to appreciate that we are the next generation, so to speak, in the family business. As such, we can have an interesting and informative viewpoint of ourselves. All psychiatrists and psychologists tell us that most of the problems in life stem from what we call self-image. How do I see myself? Self-image is made up of many different pieces, one of which is what my parents say to me or think of me. "Here comes Berel the dummy" — if they do that for fifteen years, by the time he is sixteen Berel will believe he is a dummy, even though he may have an IQ of 180. Berel may be the world's greatest but if he hears long enough that he is a dummy, he is a dummy.

My friends have a great deal to do with my self-image. We all know that peer pressure and what friends think is very important. The tragedy of life is that when we are thirty-five we rarely remember who our best friend was when we were fifteen, let alone what his influence was on us. The truth of the matter is, who our friends are when we are fifteen has a lot to do with how we are going to look at ourselves when we are thirty-five. My own opinion of myself is very important: What do I think about myself? Who am I? What am I doing here? What am I going to do with myself?

I tell my grandchildren, Zeidy doesn't know what he is going to do when he grows up. I have done a lot of things in my lifetime. Maybe I still have things to do. The self-image that a person has needs to be developed and nurtured and worked on, over and over again, day in and day out. It's the same struggle. If a person has a positive self-image in Torah, then he is a *ben Torah*. You can't be a person of importance if you don't feel that you are important. You can't be a positive person if you don't feel good about yourself.

The Torah came to make us feel good about ourselves, to give us status, to tell us the Hashem who created each and every one of us, cares about each and every one of us. He looks us up on the computer each and every day. Did Berel learn today? What did he do today? Was he here for davening? Lest you think I am making it up, Chazal tell us that, regarding a person who comes to the minyan regularly and is amongst the first ten, if he is sick and doesn't come, Hashem asks, "Where was he today?"

That means we are important. There are guys about whom no one ever asks, "Where were they?" No one knows if they were there, no one knows if they were not there. That's the worst of all worlds, if no one cares if you were not there. The Torah comes to tell us that everyone counts. That's the *chiddush* of Judaism that the goyim don't begin to understand. For the goyim there is no such thing as everyone counts. The guy working in the subway, the homeless beggar that is lying on the freezing streets of the wealthiest city in the world; he doesn't count. The Torah comes to say everyone counts. Hashem is interested in everyone. He is especially interested in the Chosen People. So He wants to know where you are, what you are doing, what is your relationship with Him.

If you forget, once in a while, that He is interested in you, then things happen in life that remind you. There are people that have to get hit over the head with a brick before they realize "Maybe Hashem is telling me something."

I am a grandfather, so I am closer to the end than to the beginning;, so I look back on a lot of things and I see everything differently now from my present perspective.

There is a famous story told by Mark Twain. Once, he got on a wagon that was being driven by a Missouri mule driver — the Egged bus driver of his day. Before they started out, the Missouri mule driver got out of his wagon, picked up a two-by-four, and hit the mule over the head with it. Then he sat in his seat, said giddyap, and started to go. So Mark Twain said to him, "You will excuse me, but what did you do that for?" The mule driver said, "First I gained his attention."

Hashem works that way, too. First he has to gain our attention. If we don't go knocking on His door, He comes knocking on our door. Most of life is about gaining our attention. A person who understands how to look at the world, he sees it. He sees everything through the prism of Hashem's eyes. A person who doesn't see, so a lot of two-by-fours have to hit him on the head before he realizes that someone is talking to him.

Hashem is talking to us, each and every one of us. Just as He talks to *klal Yisrael*, just as He talks to the whole world, but you have to be tuned in.

While in Israel I went to Yad Vashem. You want to know what it is to be a Jew, but you won't know what the world is if you don't go there. There is a memorial to the million and a half Jewish children that were killed by the paragons of Western civilization. I wept as I have not wept in years.

The memorial to the children is a room of utter darkness, with one candle. By a series of mirrors the candle becomes a million pinpoints of light. There is a voice that just reads names. I waited to hear my name. I was five years old when the war started. I could also have been one of the names. No one called my name because Hashem did me a *chesed*. My father moved from Lithuania in the early 1930s. I thought to myself, as I went out of that place of pain, Hashem left me alive, He gave me the gift of life. It is the ultimate gift.

As long as I am alive I am going to do something. I am going to build a family business. I am going to do what I can. That's how every Jew has to feel.

MALKA SHAIN

Choose Simchah!

I almost didn't go to the *shiur*. It had been a long day with the kids and I was drooping like the geraniums I'd forgotten to water outside my kitchen window. My body felt heavy, like a beast of burden with a shrunken spirit.

Rebbetzin Traub's voice was gentle, her accent exotic, and she spoke with warmth that promised me unconditional acceptance. At the end of the *shiur*, I found myself telling her my life story in two minutes.

"And so I don't know how to serve Hashem *b'simchah* — with joy," I said. "There's an inner emptiness I can't seem to overcome." The Rebbetzin didn't answer.

"I don't know why I can't break through this emptied-out feeling," I continued, "but I do accept it. I know it's some kind of test."

* To protect the privacy of those involved in this true story, all the names have been changed, except for Yaakov ben Yaakov, the hidden *tzaddik*, and Simchah, whose name is germane to the story.

The Rebbetzin made a big deal out of this. "You accept it totally?" Her tone was incredulous. "The first thing you should know is you're a *tzeddekes*!"

Very funny, I thought. "You haven't seen me when I scream at my kids, Rebbetzin."

She brushed this away with a wave of her hand. "That makes no difference," she said. "The point is you accept the tests. Most of the time, we rebel against difficulties and question Hashem. You're experiencing a *tikkun,* a form of spiritual reparation, and you should daven that it ends soon!" She curled her fingers into a fist. "You have – to ask – Hashem – for the *simchah*!" she said, almost punching out the words. "He took your tools for *simchah* away. Only He can return them to you!"

I stood outside in the cool Jerusalem air, mulling over the Rebbetzin's words and amazed that I'd had the *siyata d'Shmaya,* Heavenly assistance, to go to that *shiur.* Hashem knew what I needed to hear. I had always felt as if "*simchah*" was somehow a place I had failed to reach. I never thought it was something to daven for!

"Great *shiur,* huh?" said my friend Shuli, who was standing nearby.

She caught me in mid-thought. "Amazing lady," I said, and I told her a little of my conversation with the Rebbetzin.

For a moment, the two of us just stood there, inhaling the heady perfume of newly blossoming jasmine.

"Do you want to do something interesting?" Shuli asked. Her question seemed so out of context, as if she had plucked it, barely ripe, from the jasmine tree.

"I have a friend named Elisheva," Shuli said, without waiting for my reply. "She told me about a *tzaddik nistar* – a hidden *tzaddik* – Rav Yaakov ben Yaakov. Apparently, before he died, he promised that anyone who would make a *seudas mitzvah* for the elevation of his *neshamah* could daven at his grave, and he would do what he could to intervene on that person's behalf in *Shamayim.*"

"That's quite a story," I said. Although I was fascinated, I felt the familiar tension in my body when faced with doing something I wasn't sure of.

"Elisheva can go with us on Thursday, if you're interested," Shuli said. "It's a real opportunity for you to daven for *simchah*!"

In my nervousness, I hadn't picked up on the *hashgachah pratis,* Divine intervention, that seemed to unroll like a red carpet upon which to lay my prayers for that elusive feeling of inner joy. Shuli was right — the opportunity sounded perfect. So I resisted the temptation to stay home and do something safe, like cooking spaghetti for lunch or clicking away at my computer.

Two days later, I sat in the back seat of her car, leaning forward like a little girl straining to hear the conversation of the adults in the front.

"So you want to know about the *tzaddik*?" Elisheva said in her rich, Sephardic accent. "One time my daughter was having trouble finding a *shidduch.*" She gave me a sidelong glance. "Things got desperate and I just had to see him, you know? My daughter found a *shidduch* within a few weeks." Elisheva's hands gesticulated as the memories seemed to bounce through her body. "Another time, I had an apartment I just couldn't sell." She gave me another glance with a twist of her neck. "Our financial situation was getting impossible — you know how it is? I went to see the *tzaddik.*" Elisheva spoke about Rav Yaakov as if he was alive and well, sitting in front of an open *gemara.* "The apartment was sold within the week," she said.

Elisheva's tales were like deft brush strokes on the Jerusalem–Tel Aviv highway, casting a mystical hue over the evergreen forests and golden fields.

As we turned into the cemetery from Rechov Chazon Ish and stopped the car, it seemed as if we were alone amidst rows and rows of graves hewn from Jerusalem stone. Then an elderly caretaker appeared in a worn suit with a fraying hat.

"It's good to give him something," said Elisheva, urging me toward his dark frame.

"*HaKadosh baruch Hu* should give you *nachat*," he said as I placed some shekels in his palm. I wondered, as I do on these occasions, who was giving to whom?

Elisheva led the way to the gravesite of the hidden *tzaddik*. The name Yaakov ben Yaakov was inscribed on the stone. So he's real, I thought, realizing that until that point, in my mind he'd been more like an exotic character out of a novel.

"Here he is," Elisheva said in a matter-of-fact tone. "I'm going to see the others." I wondered who "the others" might be. She was clearly used to this — I was not. Shuli said some *tehillim* and disappeared, presumably also to "see the others," and I was alone with Yaakov ben Yaakov.

I stood there, uncertain how to ask for the "one thing" I came for. Davening, I thought, was something between Hashem and me, without go-betweens, so to speak. Here, I felt awkward, like a little girl again, about to ask the school principal for a candy and unsure what his reaction might be.

Suddenly I remembered my personal verse from *Tehillim*, the one based on the first and last letters of your name that you insert toward the end of the *Shemoneh Esrei*: "*Sameach nefesh avdecha, ki eilecha Hashem nafshi esa*" — "Gladden the soul of Your servant," my verse implores, "for to You, my Lord, I lift up my soul" (86:4).

How out of touch can you get! I thought. When Rebbetzin Traub suggested I daven for *simchah*, it never occurred to me that I'd been asking for just that every *Shacharis* and *Minchah* as I faced my bedroom wall!

It was exactly the point of connection I needed now. I bent down and touched the grave. The off-white stone felt smooth and powdery as I closed my eyes, felt the connection of my hand to my arm, my shoulder to my heart. "Rebbe," I began, bonding with my voice. Tears broke through my body like the first rains after a long drought, as words rolled from my chest, down my arm, and into my hand resting on the stone. I poured my one longing into the universe through the pipeline of prayer, where it shimmered, smooth and wet like a glistening raindrop in the deep pool of the heart.

After a while, I stood up. It felt like Yom Kippur.

I squinted into the distance for my companions, and far away I saw a group of people looking like ants. Probably, I thought, Shuli and Elisheva were there. I reached the crowd and gasped. "The others" were the Chazon Ish and the Steipler Gaon — two great *gedolim* from the previous generation!

All the calm of the previous few minutes flew out of me and into the cloudless sky. I was engulfed by a raging need to pour out my shopping list of unspoken prayers that I had suppressed at the grave of Yaakov ben Yaakov. Please Hashem, I began, the children should be successful in our *aliyah*, my husband should have more time to learn, the girls should cleave to You in *tznius* and *yiras Shamayim*, the boys should become *b'nei Torah*, You should sustain us in comfort, I should be blessed with another child who will love your Torah and mitzvos...on and on until I felt I had exhausted every longing in my soul.

By the time the three of us returned to the car, we shared a sense of satisfaction that comes from body and soul in harmony. For a while, nobody spoke.

As we drove toward the Judean Hills, Elisheva said, "If you still have time, I can take you to a very special place where you can donate the money for the *seudah*." She reminded us about the second part of the deal with Rav Yaakov.

I felt my body stiffen.

"You know Rav Unsdorf in Yerushalayim?" Elisheva asked.

Shuli and I shook our heads.

"He's a very special Rav. You should see the haven he's created in his house for the poor. Maybe you'll even get a chance to speak to him — he's a very big *tzaddik*."

My immediate impulse was to get back home. Bnei Brak had been very powerful, and now I needed to digest the experience with my feet up on the coffee table and a steaming cup of Taster's Choice in my hand. I'd had enough for one day — unaccustomed, as I was, to speaking to so many *tzaddikim* in one shot, in this world or otherwise.

On the other hand, something inside me whispered, "C'mon, let's go!" I checked my watch. It was ten thirty.

"Whatever happens, it won't take long," Elisheva said. She probably sensed my ambivalence. "Ovadia, the *shammash*, might let you both in, even though people can wait months to see the Rav. But *panim chadashot* — new faces — Ovadia normally takes."

I still didn't say anything. I needed to be back by one o'clock to fetch the kids from *gan*.

"If Ovadia lets you in," Elisheva continued, "you'll be out very soon. If he doesn't, we'll just give him the money and leave." I glanced at Shuli. She nodded.

My scared voice kicked in again. Surely we could give the

money to Elisheva who was on her way to Rav Unsdorf anyway, and be done with it? I could feel the force of my resistance rising like a mountain inside me. I hated leaving the civilization of my comfort zone and entering the wilderness of the unknown. You never knew who you might become in that wild place.

Yet, something reminded me that in a mere two days, Hashem had sent two *shelichim* – the Rebbetzin from this world and Rav Yaakov from the other – prodding me to ask what I needed of Him. Perhaps He wanted me to continue this journey to Rav Unsdorf and not just comfortably let someone donate money on my behalf. Maybe Rav Unsdorf was meant to be the third *shaliach*? What for? I thought.

"Well, okay," I said, making my voice sound nonchalant.

I don't know why I felt so shaky. Perhaps I sensed that something remarkable was about to happen. I felt as though I was about to plunge into the dark, swirling waters of undiscovered country. My heart and lungs churned, making it difficult to breathe.

Rav Unsdorf's apartment looked more like a factory than a home. It consisted of two units, one that seemed to be for cooking, and the other for eating. Mixing machines whirred from inside the "kitchen-apartment," whereas the "eating-apartment" looked as if it consisted of simple dining rooms dotted with wooden tables and chairs. Peeking through a window, I saw men in shabby clothes sitting around the tables and shoveling food into their mouths as if they hadn't eaten in days. On the opposite side of the room, someone hung through the burglar bars of a decrepit window, both hands outstretched, pleading for a morsel.

Outside, things were no less desperate. Women from all walks of life sat crowded on rickety wooden benches and hunched together in the narrow stairwells and passages. Sephardic, Ashkenazic, religious, even secular women with short skirts and painted eyelids, united in their pain and longing, sat waiting for the Rav.

"I've been coming here every day for three months now," said a young, pregnant lady standing next to me. "I still haven't been in to see him."

Suddenly, a young girl from the kitchen-apartment pressed freshly made pita with delicious-smelling omelet and tomato into our hands. "Please," she said, "wash and eat."

I was deeply moved by so much neediness and *chesed* intertwined in this small corner of Yerushalayim. Those pitot were filled as much with *ahavat Yisrael* — love of fellow Jews — as they were with food, and it was hard to say if I felt more nurtured by the food or by the care.

No sooner had we finished bentching than a burly Ovadia exploded through the door of the eating-apartment. Like a laser beam, he scanned the pool of pleading eyes that were turned toward him with desperate expectation.

Elisheva pushed forward, waving her hand with all of our money. "*Panim chadashot! Panim chadashot!*" she yelled, her free arm jerking back and pointing to where Shuli and I stood. We were embarrassed at being singled out as if we had won the lottery, and overwhelmed by the suffocating net of pushing toward the dark-skinned *shammash*.

Elisheva's prediction was right! Ovadia pointed a thick finger at us, and we crept forward self-consciously, not daring to make eye contact with those less privileged who had to remain outside.

As we stepped into the eating-apartment, we were pushed up against the wall of a small, crowded hallway, trying in vain to maintain some semblance of personal space around us. I had serious misgivings then about the sanity of what we were doing. The air was heavy and hot and I felt claustrophobic, not to mention extremely nervous. Yet below the surface of my brain crouched a foggy awareness that I had to do something here. I didn't know what.

Ovadia ushered us into what looked like a small waiting room furnished in an old-world style, with flowered wallpaper and a rickety, threadbare couch. Until then I hadn't believed we were actually going to meet the Rav. Somehow, it had been easier with Yaakov ben Yaakov. He hadn't stood opposite me, his eyes piercing through every botch-up of my limited personality!

But there was more than this. My brain buzzed with the question of what in the world I would ask when I met Rav Unsdorf face-to-face. I had poured my "one thing" request into Yaakov ben Yaakov, and I'd asked for everything else at the graves of the Chazon Ish and the Steipler. I felt I was making some sort of spiritual pig of myself!

On the other hand, this was clearly not an opportunity to be missed. We had traded in that exalted status of "*panim chadashot*" and might have to wait months, like everyone else, to stand in this privileged spot again. I felt perspiration down my back. We were the next ones in, and I had no idea what to say!

Then a strange thing happened. My brain began to revolve, slowly at first, and then with increasing speed like those crazy spin-a-rounds at the amusement park. As my head spun, a fiery energy seemed to swirl around with it, carrying the rest of me in its wake. The room began to throb, intense and alive. A new knowledge burned through me, almost branding me with the words "You Are Not Here For Your Own Benefit!"

"*Bo'u,* come inside!" Ovadia commanded with a flick of his wrist.

In what seemed to be a twirling haze of mist and light, I followed Shuli into the room.

The Rav looked shrunken, so frail it seemed he hardly had energy to hold himself up. He sat on a low couch, his shoulders stooped over hands that he clasped together. I barely heard what Shuli asked. The Rav gave his *berachah*. It was my turn.

Rav Unsdorf looked up at me. His eyes burned into my brain like a furnace of raging power. I felt almost thrown backwards by the force in those eyes. In that moment, I knew what I had to say. Hot tears tingled in my sinus cavities as if this pain that had suddenly entered my body was my own.

"I have a friend, Rabbi," I said. My voice didn't sound like mine. "She has three girls. She has struggled for many years to have more." I was inside this pain now, this longing. I could feel it bearing down on my shoulders, pulling at my chest. "I ask the Rav for a *berachah* that she be blessed with more children."

The Rav stared at me with his blazing eyes. "Her name?" His voice was soft.

"Yaffa bat Simchah." That word again, I thought, *simchah.*

"Yaffa bat Simchah!" Ovadia repeated, so that the Rav heard clearly.

The *tzaddik* closed his eyes. His fragile form seemed to quiver. His lips shook. He looked up at me again and in that moment my head stopped spinning as suddenly as it had begun. The pulsating whirl around me disappeared and the pain in my chest eased. It was over.

"What was that all about?" Shuli asked, incredulous, when we left the room.

"I have no idea where it came from, Shuli!" I said, as amazed as she was. "I had this incredible sense of compulsion — I knew what I had to say, that's all."

It was weird though, because I hadn't been thinking about my friend until the moment I spoke to the Rav.

"Can I tell her what happened?" Shuli asked when we reached Elisheva who was waiting outside.

"Go ahead."

Elisheva listened and then thrusted a pointed finger at my nose. "It will come to you first!" she said. "Whenever we daven for someone else, the *berachah* travels through us before it reaches the person we've prayed for!"

Well, I hadn't actually prayed for her – not in the usual sense. In fact, I didn't pay much attention to Elisheva's conviction that Rav Unsdorf's *berachah* would take hold in reality. My friend, Yaffa, had struggled for over ten years to have another baby. She had been to countless doctors and many rabbis for *berachos*. There was no reason to think that my humble visit to this Rav – as unusual as the circumstances had been – would be different.

How little I understood the significance of that choice I made in Shuli's car. Yaffa's baby was born nine months after I asked for the *berachah*!

I was stunned into silence when she phoned, long distance, to tell me she was expecting. Not because I didn't believe that it could happen. I was dumbstruck to think I'd been her *shaliach*, after so many years of countless prayers! I had no doubt that Rav Unsdorf's was the culmination of a series of *berachos* – all of which had been necessary in this process. To be the final messenger for her was a mind blast and completely overwhelming!

And what of Elisheva's prediction? The *berachah* did not pass through me first. My daughter was born two weeks after Yaffa bat Simchah's son!

So, what was I to make of all this? How were the puzzle

pieces connected – telling Rebbetzin Traub about my perennial feeling of emptiness, her directive to daven for *simchah,* the invitation to daven at the grave of Yaakov ben Yaakov, donating money for the *aliyah* of his *neshamah* to Rav Unsdorf, the almost out-of-body experience I had in his apartment, his *berachah* – and then the crowning glory of its fulfillment?

For a long time I wondered about this. Then one day, it's meaning shone like the rays of the setting sun on Jerusalem stones, transforming a humble abode into a golden palace. A suggestion to do "something interesting," as Shuli had it that fateful evening, was a Divine invitation to plunge into the deep space of miracle. I could have said no – I nearly did many times during the course of that saga. Hashem would have found another *shaliach.* My feeling, though, is that Yaakov ben Yaakov intervened quickly for me in the Heavenly realm, increasing my *siyata d'Shmaya* so that I would "choose life" in the back seat of Shuli's car.

By saying "yes," I emptied myself of the illusion and let in the flow of wisdom that *simchah* is not a faraway destination, but a way of interacting with the miraculous world. Looking anew at the emptiness I'd perceived as negative, I saw that in the emptying out of ego we fill up with Hashem. That realization was the *simchah* – my *simchah* – my key to living the way He wants me to live!

RABBI Y. Y. RUBINSTEIN

Gedolei Yisrael — Men of the World

After the death of Sarah, Avraham is faced, according to Rabbeinu Yona, with the tenth test: the acquiring of the cave of Machpelah. Even according to all other opinions, which state that the binding of Yitzchak was the last test, Avraham's encounter with Efron still provided a challenge.

There is a commonly held belief that religious people in general and spiritual giants in particular are other-worldly and remote from normal concerns. This encounter, which occurs after Avraham has achieved his spiritual zenith, disproves this myth.

There are two keys to unlocking what really occurred. The Ramban explains that the city of Kiryat Arba, the original name for Chevron, wherein lay the cave, had a law prohibiting foreigners from being buried within its territory. The second key is the Hebrew word "*es*." The rule is that the occurrence of this word in the Torah hints that something in addition to the subject being spoken of in the verse is also included. The classic example is the verse "*Es Hashem Elokecha tira'u*" – "You should fear the Lord your God." The inclusion of the word "*es*" means that somebody else is to be included. The Talmud tells of a Rabbi who explained the significance of every "*es*" until he arrived at this verse. Who could a Jew possibly fear like God? With this question he abandoned his project. Along came Rabbi Akiva and completed it, explaining that it refers to Talmud scholars; they are to be feared as one fears God. With those two keys we can open the door.

In chapter 23, verse 3, Avraham petitions the B'nei Cheis, stating that he is a foreigner and asking for a burial plot, and then "*V'ekebarah meisi milfanai*" – "And I will bury my dead from before me." It is significant that even though Avraham knows exactly where he wants to bury Sarah, in his initial approach he does not specify the place. The B'nei Cheis answer favorably, saying in verse 6, "We consider you a prince of God... *kevor es meisecha*" – bury your dead, none of us will refuse you the right "*mikvor meisecha*," to bury your dead.

Avraham's request was unclear. Did he require merely one plot for Sarah or a larger plot for all of his family? They therefore state that both are available. The first offer includes the word *es* – not just Sarah but others too. The second offer omits it.

In verse 7 it states that Avraham rises from this encounter and bows down to the B'nei Cheis and to the ordinary people who were observing this encounter (the debate took place at the city's gates).

Avraham knows that if he approaches Efron immediately and requests the cave of Machpelah, then his request can be denied simply on the basis that it would break the law. The B'nei

Cheis who sit at the city gates were the rulers and government. He first secures the support of the legislators before approaching Efron. But Avraham is wise in the ways of the world and society. History is littered with countless examples of people who have passed laws which, although binding, lacked popular support. Avraham realizes he must also secure the endorsement of the general population. In bowing to them he includes them in the agreement.

In verse 8, he "shows his hand": "If it is your will to bury my dead — *likvor es meisi* — then entreat Efron ben Tzochar." Avraham is stating that his request is for a place to bury his entire family in perpetuity not just his newly deceased wife.

Armed with our keys, the exchange between Efron and Avraham now looks in many ways like two chess grandmasters positioning their pieces. In verse 9, Avraham offers to buy the cave of Machpelah for a good price. In verse 11, Efron makes his first move. "No, my master, listen to me — the field I give to you and the cave within it I give also. "*Kevor meisecha,*" bury your dead. There is no "*kevor es meisecha*" here. Efron appears the generous and kind friend but what he is offering is what he knows Avraham does not want, a place to bury only Sarah. One cannot but admire Efron's chutzpah in offering to give the field as well as the cave. Avraham did not want the field but Efron wanted to be rid of it.

So in verse 13, Avraham demonstrates that he understands the significance of Efron's move, and replies, "Please listen to me, I will give you the money for the field — *v'ekberah es meisi shamah,* and all my dead I can bury there."

In verse 15, Efron makes his final move. "My lord, listen to me, a piece of land, 400 silver coins in value [a vastly overpriced sum] between you and me, what's that? *V'es meischa kevor,* and all your dead you can bury there."

Upon hearing this, Avraham concludes the deal, paying the exorbitant fee but securing what he needs.

The idea that the spiritual giants of Jewish history were remote from the values and difficulties of this world is exploded here. Avraham has finished all ten tests. He is, in every sense, a finished product, yet he is perfectly aware of how the world works and how to deal with the world and its scoundrels.

When a person goes to a great Rabbi to ask for advice, the Rabbi has to be able to understand, and to empathize with the problem. If the greats are cut off from the everyday worries of ordinary people, then they would not be able to give advice; and the advice, if given, would not work.

Avraham is showing that no matter how great the greatest of Rabbis are, they are still in touch with the realities of this world.

CHAVA DUMAS

Finding My Branch on the Tree of Life

When I first became religious, it was very important to me to study as much as possible. I had so much catching up to accomplish, and I yearned to connect with Hashem in every way and do what was "kosher" in His eyes. I longed to actualize Torah principles in my deeds, speech, dress, and every action. I hoped to daven with *kavanah* and embody eternal Torah values. How would I know what was right if I wasn't learning the Source itself, the Torah and all its commentaries? I'd read the Bible for years in English, with all the disadvantages of mistranslation that that entailed. Now I wanted to study in the original Hebrew, the real thing, where true *kedushah* could be uncovered and understood. And so, like many others, I was drawn to Jerusalem, the city of holiness.

The first two years, I attended classes in the morning, participating in a *chevrusa* with a study partner, where we painstakingly translated word by word the *Rashi*s and *Ramban*s on *Chumash*. This was followed by the exhilarating moment of putting it all together and having an insightful discussion with our teacher. How many layers of meaning we extracted from each *pasuk*! The effort we expended almost guaranteed that whatever we studied would be retained in our memories forever.

There were also Jewish philosophy, halachah, chassidus, and *tefillah* classes, not just in my particular seminary, but all over Jerusalem. I'd gotten a late start, but here in Jerusalem my *neshamah* could flourish, not only in the wealth of courses offered, but with the profoundly deep people that made Israel their home for the same reasons I was attracted to being here. Being in a city where the search for and the actualization of truth were first priority was a refreshing change from the superficiality I'd left behind in secular society, where even the basic questioning of "Why am I here?" and "What is my purpose?" was often mocked.

I was initially very resistant to any talk of gender differences and a woman's role. My afternoons were spent digesting what I'd learned in the mornings by hashing things out with outstanding, brilliant women, most of whom I met by being graciously received at their Shabbos tables. I greatly appreciated what these women gave of themselves, to help open my eyes to see with clarity what the Torah and its accompanying lifestyle offered to the modern, "liberated" woman. We spent many precious hours arguing, discussing, and dissecting what was the real truth on so many pertinent, personal issues.

But these women weren't just intellectual scholars ensconced in private libraries. They were active, busy mothers balancing many people's needs; natural teachers by virtue of their ability to express involved concepts to beginners like myself. They were both selfless and self-sustaining, doing outreach with others and inner work on themselves, involved in the *chesed* their communities and families needed, while nourishing their own *neshamos* with prayer, study, and constant growth. I felt privileged to see their lives up close and thoroughly impressed with what I saw.

While I still wanted to know everything in *Chumash*, exploring each verse in great depth, that brief but satisfying period of formal learning in seminary ended, and my Hebrew skills were not adequate to continue studying on my own. Once I was married, working, and eventually occupied with raising a family, I found my time for learning was extremely limited. I couldn't just attend classes whenever I wanted. My schedule became more demanding as the years went by and the needs of those who were entrusted to my care grew exponentially. Torah study didn't quite fit into the hours of the day. There were rambunctious kids to take to the park in the afternoon, feed and bathe in the evening, read stories to at night, and tuck into bed. There were more dishes to wash, laundry to clean, fold, put away, larger quantities of food to buy and prepare, many errands to do, appointments to keep. My days were full to the max. Juggling everything, who had time to review *Rashi*s?

Connecting with Hashem couldn't come from full-time studying, but I had to find some way to incorporate regular learning into my life. No one, including myself, was expecting me to be a Torah scholar, but I was disappointed that I hadn't mastered the written Hebrew language enough for independent study of the original texts. By living in Israel, my ability to speak Hebrew had improved, but there wasn't any extra time for more *ulpan*, and all those little letters without vowels on the printed page made my eyes swim. I was very reluctant to read *sefarim* in English, despite the plethora of obtainable books, as though that was not genuine enough to slake my thirst for "the Real Thing."

My inner dialogue went something like this:

> "Well, if I don't have time to translate the Hebrew, what's the point? Reading in English is cheating."
>
> "But at least you'll know what the parashah is about!"
>
> "Not really! Every Hebrew word has so many nuances of meaning! I'll miss all that in English! If I can't study in Hebrew, it isn't worth it. What's really great is doing it *b'chevrusa* like when I was in seminary. That was Torah! That was great!"
>
> "Yes, but that isn't happening now! You want to remain an *am ha'aretz*?"

My husband tried to encourage me by saying that I was just giving in to the *yetzer hara*'s ploy to keep me ignorant, if I refused to benefit from the wealth of Torah literature available in English. If I had only a limited amount of time to review something of significance, often late at night when I was already tired, then using English *sefarim* was a reason to rejoice, not to complain.

My situation wasn't unique. There were plenty of mothers who didn't have serious study sessions scheduled into their busy lives, and lots of *ba'alei teshuvah,* new immigrants whose textual skills weren't up to par. What was our portion in the Torah? Growing up exposed to the Western world's viewpoint of what is considered important, it was essential to find an inspirational addendum to inject into one's life.

Stagnating in Jerusalem is nearly impossible. The soul starts to feel restless, and you know it's time to find something suitably life-sustaining for spiritual nourishment, that special Holy Vitamin to ingest every day to keep spiritually balanced and healthy. Since the Torah is God's way of speaking to us, I needed to grasp my own personal branch of the Tree of Life that would support me in my daily endeavors, with the aim of infusing meaning into every mundane action, elevating the physical to spiritual heights.

So eventually, after I finally overcame my negative attitude toward studying in English, I found some favorite items to focus on: Rabbi Pliskin's *Guard Your Tongue, The Chofetz Chaim – A Lesson a Day*, and Rebbetzin Samet's *The Other Side of the Story*. *Shemiras halashon* became a crucial avenue for connecting to *kedushah*, with the emphasis on the tongue's ability to uplift and edify, or break down and destroy. Judging others favorably, striving to be an *oheiv Yisrael*, to love my fellow Jews, focusing on how all Jews are really One, were remarkably relevant for my life as a woman and mother. The immediate effect of applying these words of wisdom could be seen in the faces of the people around me. One uplifting word and the response was joy, while a negative utterance could crush someone's spirit. I was grateful to the authors of these books for providing the sound guidelines for what constitutes acceptable speech.

I joined a women's discussion group on *Pirkei Avos* that emphasized using the text as a tool for spiritual growth. We were encouraged to start keeping a journal of "success stories," when constructive *middos* conquered impulsive negative reactions. Daily challenges became opportunities for introspection, as we were encouraged to analyze our actions and look for glimmers of how to respond better if we were confronted with the same difficulty in the future. We could, with practice, even learn how to stop ourselves mid-yell, calm down, and change our tone of voice to one more positive, without the kids even realizing what had happened!

On the recommendation of Rebbetzin Ruchama Shain, I also began recording *hashgachah pratis* events whenever they occurred. Now I had a unique way of keeping track of my "progress," measuring myself as a person from day to day, actively keeping my eyes open to see how palpable is Hashem's presence in so many little details of our lives. More and more English books were being printed with incredible accounts of Divine providence, how Hashem's hand was openly manifest in people's lives. Over the years, these became our family's favorites for the Shabbos table and bedtime reading.

Creating a home built on a strong foundation of timeless principles is part of the "Women's Torah" which is fully ours to partake of and utilize. Once I heard a Rebbetzin say, if one has the right *kavanah* in mind while doing the dishes, it is possible to bring Mashiach. And understanding the intrinsically significant value of feeding my family physical food imbued with love can make meal preparation an uplifting experience. In *Mishlei*, Shlomo HaMelech says, "The wisdom of the women builds her house." Why is the beginning of the *pasuk* in the plural, but the end is in the singular? Because the collective wisdom of all the Jewish women, which we have a responsibility to gather and transmit to our daughters, is what helps build our individual homes.

It isn't an easy enterprise, but we aren't alone in our efforts. We are part of a transcendent community striving for a single purpose, to actually bring Torah and *kedushah* into the world. We as women have many tasks that need to be done, and what really matters is the attitude with which we view our ongoing responsibilities. We are constantly doing *chesed*, emulating Hashem,

Who is the ultimate *Ba'al Chesed,* showering us continuously with kindness. By emulating Him, we are in essence drawing closer to Him.

It is often said that the *kohanim* in the Beis HaMikdash, the supreme center of holiness for the Jewish people and all the inhabitants of the earth, were involved in very physically demanding work: slaughtering *korbanos,* building fires, washing *keilim,* clearing out ashes and debris. Our own homes are compared to the Beis HaMikdash and called a *mikdash me'at;* when our own labors are physically demanding, we have before us the *kohanim*'s historical example of how we as Jews infuse physicality with intense spirituality. We just need to open the door to let Hashem into our activities, to appreciate the eternal worth of our work as women. Then our portion in the Torah Tree of Life is guaranteed.

YAEL SUROFSKY

Candlesticks

Candlesticks,
receptacles of light,
holders of holiness,
I search for you in many places,
observe your features and forms,
discover your essence.

Silver candlesticks,
antique hues that stir up memories
of Bobba.
Their outlines
standing proudly in the background
of faded photos.
Recollections of simple shtetl homes,
of tears of longing and faith,
even during their temporary residences
at the pawnbroker.

Silver — a bridge to an ancient glorious past,
they would polish you to a high shine
of polished silver, as they worked hard
to uncover inner treasures within,
and to unveil His radiance
in every tarnished vessel.

Crystal candlesticks,
transparent, they accept light,
reflect it,
the more you empty yourself out
of ego and physicality,
of your own presence
that blocks light,
the more you open your gates
to accepting His presence,
reflecting His light.
A harmony of perfection and symmetry,
clear of imperfections,
bright as sunlight that fills
every transparent space.

Earthenware candlesticks,
humble and lowly,
they hold the flame steady,
despite appearances,
they were fired in the furnace
of the kiln,
their clay was formless material
in the potter's hand,
as he shaped it to reflect his will.

You entered weak and soft to the touch,
and you exited the fire steadfast,
with form and shape,
a strong will to hold the fire,
your appearance lowly as the desert of Sinai
willing to receive the Torah.

Candlesticks,
I search for you in many places,
I search within you,
for your potential to hold light,
I search myself to discover,
the essence of candlesticks
within me.

RABBI SHLOMO PRICE

Having Both Worlds

A Letter to an Alumnus

My Dear Friend,

It is with trepidation that I begin this letter to you. As you may know, I always shy away from giving advice, as it is a great responsibility to give the right advice to each person. Each person is different and requires advice that fits his individual situation. However, as my heart goes out to you, I felt I would try to give you some general advice that may give you some *chizuk*. So, with a prayer on my lips that Hashem should give me the knowledge and *siyata d'Shmaya* to know what to write, I will begin.

You asked me if there is a middle path between life and religion, and if you find yourself pulled from the two sides (*gashmiyus* and *ruchniyus*) can you have both?

I see a common misunderstanding of what a *frum* Jew is expected to do. Many people think that being "*frum*" means sacrificing the pleasures of *gashmiyus* (physical matters) and giving up *olam hazeh* in order to get the eternal spiritual pleasure of *olam haba*. However, this is a terrible mistake. In a beautiful essay in *Lev Eliyahu* (*Parashas Vayeitzei, "L'hisaneig al Hashem"*), Rav Eliyahu Lopian stresses that in reality those that search and strive for *ruchniyus* don't sacrifice anything. On the contrary, only they can really enjoy this world. But those that strive only for *olam hazeh* — the "*olam hazehnikers*" as he dubs them — cannot enjoy even the *olam hazeh* they get.

Rav Eliyahu starts off by analyzing an interesting conversation between Yaakov, Rachel, and Leah (*Bereishis* 31:3–16). After twenty years at Lavan's home, Hashem just told Yaakov to return to his father's home. Interestingly, when Yaakov relates this to his wives, he doesn't get straight to the point. Instead, he gives a whole introduction describing how the relationship between him and Lavan has eroded, and that he had been fooled many times by Lavan. Finally, he ends off saying that Hashem told him to return home. Rachel and Leah also respond in a strange way. "Do we still have any portion or inheritance in our father's home? And now, do everything that Hashem tells you to." They were saying that they didn't expect to get any material gain in their father's house, so now they will listen to everything that Hashem has instructed them to do.

This is quite puzzling. If Hashem has told Yaakov to leave, what is there to discuss? Why does Yaakov bother to give this lengthy introduction to explain why it is logical to leave? Wouldn't it suffice for Yaakov to relate that Hashem ordered him to leave, thus there is nothing else to consider? The response of Rachel and Leah is even harder to understand. Did they mean to say that the only reason to leave is the fact that their father's home is no monetary asset to them?

The Lev Eliyahu asks a similar question regarding *Koheles*. Throughout *Sefer Koheles*, Shlomo HaMelech describes how much he has experienced in this world and how worthless are all the pleasures of this world. "Vanity of vanities, all is vanity" repeats itself throughout the book. Finally, he concludes (12:13), "At the end of everything, when all is heard, [the final verdict is] to fear Hashem and keep His mitzvos, because this is all of Man."

Again, we have the same puzzling question. Why does Shlomo HaMelech need this whole introduction? Does he mean that the only reason to fear Hashem and do mitzvos is because the world's pleasures are worthless? What if the pleasures of the world *were* good, would that be a reason not to do the mitzvos?

The answer is that Yaakov, Rachel, Leah, and Shlomo HaMelech are all teaching us an important lesson, a foundation in serving Hashem.

A person should not think that serving Hashem and keeping the Torah comes at the expense of the pleasures of this world. This is a totally mistaken concept, and is not the path to serving Hashem. Rather, a person is obligated to understand and realize that if he does the will of Hashem, he will have goodness and blessing in this world and in the next. The main reward comes in *olam haba*, while the person "eats the fruit" in this world.

This is the explanation for the conversation between Yaakov, Rachel, and Leah. They are emphasizing that obeying Hashem's command is not coming at the expense of any physical gain. They saw clearly that it was good to leave the house of Lavan because they were not expecting any money from him. (If they had been expecting money from Lavan, then there would have been a different way to understand why they would not be sacrificing anything. The main point is: serving Hashem can lead only to good things, not to loss.)

Shlomo HaMelech is also telling us that serving Hashem doesn't involve any sacrifices because all the pleasures of this world are vanity. The greatest pleasure is getting away from the falsehood and vanity of this world.

Living a life of *emunah* (belief in Hashem) and *bitachon* (trust in Hashem), together with the concepts of *gam zu l'tovah* (everything Hashem does is for the best) and *hashgachah pratis* (Hashem is constantly guiding us) — a life where we control our *middos* and desires — makes us the happiest people around.

The Tiferes Yisrael says on *Avos* (6:2), "The only true freedom is the freedom of the soul. A person is not free if his desires are liberated and his soul is enslaved to his desires."

Furthermore, the Lev Eliyahu points out that only those who serve Hashem really get to enjoy the pleasures of this world. Those people who seek only pleasure— the *olam hazehnikers* — will not enjoy it. A person who is controlled by bad *middos* such as desire and jealousy cannot enjoy what he has. On the outside he may pretend he is living a happy life, but when you get to know him, you see how miserable he really is.

How do we conquer our desires? "If you can't beat them, join them" wouldn't work here. The Vilna Gaon compares this to someone who wishes to quench his thirst by drinking salty sea water. At first he may think he is quenching his thirst, but soon he will be thirstier than he was before. The same is true of desires: the more we give in to them, the more we will want them, and they will rule us.

The way to conquer them is to work on your *middos* and to learn to love Hashem and mankind. Once this happens, our jealousy of others will dissolve because we will only want what is best for others. The moment we understand that fun does not bring happiness, we begin to lead our lives differently. The effect can be, quite literally, life-transforming.

We can learn the lesson of happiness and jealousy from Haman HaRasha (the wicked Haman). In *Megillas Esther* (5:13), he recounts all of his greatness, riches, and children, even mentioning the fact that Queen Esther invited him along to the party. Yet there is one thing that bothers him, namely that Mordechai the Jew doesn't bow down to him. We would think that such a person would be 99 percent happy and one percent not. Yet Haman says, "All of this is worth nothing"! How ridiculous this is. The second most important person in the kingdom cannot enjoy all the riches and pleasure he has because there is onc Jew who refuses to bow down to him! But that is how jealousy poisons all of life's joys.

There is a verse from *Tehillim* (34:11) that we say in the *Birkas HaMazon* (Grace after Meals): "Those who seek Hashem will not lack anything good." The Lev Eliyahu quotes a question from the Shlah HaKadosh, who asks, "Don't we see so many people who 'seek Hashem,' and yet they are lacking good?"

The Lev Eliyahu explains the answer of the Shlah HaKadosh with a parable. A person visited two friends in their homes. In the bathroom of the first one he found a huge closet full of medicines. In the second one he found only a small medicine chest. He approached the second friend and said, "Why didn't you tell me that you are so poor and can't afford to buy medicines? I am more than willing to help you out with the expenses. Look at our friend across the street, he is so successful, he has so many medicines."

Upon hearing this, the friend began to laugh, saying, "Don't you realize that he has so many medicines because everybody there is sick and in need of medication? My family, *baruch Hashem,* is well and we don't need so many medicines."

It is the same with all worldly pleasures. You go into the rich man's house and you sink into his thick carpet and you see all the fancy things he has. Then you go to your Rebbe's house and he barely has anything there and you feel bad for him. As mentioned before, the rich man may be suffering from terrible sickness: jealousy, desires, and honor-seeking. Your Rebbe doesn't have that sickness and consequently doesn't need the "medicines."

One of the main principles in economics is "keep up with the Jones'." Everybody can be happy, but once somebody on the block gets something nicer than the others, they are all jealous. Even the commercials proclaim, "Be the envy of the block, be the first one to get it." The rich man has the sickness of jealousy...consequently he needs all those fancy things to "cure" himself. Without them he can't find happiness. (There is nothing wrong with being rich if Hashem blesses you — use it in good health. We are discussing here those who are obsessed with money.)

This, says the Shlah HaKadosh, is the explanation of the verse, "Those who seek Hashem will not lack anything good." It doesn't say that those who seek Hashem will have everything good. It says they won't lack it. There are two ways not to lack it, either by having it or not needing it. David HaMelech is telling us that those who seek Hashem won't need all these things. They will be happy without them.

May Hashem help us be amongst those who love to serve Him.

ROSALLY SALTSMAN

Pearls of Wisdom

An *eishes chayil* is considered more precious than pearls. I hadn't really thought about why the comparison to pearls, as opposed to diamonds or emeralds, until a conversation I had with a friend. We were discussing change and spiritual growth, and it occurred to me that we ourselves are pearls, and as we get older (and hopefully wiser) we add layer upon layer to our already intrinsic worth. In contrast to other precious gems that are cut smaller to be more marketable, pearls are the only gems that are cultured to increase their size, and their growth is limited only to the patience and endurance of the oyster that hosts them.

The corporal bodies we are given by Hashem at birth are oysters that house the pearls of our *neshamos*. It takes only one minor irritation, one miniscule grain of sand, to begin our spiritual growth. If handled properly, we can take each grain of sand that gets under our shells and turn it into a unique jewel. We then become not only more precious than pearls but mothers of pearl.

All the women, all the *neshos chayil*, are Hashem's string of pearls that He gives the Shabbos Queen to adorn herself with. We can be grateful that with every irritation that we rise above, we increase our worth and our value, as Hashem observes us under His highly sensitive loupe.

ORA WISKIND ELPER

The Voice of the Shofar

> And the voice of the shofar sounded louder and louder; Moshe speaks and Hashem answers him by a voice.
>
> (*Shemos* 19:19)

On Har Sinai two voices, both of them tremendous, issue from the heavens, striking awe in the hearts of *b'nei Yisrael*. For a moment they are silenced, overwhelmed by the voices they have "seen," the revelation they have witnessed. How does Hashem make His presence tangible? How does He speak with us in other voices than His own, voices we can bear to hear? And how are we to respond? I would like to speak with you about *kolos* — the voice of the shofar and our own voices, about the dialogue that informs Rosh HaShanah and its promise of a new beginning.

In Tanach, the whole world is filled with voices: the seas, forests, skies, and rivers speak, and yet it is really Hashem's voice that is heard in the guise of nature. Eliyahu HaNavi sees beyond the appearances of natural phenomena. As he stands on Har Chorev, Hashem passes before him; a whirlwind surrounds him, rending the mountains, shattering rocks in pieces, the earth quakes, a fire roars. But Hashem is in none of them, and after the fire, "*kol demamah dakah* – a small voice of silence" (*Melachim* I 19:12). This voice out of the silence is Hashem's true voice, the most intimate and direct revelation of His will.

Hearing Hashem's voice, the inward essence of nature, is the closest any person besides Moshe Rabbeinu ever comes to experiencing Hashem's presence. The voice acts as His messenger, His embodiment, yet paradoxically its form is completely insubstantial, disembodied. And so it remains mysterious: invisible and at the same time clearly, undeniably present. When Moshe reminds *b'nei Yisrael* of what happened when they received the Torah, he says:

> You heard the voice of the words, but saw no form, only a voice.
>
> (*Devarim* 4:12)

The voice of the shofar transports us back to Har Sinai, recreating for us the whole atmosphere that accompanied *matan Torah,* the giving of the Torah.

What effect does the voice of the shofar have on us, here, today? It is a primal sound, a bit like the cry of an animal (and of course it speaks for the ram it once belonged to, the great-grandson of the *ayil* that saved Yitzchak's life as he was bound on the altar). And the voice of the shofar is primal in another sense as well. As the midrash says, it echoes the shofar that sounded as Hashem created the world. In a more immediate sense, it is a summons, a strident voice calling us to action. The Rambam hears it say:

> Awaken, sleepers, from your slumber. Search your deeds and repent. Remember your Creator!
>
> (*Mishneh Torah, Hilchos Teshuvah*, ch. 3)

This voice, shaking our drowsy shoulder, beseeching our unconscious ear, addresses us as individuals and speaks to all of *klal Yisrael* as well.

Since the beginning of Elul, the prophet Yeshayahu calls Yisrael, described in human and in female form, to awaken after the long slumber of exile. In the Haftaros his voice rises with excitement, a harbinger of her new life, the end of suffering, her ultimate redemption:

> Awaken, awaken, dress yourself in strength, O Zion; shake yourself from the dust...
>
> (*Yeshayahu* 52:1)

> Arise, shine, for your light has come.
>
> (ibid. 60:1)

But Yeshayahu's urging is not only to some abstract entity; it is not only *klal Yisrael* who are in a physical *galus* from Eretz Yisrael. Each one of us is bound in the chains of our own spiritual exile. Just as the sins *b'nei Yisrael* committed caused them to be driven from the Land, our own sins have estranged us from Hashem, driven us to some strange land where we only faintly recall the grace of His countenance. How can we return from this great distance? How can we regain the intimacy we once had with Him? This is where the second voice of the dialogue comes in, the voice answering the summons of the shofar. The prophet Yirmeyahu speaks of that human voice in the Haftarah for the second day of

Rosh HaShanah, born of pain and of longing and full of love.

> A voice is heard from Rama, lamentation and bitter weeping; Rachel mourns her children; she refuses to be comforted, for her children are no more.
>
> (*Yirmeyahu* 31:14)

Rachel Imeinu, the great mother of the exile, weeps for her lost ones. All of her being wants only to find them again, to bring them back from the land of their enemies. And her mournful voice, all that remains of her, awakens Hashem's mercy; she need weep no more, for all who have been driven away will be restored to her, will be drawn into her home once again.

> Thus said Hashem, keep your voice from weeping and your eyes from tears…for the future holds hope, says Hashem, and your sons will return to their borders.
>
> (*Yirmeyahu* 31:16)

But how are we to return from our existential exile, how can we feel Hashem's embrace after so long? We must recognize and admit just how alienated we have become, just how much we have driven ourselves away, and we can only appeal to Hashem:

> Bring me back, and I will return.
>
> (*Yirmeyahu* 31:17)

The shofar demands our verbal response, demands that we draw our thoughts and fears out of ourselves and express them objectively. The Rambam speaks of *vidui devarim* – the necessity of expressing our wrongdoings in words. The act of *teshuvah* requires more than good intentions, more even than a sincere will to repent. Hoshea, in the Haftarah of Shabbos Shuva, wishes to impress his people with the importance of verbal confession. He exhorts all of Yisrael to undertake the journey back to Hashem and to offer Him, not sacrifices, but rather a much more intimate gift of themselves:

> Take with you words, and return to Hashem.
>
> (*Hoshea* 14:2)

Our desire to come back to Hashem consumes us, transforms us. Ultimately, we wish to become completely and only voice, like Rachel's voice, unimpeded by any body, any physical bounds. "I am my prayer" (*Tehillim* 69:14) — all of my being is expressed in the words I offer up to You.

It is said that David HaMelech's harp hung at the foot of his bed, and at midnight, a north wind blew through the strings and the harp played by itself. In the same way we too can aspire to be an instrument, to let our soul's voice speak for us, and to believe, if it can only be pure, that Hashem will hear us, and answer.

This, then, is the dialogue of Tishrei, really of all year long, but especially audible in these days. The voice of the shofar, the shadow or intimation of Hashem's own voice, awakens us, and our pleas awaken Him, so to speak.

In *Shir HaShirim* (5:2) there is a passage that perfectly describes and reflects our own spiritual state in these first days of the New Year, the waiting, the promise, and the danger. It begins this way:

"I sleep," still imprisoned in the exile of my sins, "yet my heart is awake." Deep inside, I know I can return... And then, in the silence of the night, without warning:

> "The voice of my beloved knocks."
> And what does He say, this voice beyond the door?
> "Open for Me," open your heart, don't turn Me away.
> This voice speaks to us now as well.
> Let us get up, before it is too late.

RABBI PINCHAS WINSTON

A Chanukah Story

This is a Chanukah story. I tell it every year, if only to proclaim the miracle. I can confirm its veracity, because it happened to me personally.

In my second year of marriage, we lived in a neighborhood of Yerushalayim called Har Nof. At the time, I was learning in a *kollel* in the Old City, some forty-five minutes away by bus. On Fridays I used to go in for the morning to learn, even on short winter days such as *erev Parashas Mikeitz,* which happened to fall that year during Chanukah.

We were having important guests for Shabbos, my father-in-law and mother-in-law, and I wanted to prepare a special *d'var Torah* for the Shabbos table. As was my custom in those days, I would begin learning the parashah the last fifteen minutes before leaving for home. I would search for a question to ponder on the bus ride home, which, I hoped, would form the basis for my Shabbos table *d'var Torah.*

I do not recall how many times I had learned that week's

parashah. But I do know that I had never before stopped on the *pasuk* that caught my attention that morning, the verse that has the freed and cleaned-up Yosef standing before Pharaoh: "Yosef answered Pharaoh, saying, 'Not I, but God, will answer the peace of Pharaoh' " (*Bereishis* 41:16).

All of a sudden it occurred to me: How could Pharaoh talk seriously with Yosef, let alone trust his interpretation of the royal dreams? Wasn't Yosef accused of being an adulterer? And if you tell me, So what? Egypt was an extremely immoral place, I'll counter by telling you that we learn from Avraham that although the Egyptians didn't mind murdering people, they did hate adultery. (That's why Avraham told Pharaoh that Sarah was his sister and not his wife, for fear that Pharaoh would kill him in order to take Sarah and avoid adultery!)

As I closed my *Chumash* and prepared to make the long journey home, I was satisfied that I was on to something big, and I began pondering the question as I left the Old City for Har Nof.

From the main post office outside the Old City, I could catch either the 15 or 11 bus, both of which go directly to Har Nof. Both buses showed up at the same time, both equally crowded. I'm not quite sure what steered me, but I headed for the number 15. I began my odyssey to the back of the crowded bus, hoping to find a safe place to hang onto my groceries and a pole for balance. As I made it to the back, I saw a seat in the corner that was empty. Not wanting to seem selfish and make a *chilul Hashem* (profanation of God's Name), I let the seat remain empty, just in case someone else had precedence over me. No one sat down. I checked the seat for bubble gum, but it was clean. Feeling safe, I sat down, parked my groceries under the seat, and silently sang praises to God for my little island of calm in the midst of all the pre-Shabbos pandemonium.

I opened my pocket *Chumash* to think through my question while the bus made its way to Geula. It finally reached the main stop on Malchei Yisrael, letting off many people, taking on even more. I was engrossed in my *Chumash* and barely noticed that the only available seat was the one next to me. In the back of my mind I was somewhat conscious of the *krechtzing* of a tired, middle-aged man as he dropped down next to me. I had this eerie sense that he was the talkative type, and I turned myself toward the window and made my *Chumash* even more obvious. The only thing missing was a "Do not disturb" sign.

I should have gone for the sign, because nothing I did deterred this American tourist, who seemed bent upon striking up a conversation with anyone who would listen, or not listen for that matter.

"I see you're learning *Chumash,*" he said.

"Yes," I said politely but curtly, hoping to indicate that that was to be the end of the conversation. There was only twenty more minutes to Har Nof, and I had yet to find a satisfactory answer for why Pharaoh was prepared to overlook the charges of adultery against Yosef.

However, the man was politely insistent. "Where do you learn?" he asked next.

I told him the name of my yeshivah, expecting little in return, but again I was wrong. Like Yehudah in that week's parashah, I was blind to the unfolding Divine providence.

"Really? I know your *rosh yeshivah*. In fact, his brother is my Rav back in the States, and his son made my son's *shidduch*. It's a great story. Let me tell you how it goes..."

And so he did, and did, and did. Defeated, I closed my *Chumash* and slipped into captive audience mode. The truth is, it was a remarkable story. Had it been any other time, and had I already developed a novel *d'var Torah* for the Shabbos table, the story would have thrilled me. It was hard to feel both frustration and excitement simultaneously.

As the bus made its final approach toward Har Nof, the story ended, and the man said, "I'm sorry. I know you were learning *Chumash* before I interrupted you. At least let me give you a *d'var Torah* on this week's parashah."

"You might as well," I thought to myself, sarcastically, "because I sure don't have one!"

The man continued to speak. "In fact, it is right on the *pasuk* that you had your finger on, before you closed your *Chumash*..." My eyes, for the first time that trip, lit up. He continued, "That verse contains an extra word. In the *pasuk* before it, it says, 'Pharaoh said to Yosef: I had a dream and no one can interpret it, and I heard about you, saying (*leimor*), you can hear a dream and interpret it.' The next *pasuk* says, 'Yosef answered Pharaoh, saying (*leimor*): Not I, but God, will answer the peace of Pharaoh.' It seems to me that at least one of the *leimor*s is extra."

"Well, the Torah often speaks like that," I said.

"I know," he jumped in, "so I went to many rabbis in my city to see what they thought, and they all agreed that there is an extra *leimor*, but had no interpretation for it. However, one rabbi I went to had already noticed the extra word on his own, and did have an interpretation to offer, which I found very interesting. He told me that the *leimor* was an allusion to a sub-dialogue between Pharaoh and Yosef."

"A what?" I asked, now feeling the pressure of my stop fast approaching.

"The rabbi was basing his *peshat* (interpretation) upon the Talmud, in *Sanhedrin* 56b, which finds sources for the Seven Noachide Laws in the Torah. It turns out that, according to the

Oral Law, different words allude to different mitzvos. The word *leimor* is the word that alludes to the mitzvah not to have illicit relationships!"

Boinggggg! "Like adultery?" I asked hesitatingly, feeling the finger of *hashgachah* touching lightly upon me.

"Exactly," he answered. "Pharaoh's *leimor* alludes to Pharaoh asking Yosef, 'How can you be an interpreter of dreams? You're an adulterer! Even your own God hates such illicit behavior...why would He want to work through you?' Yosef's *leimor* means, 'That's exactly the point. The very fact that I can interpret dreams correctly, which only can be done with God's help, proves my innocence!' " (After the fact, I noticed that "*leimor*" also appears in the episode of Yosef and the wife of Potiphar, and Rashi makes reference to the *gemara* itself there in 39:9.)

"Yosef's point was accepted by Pharaoh, which is why he felt confident raising Yosef to the position of viceroy of Egypt! A great answer, no?"

My jaw dropped open. Shivers went up and down my spine as I pondered the odds of such a coincidence. Seconds before arriving at my stop, I quickly explained what had just happened. The man laughed, and finished by saying, "To think! I came six thousand miles just to answer your question!"

I smiled warmly. We said good-bye to each other and thanked one another for what had obviously been very, very *bashert*. As I got off the bus, with a far better, more fascinating Chanukah *d'var Torah* than I had ever bargained for, I looked heavenward and thanked God for what was the most important message I could ever learn:

Answers are from God. It is only up to us to formulate the questions and to be available to receive that holy, hidden Light of Creation, when God decides to send it down to us.

BRACHA GOETZ

To Barbara, Wherever I May Find Her

Barbara, you were angry and you were Jewish – but what could I say to you way back then? What would I say to you now...if I had the chance?

You hated men vehemently at the time. They were the ones who had put you down, kept you "in your place" for all these millennia. Remember how we all used to hang out in Bread and Roses restaurant – all the angry feminists of Radcliffe, who were mostly Jewish, and who could see so clearly that men were the culprits and women the victims. I was there too, but if you remember, I never had much to say at any of our meetings. I didn't see it all so clearly. Something bothered me with all this talk about the good guys and the bad guys...and most of all, it seemed so full of anger.

Now here I am, many years later, finally feeling ready to say something back to you. What I have to say will sound strange at first, and that is why a part of me doesn't even want to bother. At the same time, I know it is important for me to let you hear my thinking now.

Remember the disgust we used to feel when we were considered nothing but a pretty face by all those men out there? Those were our souls reacting. When we were striving to be treated with the same respect that men were afforded, when we were fighting to have the opportunity to fulfill our greatest potentials as women — and even when society's stress on skin-surface beauty was making us sick deep down inside — all of those times, it was our Jewish *neshamos* that were crying out to be recognized by us.

I know what you'd think of me if you saw me. Not usually barefoot, but often pregnant — and baking bread (challah) periodically. Right away you would probably classify me as one of those who had given up. But it's more the other way around. I turned away from all the anger at Bread and Roses because it was a dead-end street. All I knew then was that it couldn't be the way for us to get somewhere.

Last time we saw each other, I was headed for medical school in Virginia. The summer after my first year there, I took a trip to Israel. I had just six weeks of vacation until my second year of medical school would begin. I was coming in search of something that was missing in life, and I knew that this was the last stop I was going to make before resigning myself completely to the cynical, desensitized way of life I was finally getting used to. I could not understand at the time that the constant, unsurrendering force inside that kept pushing me onward and wouldn't let me rest was Jewish. The drive to meet our spiritual needs is in all of us, but we don't usually recognize where the deep and unfulfilled cravings are coming from.

We had dismissed Judaism early on as being unable to provide any solutions to the problems that were important to us. The graduation ceremonies from Judaism were held at gaudy bar mitzvah receptions. There was more than plenty of good food — but nothing that lasted. Then, later on, we all heard stuff about how the status of a woman was inferior to that of a man in Judaism. Someone once even showed us some Jewish laws to prove it. We didn't hear much, but what we did hear seemed to make a lot of sense. After all, it was exactly what we had suspected.

Well, now I wish I could ask you to take a second look. I would ask you to look from the place that lies even deeper than your anger. From that pure part of you — still unmarred from long years of hating — I would ask you to look at me and see what there is to this woman doing dishes, changing diapers, and making dinner for her husband every day. You never wanted others to judge you at face value. Now, I'm asking for that too.

An understanding of the woman's true role in Judaism can only be obtained by suspending your usual way of thinking for awhile. From the very start, we have been taught to believe that public recognition is what counts. We saw men out up front in prestigious positions getting a lot of recognition — and we wanted it too. It seemed that men were having all the fun, living life in the most exciting way. But who told us that out in public is "where the action is"? Who was telling us that success in the public arena would make us happy? And who got us thinking that being a homemaker was a drag? What I'm trying to say is somewhere along the line most of us accepted an assumption which no one ever proved to us. We believed it when "they" told us that getting public recognition would bring fulfillment, and yet we never saw even one living example of it.

In these intervening years, through exploring authentic Judaism, I've had the chance to discover a fact of life that was never disclosed to me before. Simply put: What's up front is not what counts. It's still very hard for me to accept that thoroughly, however. It will take a long time for me to adjust to this view of life, completely topsy-turvy to the one in which I'd been indoctrinated.

In a sense, though, I think this topsy-turvy view of what really matters in life can be considered a truly feminist way of thinking. It requires recognizing fully that the man's role is not the preferred role. Once this readjustment in thinking can be integrated at a deep level within, it finally becomes possible for a woman to realize her greatest potential. Once freed from the burden of wanting to be like a man, she is able to be a woman wholeheartedly. We are then able to taste the many pleasures inherent in creating a home. Pleasures of the deepest sort, that we would never have permitted ourselves to accept and experience as pleasures before.

I'm not trying to say that in order for every Jewish woman's *neshamah* to achieve fulfillment she has to be a full-time homemaker. What I believe is that we have to be open to enable the spiritual nourishment that we all need to get in. When creating a holy environment in which love can grow is a woman's top priority, the spiritual nourishment gets through in a steady flow.

I'm also not trying to say that every minute as a Jewish homemaker has been a delight. I mean, it could have been if I had let it — but some old thoughts still hold me down. There are times when I wish that my children would just leave me alone and let me do what I "feel like doing." But they are always there, wanting me to help them with their homework, or read to them, or simply hold them. Boy, does that push me to grow in ways that I never would have been able to before. Then there is my husband. It is even harder to be giving to him. I hear all these old whispers when I am doing things for him. I bet they're coming from brain cells still lodged in there since Bread and Roses. "What are you, his servant?" or "Men! They're all alike!" those brain cells hiss, and sometimes I succumb.

It's pretty futile to try to argue with these subliminal voices directly. They'll say something that still stings, and then fade away with a mocking, condescending laugh. The best way for me to quiet that kind of irritating chatter is for me to fill my mind with higher things. Little by little, as I learn more about myself, more about what the purpose of life is, and more about which pleasures in life are the greatest and most lasting, the resentful voices slink away, ineffective.

One of the biggest obstacles we have to get beyond is that we've actually been taught to see giving in a negative light. Our secular training tells us that it's the women who are the givers and the men who are the traditional takers. I don't understand why this creates anger, though, since God, the One we all seek to emulate, is universally recognized as the Ultimate Giver. Still, I wish I could somehow get you to come and visit with families whose homes are built solidly upon a Torah base. Both the men and the women are clearly trained from the very start of their lives to strive to become givers. In fact, a man gets married, according to Torah opinion, so that he will have the opportunity to give during the course of his life in the most significant way.

The role of the Jewish people is to make clear the spiritual essence of every single physical entity in this world. A Jewish woman can choose to be at the very center of this most holy work. We are the ones who largely determine whether or not the spiritual potential inherent in all things will be brought out. Seemingly mundane actions are transformed into uplifting, limitlessly inspiring experiences when a Jewish woman's body and soul move in sync, with clarity.

Does my being a woman devoted to creating a truly Jewish home still make me seem like some kind of martyr to you? But, a martyr to what? Really, when you think about it, what am I sacrificing? Am I sacrificing myself to become a better person? What am I losing? Can you imagine how much there is to be gained?

One last thing I want to ask you. Have you ever wondered about how Judaism has managed to be preserved through thousands of years? I think the answer is that what is most sacred about it — its greatest treasures — are not left out for public display. We turned away from Judaism when we were both in college, but we had actually never even met Judaism, only some very cheap imitations of it. And yet, that is exactly what has been its protection device. In order to get at the core of Judaism, at what makes it infinitely valuable, we have to invest a great deal of intellectual, emotional, spiritual, as well as physical effort, putting ideas into action — actualizing potentials — through mitzvos.

The essential ingredient in Judaism that we were never offered a taste of is its modesty. That is what has kept it from being totally depreciated by a mass consumption that was effortless. The status of the Jewish woman in a Torah lifestyle has been preserved on the high and powerful level that it was always on because of the modesty inherent in the role. Without it, there is a tremendous sinking, and the power, as we saw so starkly, becomes lost.

Remember that detestable little expression, "Women

should be seen and not heard"? In Torah-true Judaism, we are striving for the reverse. The aim is not to wrap women up in rolls of adhesive tape so that no one will ever see them. The stress is on developing inner beauty, and not focusing on externals. What is internal — what is hidden and lasting and requires an enormous amount of effort to develop — is what is valued. So many of the superficial social games we used to play are absent. Voices are coming from deep within, and so that is where the attention gets focused.

The goal of Judaism is to have the voice that comes straight from the heart of a Jewish woman penetrate every imprisoned heart that still yearns to be set free. Jewish women were created along with Jewish men to be lights to the world, to make clear the way to come close to God and derive the greatest and deepest pleasures from life. Yet for some time now, many Jewish women have not even heard their own voices speaking. We've been listening to the loud and pervasive voices of those raised with values which are foreign to our own, and they have affected us deeply. I hope that somehow, you will hear my voice now, Barbara, as I finally found something I wanted to say. And I pray that one day, God willing, I will hear yours.

ESTHER SUTTON

Emunah — Learning How to See

It has been said that the main test of the pre-Messianic era will be one of *emunah. Emunah* means more than any of its usual English translations. It is more than faith or belief because it must be based on knowledge. It is more than ordinary knowledge because it must come from the core of one's very being. Rav Mordechai Neugerschal, *shlita,* has used the phrase "*imunim be'omanut ha'emunah*" (practice sessions in the art of *emunah*). It is beautifully apt that *emunah* and *omanut* (artistry) share the same root. Just as any art must be practiced and developed, so it is with *emunah.*

As Rav Shlomo Wolbe, *shlita,* explains so poetically and poignantly in his modern classic *Alei Shur,* the universe is actually a living laboratory, a workshop in *emunah*:

> There is nature. Sunrise, sunset. The rising of the moon and stars. Lightning and thunder. Flowers and trees. Mountain,

hill, and plain. Birds, animals, wildlife. It's incredible that all these creations don't speak to us!

"The heavens declare the glory of Hashem" (*Tehillim* 19:1) – but we don't hear their story. We walk about in the world like blind people, and we simply don't see. The sages learned modesty from the cat, boldness from the leopard, lightness from the eagle, quickness from the deer, strength from the lion. Every living creature spoke to them.

With the renewal of the moon's cycle, they set for us a time and a blessing for receiving the *Shechinah*. The renewal of the moon meant something to them; it spoke to them, stirred them.

The Rambam acquired love and reverence for Hashem from contemplating His wondrous creations, and so he instructed us to do. Will we one day open our eyes and actually perceive something (Hashem's presence) within the creation?

Within the context of this spiritual work [waking up to the incredible, spiritual gifts of life], our Sages came to our aid and established the blessings of pleasure.

It can't be stated any more plainly: we need to wake up! We can't just go through the motions of life – even of a Torah-based lifestyle – mechanically anymore. If there is anything that we can gain from all the complex problems and difficulties that confront *am Yisrael* right now, it is that we must wake up to the preciousness of life, to the value of every moment, to the potential spiritual treasure that lies within every mitzvah that we do, and every line of Torah that we learn.

The whole point of all the blessings we constantly say on food and drink, or upon seeing the ocean, or hearing thunder, is for us to remember, recognize, and relate to the one Creator who brought all these things into existence,

> including our very selves.
>
> Our great sages were stirred and touched by nature and creation, and it moved them closer to their Creator. They formulated the blessings so that we, too, could be moved and stirred by the world in which we live – and use the beauty, the complexity, and the mystery of the universe to bring ourselves closer to the *Ribbono shel Olam*.
>
> (*Alei Shur*, vol. II, p. 297)

Rav Wolbe goes on to speak about the blessing of *HaMotzi*, how we ignore all the stages of man's laborious efforts – planting, sowing, grinding, baking – and instead declare: "Blessed are You, Hashem, our God, King of the universe, who brings bread forth from the earth!"

It is all Him. Not the farmer, not the grinder, not the baker, and not the storekeeper, but Him, blessed is He, and no one else.

> It's possible that we have to work for weeks and months until we actually can truly "acquire" the blessing of *HaMotzi* – and it is impossible to shirk this *avodah* [the responsibility to do this work]...
>
> It is impossible to limit this contemplation to things which require a blessing. ...We must take time to contemplate creation, to accustom ourselves to perceiving something of His blessed loving, kindness, goodness, and wisdom, and to arouse ourselves, through this, to greater love and awe, as the Rambam wrote.
>
> And because we are speaking here of two of the "constant mitzvos" of love and awe of Hashem, it is only right to transform this practice into an integral part of our lives.
>
> (ibid., p. 298)

Emunah, then, is not something that we can take for granted. It is rather a pro-active, ongoing process of seeking out

Hashem's hand behind the phenomena of the physical world, within history, and within each of our own personal sagas.

I think of it as something like learning how to draw. My art teacher says, "I teach people to see." We think we see. Until we really begin to look. And then we realize how much more we could have been seeing.

I remember learning about dark and light – how you look at an object and you begin to take note of where the light is touching it, where its brightest area is, and where it is bathed in shadow.

At first I had to make a concentrated effort to perceive this. Then, one day, as I was coming home on the bus from Yerushalayim, I remember looking out the window at the wooded browns and greens of Harei Yehudah, and I realized I was thinking – dark, light, dark, light, dark...

I was suddenly, naturally and without effort, aware of the patterns of light and shadow. Before, I had been aware of colors, forms – trees, hillsides, sky. Now, I saw another dimension: I was conscious of light and dark, as well.

We can train our eyes to see more subtle levels in the physical world. We can also train our eyes and minds and hearts to look beyond the physical, to perceive Hashem, Creator of all life.

Beyond Seeing — A Personal Postscript

Women were gathering from all parts of the neighborhood. It was a warm, clear morning in Harei Yehudah. The mood in the bus was up-beat, anticipatory. Despite all the difficulties we were experiencing in our precious land, we could still do this, thank God. We could travel together along incredibly scenic roads through Harei Yehudah into Yerushalayim the holy city, up past the lovely neighborhoods of Ramot, into the hills overlooking all of Yerushalayim and Midbar Yehudah.

Shmuel HaNavi is truly one of the guardians of Yerushalayim. His grave site is high up on a hilltop from which one can see panoramic vistas in every direction. By the time we arrived there, I was already feeling strengthened. Simply being on the bus with other women, on our way to daven, was encouraging and empowering.

> These may believe in the power of their chariots, and these in the power of their horses, but we need only mention the name of Hashem!
>
> (*Tehillim* 20:8)

The structure over the *kever* is a citadel with a tower. And the whole theme of the area seems to be that of heights – of reaching up.

Standing there, outside the building, you are struck by the overwhelming brightness of Israeli sunlight. But in order to get to the *kever*, you leave that form of light in order to "see" in a different way. You pass through a large room with a vaulted ceiling, then through a small corridor. Finally, you descend a steep flight of stairs. Without any effort, without even realizing what is happening, you are transported to another dimension. There is no electricity there, no media, no outside world. Only ancient stone walls, the glimmering lights of the candles, and then soft darkness. I couldn't see any details, only the forms of women half enveloped in darkness, women crying, women praying. I stood by the doorway, transfixed by the scene before me, and burst into tears. It was as though all of our fears, concerns, worries, hopes, and fervent love for this land, for our people, for our precious children, could finally be, not only released, but offered as a prayer.

"Please Hashem, let us live to serve You. Please Hashem, let there be no more deaths. Let us choose life. Let our children choose life. Help us to truly live. Help us to wake up and know with our whole being the value of the every moment. Help us to know the difference between what is important and what is trivial. Please Hashem, in the merit of the great prophet who anointed David, King of Israel, send us his descendant! We need him so desperately!"

In that darkened room of shadows and candles, I felt the presence of our prayers. I felt the prayers of the holy women there, and knowing a small part of some of their individual stories and struggles, I could sense the depth of their prayers. When we left, my cheeks were wet, and a taste of redemption was in my heart.

If only we really knew. If only we really understood how close He is to us. If only we really could sense and feel that He is here, at hand, next to us, surrounding us, waiting for us to notice Him — to speak, cry out, give thanks, love...

If only we could remember that the purpose of all that transpires, of everything that we go through in this universe, is to prod us, to present us with our choice: do we choose life, goodness, and closeness to the Holy One, blessed be He, or...?

LIBBY LAZEWNIK

The Sticky-Fingered Boy

A long time ago, when the muse was upon me, I wrote a poem in which I compared Time to a "fat boy," greedily plucking the years from us like so many sugary sweets. I called him "sticky-fingered," and made it clear that I did not regard him with anything resembling warmth or affection.

At other moments, I have drawn parallels between Time and the wind that scatters the days like the brittle leaves of autumn. I have compared it to water, slipping through our fingers despite our most earnest efforts to cup and contain it; to an all-consuming fire; and to the earth, which swallows everything in the end.

Time, in other words, is the enemy. Unfortunately, it is an enemy that always wins.

I have regarded the whole setup as a personal outrage. Is it fair, my being thrust into this arena, this life, as an ill-equipped lightweight facing off against a rock-muscled champion whose lightest tap will fell me? It is an unequal match, a fight I am doomed to lose. In a vain effort to delude ourselves that we have any power at all to stay Time's hand, some of us take up photography, or videotaping, or journal-keeping, pretending that there is the remotest possibility of dominating even a splinter of Time's great and unyielding tree — of capturing so much as the fleeting breath of its passage within a picture frame or two notebook covers. But the most assiduous record-keeper will wind up with just that: records. The days themselves, and the years, are irrevocably gone. What we may be hoarding in the cedar chests of our minds is memory, not the real thing. That is lost to us forever, stolen by the fat boy with the insatiable sweet tooth. The battle was lost before it was begun: a foregone conclusion. And when the bell rings to signal the end of a round, Time will be standing in his corner, brushing off his pants and wearing his customary tired grimace. Winning can be such a bore.

Time broods darkly in the background of our lives always, but birthdays are the worst. Birthdays are Time's trophies. He lines them up on his mantelpiece, to gloat over, while we anxiously inspect the mirror for gray hairs and scratch yet another year sadly off the calendar. I remember when I turned eighteen and moaned along with my friends about how ancient we were all becoming. When my father, *z"l*, celebrated his own next birthday, I asked him if he was depressed.

He looked at me as though I had suddenly begun to converse in Chinese.

"Depressed?" asked the man who had survived the Holocaust by the skin of his teeth, and lost so very much along the way. "Depressed?" he asked, bewildered. "Depressed, about having lived another year?"

It was as though we were inhabiting different planets. He had something valuable to teach me, my dear father. Perhaps the most valuable lesson of all. But I was not ready, then, to hear it.

Nor did I become ready for many a long year afterward. Perhaps I am still unready. I still harbor an uneasy mix of feelings regarding the march of Time — a mix that tends to leave behind an aftertaste more unpleasant than otherwise. I ought, at this stage of my life, to be dignified in the face of the inevitable. I ought to regard the steady, hissing escape of the years — like steam from a boiling kettle — with equanimity at least. If I can't make Time my friend, I ought to at least be prepared to shake his sticky hand and let bygones be bygones.

And yet, I still find myself holding my breath at particular moments, imprinting their beauty, their poignancy, upon my memory as though to seal them there forever. Like an ice-storm that imprisons every blade of grass, every sparkling bush and tree and branch, in a frozen, immutable sheath of glass, I long to store the days of my own life in an unbreakable glass case and keep the key tightly in my hand forever.

But nothing can grow in an ice storm, and faces smiling out of picture frames are lifeless. It is the changes, inner and outer, that define human progress. And, much as I hate to admit it, Time is our ally here. Without Time, there can be no change.

I once considered writing a science-fiction story in which a woman with a couple of adorable babies longs to keep them that way. By some marvellous alchemy too complex to describe here, she gets her wish. Her babies will remain babies forever. She will be the quintessential mother always.

Her first reaction, naturally, is one of delight. But when the years pass with no diminution in the number of diapers to be changed, no increase in her babies' vocabularies, no sign of progress in the cute little tricks they do, she begins to wonder if the blessing she'd so desired was not really a curse in disguise. It is the knowledge of impending and inevitable change that makes each moment in our lives so exquisitely sweet. Precisely because we know we can't hold onto them, we are driven to pack the years to the maximum, like expanding duffel bags. Endlessness produces, mostly, ennui. It is the glimpse of a distant end that makes the beginning and the middle so very delicious... if we let it. As long as we insist on fighting Time, we are not letting it.

Looking back over this article, I see that I have used upwards of half a dozen different metaphors for Time. Metaphor seems to fit this tricky antagonist, too slippery to catch hold of (like the water running under that proverbial bridge). Time is unyielding as the earth itself. It is fleet as the wind. Like an inferno, it devours everything in its path. Time is a heavyweight boxer who packs a mean punch. It is an unfellable tree. It is all of these things, and a thousand things more. Time, in a word, is unconquerable.

And yet, despite this truth, Time has one very endearing characteristic. It has absolutely no objection to being harnessed.

Another metaphor to add to our list: a horse, or even a pack-mule. Time will bend a docile knee to let us mount whenever we like. Should we show an inclination to throw a saddle over its back and take up the reins, Time will let us lead him around like the most tractable farm animal. A five-year-old could do it.

The trick, I think, is to stop whining and start winning. Instead of sitting on the years like a miser on his pile of money, we can spend them instead, wisely and beautifully. And I've come to the conclusion, much to my chagrin, that the only way to do that is by joining forces with the enemy.

We must become farmhands, rolling up our sleeves and

hitching the mule to plough the field of our own lives. Each year is a furrow to be dug together with Time. The seeds we plant with his help are guaranteed to sprout, and then burst into glorious blossom — if we go out there and get the job done instead of boxing at shadows.

Because that, in the end, is all Time can be for us: a shadow (another metaphor!), it trails us everywhere, coughing discreetly over our shoulders from time to time (those gray hairs and birthdays) to remind of its presence. Like a good butler, it never intrudes. It merely serves. It is up to us, masters and mistresses of the manor, to decide the day's menus and which silverware to use for the guests.

Here he comes again, the lad with the sugar-smeared lips, greedy hand outstretched for more. He's just stolen an hour of my time... or has he? For whatever they're worth, I've got these pages to show for that hour. He, on the other hand, has got the candy he came for.

I think we can work together, this kid and me.

And in the end, I just may emerge a winner from our partnership, too. While I will not outlast Time, I can change and grow with it. I can wear those gray hairs with dignity when they come, and speak the wisdom I have gained with the years. I will relish the companions I've picked up on the journey. Though my closet be crammed with regrets and disappointments, its shelves spilling over with half-formed plans and abandoned dreams, in a larger sense I will bask in the knowledge of a job well done.

And in this way, perhaps, the years will taste even sweeter to me than they do to the sticky-fingered boy in my poem.

Travel

GERSHON GLEICH

In the Streets of Krakow

Walking down the streets of Kazimierz, formerly the center of Jewish life in Krakow, has always fascinated me. Empty streets, once so full of life... As a child, I used to wonder who were those people who had been torn so viciously from our community, the community of Krakuses, Krakauers, or simply inhabitants of Krakow, or Kroke, whatever you'd call it. They had lived their lives, children were born, marriages arranged, others died and were buried… This exceptional city has suffered an irreparable damage to its identity – the barbarians from German tribes have eradicated an important part of its history and present.

I am still walking the streets of Kazimierz. Something, however, has changed this year, and it's not only the fact that the streets have slowly begun to fill up with people – both tourists and local citizens, visiting the synagogues, the museums, frequenting the Yiddish-style restaurants and cafés, attending concerts of Klezmer bands and lectures of historians. What has really changed is hidden within me – since I've discovered the great secret which was kept hidden from me for more than thirty years, since the very moment I was born. I know now there is something more that connects me to those who tragically passed away so many years ago – in fact, I am one of the descendants of the rich and ancient culture which flourished in this country for many centuries.

I've walked a long path during the last few months, from the moment my father told me about my Jewish roots, to the discovery of my real ancestors – parents and grandparents of my late mother. The stories I was told by my mother and my grandmother have become suddenly more clear. I had asked myself many times since I was a child, why did my grandmother have to hide herself and her two daughters from the Germans in a small village near Tarnopol in the Ukraine and spend the whole fortune she could take with her on food and milk to keep them alive? I had asked myself, why had my grandfather, an esteemed pediatrician in Lwow, walked out one day when the German-Soviet war broke out and since then has never been seen again?

The first time I heard about my roots was in early May of this year. My father had been doing some business with Israeli businessmen and during a meeting, he mentioned briefly that my brother and I also have Jewish forefathers. I was astonished, and, to be honest, I thought my father was joking. I asked him and he told me that my mother was in fact Jewish and that her family changed their real name to a "polonized" one in order to stay alive during the horrible time of World War II. He didn't remember what the real name was, and after a couple of days of researching through the Internet I gave up. I slowly started to forget the whole thing.

Sometime in late June, my mother's cousin, who lives in the USA came with his family for a few weeks to spend his vacation in Poland and Europe in general. We met for dinner and after leaving the restaurant, we all decided to go to the Market Square in the center of Krakow, to sit down in one of the summer-gardens to have some beer, with ice-cream for the kids. It was a lovely, warm summer night. After a while, it popped up in my mind that my mother's cousin might know something about the revelations my father had told me earlier. Uncle Andrew seemed confused for a while but then told me the real name of his and my mother's family (my grandfather and his father were brothers) and briefly presented me with the family history. He told me about my grandfather Pawel and his father Adam, and the grandparents Filip and Helena.

After I returned from the family meeting, I immediately switched on my computer and started to search the Internet. However, the name didn't bring me much further — I didn't find any Pawel with that family name, who was a physician in Lwow before the war. There was no reference to his brother Adam either, who was a lawyer and should have been mentioned in the records.

I decided to visit the library and search for any records that referred to pre-war Lwow. I assumed that I'd find at least a phone book. In fact, I was able to locate an address book of Lwow from 1935, and soon I held it in my hands. I quickly browsed the yellowed pages of the register, then I found it — there was a match! In 1935, there were both a pediatrician and a lawyer with the same family name in Lwow; however, the first names, as I knew them, didn't match. The pediatrician's first name was Peretz and the lawyer's first name was Adolph. I was confused, so I wrote an e-mail to uncle Andrew. He confirmed that the real first names were indeed Peretz and Adolph. I was triumphant!

The coming days and weeks, I barely ate and slept, and tried to spend as much time researching as possible. Thanks to numerous genealogists around the world, I soon learnt more about my grandfather. I received an e-mail from Israel with a quotation from a book on the martyrdom of Jewish physicians in Poland. This short record gave me the year of my grandfather's birth as well as a final confirmation, which matched the stories I'd been told as a kid — my grandfather was killed by a Ukrainian band in 1941. Later I read about the history of persecutions of Jews in Lwow, and now I am quite certain that my grandfather was killed around July 1, 1941 in Lwow during the first *Aktion*, called the *Prison Aktion*, when thousands of Jewish intellectuals were murdered by the Ukrainians under the watching eyes of the German conquerors. He lived merely a few hundred meters from the prison of Brygidki, where most of the killings took place.

I received the Pages of Testimony from Yad Vashem, filled out by friends of my grandfather, and I was able to find some notes made by my mother — it seems that she started her genealogy research a long time ago, but didn't want or couldn't receive more information from her uncle and aunt. Thanks to my mother's notes, I learnt that my grandfather had more siblings. I also learned of the probable names of my great-grandparents (my mother's notes included only the Christianized first names). The database of JRI-Poland, an astonishing source of genealogical information and a searchable source of vital records, contained information about my grandfather's elder brother — I was able to order and receive a copy of his birth register, which in turn led to the discovery of my great-grandparents', Fischel and Hencia's, marriage record.

From this record, I am aware now of the first names of my great-great-grandparents: Henoch and Brajdel from Janow and Abraham and Malke from Mosciska. Although the search has become considerably harder, I am not giving up. I am looking now for their siblings, who in turn will let me find, as I hope, cousins living around the world, people whose existence I wasn't aware of. This year, for the first time, I even visited Lwow and Zolkiew, cities where my ancestors once lived and died, and walked the same streets they walked too. It was an unforgettable moment.

I am currently reading a lot about the history of Jews in Poland, their traditions, culture, and religious life. Apart from the fact that Nazi fanatics made Poland into the largest Jewish cemetery of all times, they succeeded also in one more point: to convince the Israelis and Jews around the world that contemporary Poland is a country of ashes, graves, concentration camps, and anti-Semitism, and to make both Jews and Poles forget the centuries of common history of Christians and Jews living side by side in Poland, sharing common traditions, habits, and even cuisine. I know also that according to estimates, there are tens of thousands of people like me in Poland, who don't know anything about their real identity, until somebody helps them to uncover the secrets of the past. That's also a subject I would like to devote my spare time to.

Thus, although I have been a Krakauer all my life, walking the streets of Kazimierz makes me feel even more at home.

JENNIFER HALL
Librarian of the Telshestone English Library

Nowhere Is Very Far in Israel

Nowhere is very far in Israel. Certainly Kiryat Ye'arim Telshestone is not far from Jerusalem, fourteen miles on the Jerusalem–Tel Aviv highway.

It is Chanukah. No morning *shiur* — a free morning. I decide to go to the Old City to see if the Moriah bookshop, close to the Kosel, has any books that the Telshestone English Library doesn't have.

The 8 a.m. bus to Jerusalem has not appeared. A friend rushes out of her flat to catch the bus. "It hasn't arrived," I tell her. "Perhaps I have time to make a sandwich to take to work," she gasps before running back into her flat.

Thereupon the Egged 185 to Jerusalem appears in view and slowly lumbers up the hill. I wonder if my friend will be back in time. When she doesn't appear I cross the road, look up to her first-floor flat, and call, "The bus is coming!" Will she hear? As the bus makes a swift descent down the hill she breathlessly runs across the road. "Did you hear me calling?" I ask her anxiously. After all, this situation could arise again. "My daughter heard, thank you. I was busy clearing the kitchen table."

We sit together on the bus while she discusses the subject of *shidduchim*. The conversation takes us to Geula, where I alight to catch the no. 1 bus to the Kosel. It is not long in coming.

Bus no. 1 takes a route skirting the edge of East Jerusalem. It's not often that I take this bus, and I look with interest out of the window. I see a picture of the Middle East, with the sights and sounds of the Middle East. The horses tethered to the nearest post, the Arab women dressed in their traditional garb, and a sight I never ever see in Telshestone, elderly Arab men just sitting around, or simply standing. In Telshestone the elderly men are rushing to a *shiur*, or a minyan, or a session with a *chavrusa*. No one ever, ever, just sits.

As the bus follows the line of the ancient walls of the Old City, we pass stall after stall of every item imaginable, stacked cheek by jowl on the pavement. Are there enough tourists to give all these Arabs *parnasah*? I notice the gravestones in the local cemetery placed very close to the ancient city walls. Not something that planning permission would allow in England.

As the bus approaches the entrance close to the Kosel, we return to the twenty-first century. The bus stops, the front door opens, and in comes an enormous gun followed closely by a soldier. He walks slowly along the aisle and searches the bus thoroughly before leaving by the back door, which is opened by the driver as if on cue. The bus continues its journey to the Kosel.

It's 9:05 a.m. Nowhere is very far in Israel. The Moriah bookshop doesn't open until 10 a.m. I go through the Kosel security. The metal detector doesn't realize that I have two metal and plastic hips. I make my way to the Kosel plaza. There is plenty to interest the casual observer. Say a few *tehillim* perhaps, or sit in the hot winter sun, or just contemplate the 2,000 years of history. A group of American tourists pass by. One says, "I am a Jew at heart." Is that enough? I ask myself, at the same time delighted that tourists haven't abandoned the Holy Land.

I make my way up the long flights of steps to the bookshop. There are two men sitting on the steps trying to eke out a living from selling *segulah*s for good luck to the tourists. An elderly distinguished Arab gentleman approaches me. "I have lived seventy-five years in Jerusalem..." he begins. I congratulate him and hurry on. To my delight the bookshop opens ten minutes early, and I enter with gratitude and alacrity.

With an experienced eye I peruse all the English titles. Does the shop have any books that the library does not possess and that the readers would thank me for buying? These are my criteria. I find a children's book and a small paperback Holocaust biography. As I stand at the counter to pay I hear a voice asking an assistant, "How has the book sold?" Ever alert for possible authors for this book (I did meet a distinguished author in a bookshop and he asked me if the library possessed all his books), I listen to the conversation, but he isn't the author of the book concerned, and I hurry out of the shop.

To reach the no. 38 bus back to the city center one needs to walk between tall buildings along narrow alleyways, where the channel for rainwater — and sewage in a past millennium — has existed for 2,000 years. The bus is standing, driverless, at the stop. By the time the driver arrives there are enough passengers for "standing room only." When my husband and I first visited the Kosel after we made *aliyah*, he stood at the bus stop, the consummate English Gentleman that he is, allowing passenger after passenger onto the bus first. On that occasion, as I pushed my way onto the bus, I told him that it would take him three weeks to get home if he didn't exercise his right to board.

Since on this occasion I have arrived at the bus stop before any one else, I have no hesitation in trying to be the first to exercise that right. The bus is crowded, even as we make our way to other stops. At one stop an elderly *frum* gentleman berates a young boy for not giving his seat to a *frum* lady who has just boarded. At the next stop a passenger helps a mother off the bus with her pushchair and the entire bus shouts at the driver as he attempts to close the door before the passenger boards again.

As we leave the environs of the Old City, by a different route from that of the no. 1 bus, I stare at the magnificent scenery of the hills of Jerusalem, replete with thousands of years of biblical history, grateful that I have the *zechus* to live here, grateful to the library that I am making this journey on this day.

Since nowhere is very far in Israel, it's not too many stops before I alight on Rechov King George opposite a secondhand book shop that I have yet to explore for the library. There are two sections: one packed floor to ceiling with Hebrew books, the other spilling English books onto the pavement. I ask the assistant, "Where do I start?" I know that readers will rush a book to the library Rabbi if it isn't "suitable" for the library, and I exit empty-handed.

It's now 10:55 a.m. Do I take a bus to Geula, or do I walk? The decisions one makes affect the lives of other people. Since nowhere is very far, I decide to walk. As I cross one of the small parks on Rechov King George, I hear my name. In making the decision to make *aliyah*, one leaves behind family and friends.

Here in Israel, everyone is family.

I look toward the call. One of the readers from the library is sitting on a bench next to a girl and motions to me to come and sit with them. I glance at my watch. I have plenty of time before the 185 bus leaves Geula. I walk over and she introduces me to her daughter. "She lives in America," the mother explains.

"Why do you live in America?" I ask her. She gives me the usual answers. She will come eventually, when she gets married, but not now.

I tell her the story of how we bought our portion in Eretz Yisrael. Our daughter in Jerusalem was due to give birth at the same time as our daughter in Paris. We decided to make the round trip, spending the first half of Pesach that year in Jerusalem, and the second half in Paris. Since our son was also living in Jerusalem, having no intention of leaving, I told my husband that I can't be a Granny living in England. We were taken to Telshestone. No one can find it on their own, nestled as it is in the hills of Judea. On the spur of the moment, we bought a house in Telshestone that has the most magnificent view of those hills.

How do people make plans for years? We then had to sell our house in England. Upon our return, via Paris and our second granddaughter in five days, my husband went to see the Manchester *rosh yeshivah*, who was taking a post-Pesach vacation in our hometown. My husband told the *rosh yeshivah* that we had to sell our home in England urgently, because we had to pay for the house in Telshestone. He told the *rosh yeshivah* that there is negative equity in England and the economic situation there is so bad that houses are not selling.

The *rosh yeshivah* — to whom, it is said, the keys to *berachos* were given after the passing of the Steipler — gave my husband a *berachah* to sell our house in England quickly.

I notice that at this point the daughter has lost interest in the story, maybe because I am not saying anything she wants to hear. But her mother is sitting on the edge of the bench. "What happened next?" she asked.

Five days later my husband telephoned the *rosh yeshivah,* who had meanwhile returned to Manchester, to tell him that the house had been sold. The *rosh yeshivah* asked, "Is property selling in your area?"

I tell the daughter that no time is the right time to make *aliyah,* but if you take the first step then Hashem will take the next. The mother kisses me as she thanks me profusely for telling the story. The daughter is less enthusiastic.

I continue on my way and arrive at the bus stop in Geula shortly before the bus. The journey home is swift and uneventful. As I stand at the door of the bus waiting to alight at my stop in Telshestone, a passenger starts a conversation. He is starting a boys' choir and wants the choir to raise money for the library.

Israel. It's the only place for Jews to live. It's 12:15. In just over four hours I have been back in time 2,000 years and returned home.

Nowhere is very far in Israel.

RACHEL GREENBLATT

Israel, the Place They Call Home

The concept of being a stranger in your own land is an unusual one, particular to this generation of Jews who have been privileged to see the rebuilding of the Land of Israel in their lifetime 2,000 years of exile.

Deciding to visit for the first time, the so-called "secular" Jew can find it somewhat like growing up with a family you thought was your own, only to discover in later life that actually your real home and family live elsewhere and it's time to go home. Initially you think you'll just take a chance, out of curiosity, and see exactly who it is you really belong to. But you make it quite clear to yourself and to those around you that you'll be back soon.

In the beginning everything is strange — the people, the dress, the language — and you feel like a complete alien, waiting to leave. You stay close to places with others like yourself, the beach, the hotels, and the restaurants

If you are lucky to be here in early December, you might be moved to see menorahs blazing into the night atop every large building. Most probably, you will put this down to nothing more than an old custom. Your tour guide mentions something about the victory of the Maccabees over the Greeks. Unfortunately, he neatly ignores the powerful message behind the Chanukah celebration, and he omits to mention the miracle of the oil for the holy lamp which had been defiled during the tragic destruction of the Temple. The victory of the few against the many, the weak against the strong, and the pure against the impure, are only a part of the miraculous chain of events so deftly swept under the carpet in the hoopla of an impressive military victory.

Or, if your visit comes about during the festival of Sukkos, you might find yourself fascinated by the plethora of small wooden huts hanging from every balcony and waiting around each corner. You will notice Orthodox adults and children scurrying in and out, and you will be told that these structures are a reminder of the Jews' wanderings in the desert thousands of years ago. "Interesting," you mumble, anxious to get on to more exiting things. The tour guide probably does not mention that the Jewish people, a nation of 600,000 adult male souls, in addition to old men, women, children, and animals, were miraculously saved through forty years of journeying in a desert true to its name – deserted and barren.

Maybe years later, on your second visit, you begin to tour around. People tell you this is the "land of your fathers." You didn't realize you had all those ancestors, or that they were relevant to you at all. Your guide takes you to see the "sights" – stone buildings, ancient fortresses, old *mikvahs* (whatever they are!), towns whose history dates back to biblical times. The strangest feelings waft over you. "Is this really mine?" you ask yourself. The people are so different, the environment almost hostile, and yet...

Later still, you are taken to places that speak of more recent history. Of wars where young Jewish soldiers gave their lives for the Jewish land; of heroism in the face of great danger; of bravery against marauding Arabs; of uncaring British soldiers; of immigrants fresh from the concentration camps.

Before you know it, you are crying. But you will not be deterred. You are, after all, from a different world. You know you're Jewish, but not this kind of Jewish. You are a one-day-a-year Jew, and that's how you're going to stay. Your home is elsewhere, your job, your family, your life — your lack of religion.

You even visit the Western Wall. Watching the crowds who gather here in search of their Creator, you marvel. Before you know it, you too find a scrap of paper and scribble a message. "Please God," you write... It is a private wish — who knows, if there really is a God who hears, maybe He'll listen to my prayer too. You are painfully aware of your distance from Him and from many of the swaying bodies in this wide open plaza. You relate better to the girls who are awkwardly covering their hair with their cardigans or borrowed scarves in an effort to show respect to the place. Yes, this is all very quaint. But enough's enough.

But your trip has not ended yet. Your guide shows you newer places, memorials from bus bombings, gravestones of murdered youngsters, and you are greatly moved.

Then again, this has little to do with you, and you reason away your growing emotionalism with justifiable excuses. Every country has its stories and its struggles.

But there is one place that you visit on your trip which will stay with you forever. It is Yad Vashem, the Holocaust Memorial Museum. The bus drops you off at the beginning of a long tree-lined boulevard. It is eerily silent, and you are uncertain which way to walk. "Put one foot forward and move," you tell yourself. But it is a long, long walk. You didn't bring water with you and you're getting tired. In the stillness, with only the birds to keep you company, you suddenly feel you are traversing a path your great-grandparents might have taken... Aching feet, destination unknown. The German officer screaming unintelligible commands from the back. You stumble, and get up. You wonder what happened to your parents, your brothers and sisters, the Rabbi... Suddenly, you reach a clearing and you see a squat grey building. You walk into the dark cold building bracing yourself for what you might find in there.

The gaunt faces stare back at you. Jewish faces, any one of which might have been members of your own family — who knows? Jewish mothers, Jewish children, Jewish babies... You see the vicious laughing faces of the German Gestapo. You almost hear the click of their boots, the barks of their dogs, and you are cold with terror. Your feet take you around the inside of this place of awful memories and you are stunned. "Six Million," it says. All gone.

You cannot fathom it. How did it happen? Why did it happen? The questions remain.

In a large dark hall, you suddenly join up with the other people who also walked around here alone. The stone floor is scattered with engraved words. It is dark and you cannot make out the names. With difficulty you read "Maidenek," "Auschwitz," "Buchenwald" — names of infamous concentration camps.

The Cantor raises his voice in quivering prayer. In the loud silence he chants *"Ani ma'amin."*

"I believe"... This is the answer!

The Jew believes. He believes that there is a reason for everything; he knows there is reward and punishment in this world and the next. He knows that he doesn't see the whole picture. He knows that a Jew is above reason, and his relationship with his Creator is more vital and more is expected of him. Most of all, he knows now that a Jew is always called to account for his actions. Yes — he sees that each Jew is responsible for his actions, and for those of his community. With time and study, he might come to see that no Jew is alone in this world. He can run to the ends of the earth, he can reject the religion of his forefathers, he can even embrace another religion. He can worship other gods — gods of Music, of Money, of Information, of Science. But when he dies he dies a Jew. He is remembered as a Jew, he is buried as a Jew. And if he should by chance forget, the nations of the world will never cease to remind him...

You stumble out into the bright sunshine. It is all so surreal. Could this really be possible? Even seconds later, in the light of day, you are inclined to want to reason this all away. But this will never go away, never...

It is a different you who goes back. The sights and smells of the Jewish land travel with you. You have truly been home. Suddenly the people you grew up with seem strangely distant and lacking real understanding. All that was once familiar, now feels odd. You are quite tempted to stay there, but you simply cannot, for you have found your true home and you cannot wait to get back...and be embraced in the warmth of truth.

NOACH HALTRECHT

Color Coding for the Kohanim?

No visit to the Holy Land of Eretz Yisrael is complete without a visit to the Kosel. Morning, noon, and night, there is a special and often unfathomable emotion from the first sighting, which increases as one approaches the Wall itself. For those of us fortunate to be "locals," the easy feeling of familiarity on a visit is offset by the knowledge that we are sharing historical moments of the Jewish people over many centuries.

The present-day "concourse" is a modern construction. In the time of the British Mandate (1917–1948) the Kosel area looked very different. Access was restricted and there was no seating. The Palestine Wailing Wall Order in Council (from Buckingham Palace, no less!) dated May 19, 1931, stated:

> The temporarily enacted prohibitions against the bringing to the Wall of benches, carpets or matting, chairs, curtain,

> and screens, etc., and the driving of animals at certain hours along the Pavement are to be made absolute... No benches, chairs, or stools shall be brought to or placed on the Pavement before the Wailing Wall. No screen or curtain shall be placed on the Wall or on the Pavement for the purpose of separating men and women or for any other purpose.

Over the generations the panorama at the Kosel has altered and it has been the scene of dramatic events recorded in a multitude of history books.

Throughout our exile, we have mourned the loss of our Beis HaMikdash, our Holy Temple. We yearn for the coming of the time when we shall have our Third Temple. So rightfully we visit the Kosel whenever an opportunity presents itself or whenever we need to feel close to Hashem, and hope our *tefillos* will be heard in *Shamayim*.

The Kosel attracts all sorts of visitors who gather on the concourse for their own private reason. Black hats and long coats mingle with those who collect a cardboard head covering as they approach the Wall, today known as the holiest spot in the world for the Jewish people. Tourists from many countries listen spellbound to the tales of the Kosel related to them by their guides. The Kosel has influenced us in so many ways, some positive and immediate, some slow but certain, increasing our awareness of the true concept of the Beis HaMikdash.

No one who has ever been to the Kosel for *Birchas HaKohanim*, the Priestly Blessings, can remain untouched by an emotion that stirs the deepest feelings inside a Jewish *neshamah*. If we take our imagination back in time and visualize the tremendous hustle and bustle of activity constantly taking place inside the Beis HaMikdash, we can bring alive our daily *tefillos* in which we highlight the *korbanos* – offered daily, weekly, monthly, and for the *yamim tovim*, through the *kohanim*. If we stand by the Kosel and close our eyes we can almost hear the bleating of sheep and goats, the noise of cows, and the twitter of doves and pigeons.

If we squeeze our eyes shut even tighter, we can smell the odor of the offerings from the *mizbe'ach* and the fragrance of the *ketores* sweetening the pure air of Yerushalayim. We can visualize the *kohanim* scurrying about, under pressure, performing their tasks. Their service in the Beis HaMikdash was exact and detailed, with time factors and the right mental approach. The results would bring forgiveness or otherwise effect the outcome of the sacrifice for the individual and for the community.

Is it possible to bring alive in our imagination the flood of activity on the eve of Pesach, when everyone brought their Pesach offering and their *chagigah*, too, when appropriate. The *kohanim* had to "process" literally thousands of animals as *korbanos* in a short time, ready for the Seder night eating.

There were so many things all happening at once and the possibility of error was always present. The chance existed of mixing up essential features of one sacrifice with those of another sacrifice. During one *Daf Hayomi* shiur on *Zevachim* it was suggested that maybe the vessels utilized could have been color coded to minimize the risk! Furthermore, the hazards of a side of meat flying off the *mizbe'ach* (the meat would have been hardened in the fire and thrown off by the effect of the combustion) seemed a valid reason for a *kohen* to claim "danger money," or at the very least to have an Industrial Injuries Insurance Policy as part of the terms of his employment! Maybe "protective hard hats" could be color coordinated with the color-coded vessels!

The conscientious *kohen* is described as *zariz*, meaning

"quick." He had access to lots of meat to eat! Furthermore, he could bring in the seasoning of his choice to make it even more palatable. Even so, digestive problems were also an occupational hazard. He had a heavy work schedule during the time his "watch" was on duty.

Can one really imagine all this, standing beside the Kosel with eyes tightly shut? Can one fully internalize the real Beis HaMikdash? "Virtual reality" should allow us to do this with ease!

A walk through the tunnels beneath the existing concourse reveals another dimension to the splendor and miracles contained within the Temple boundaries. The sign directing us in mind, emotion, and hope towards the *Kodshei Kodashim,* the Holy of Holies, surely leaves us inspired and elated. The bricks and the pavements become alive, and our ears hear the sounds, and our mind opens to the enormity of the loss we have sustained.

The garments of the *kohanim* and of the *kohen gadol* worn during the *avodah* affect atonement for certain sins in combination with repentance by those guilty of the sins. The tunic atones for bloodshed, the trousers for immorality, the turban for those who are arrogant, and the belt for improper thoughts of the heart. The *efod* atones for miscarriage of justice, the *me'il* atones for sins of *lashon hara,* and the *tzitz,* the golden head plate worn by the *kohen gadol,* for brazenness.

In *Tehillim* 84:2, David HaMelech says, "How beloved are your dwelling places, Hashem of Legions." The Gemara in *Menachos* teaches us that anyone connected with the construction of the beloved dwelling place of Hashem is also called beloved. Avraham, the founder of our nation, is called beloved. The Children of Israel are called beloved. The Temple was mainly built on the territory of Binyamin, who is called beloved. Shlomo HaMelech, who built the Beis HaMikdash, was named the beloved of Hashem because Hashem loved him. What's more, the atmosphere of the Beis HaMikdash fostered a feeling of love and fellowship among the Jewish people. Even if there was strife, when they entered the Beis HaMikdash, they were united by a spirit of peace and brotherhood.

Our "virtual" reality is now ready to become "actual" reality. Whilst we keep alive the wonders of the activities within the Beis HaMikdash by means of our daily recitation of the passages of *korbanos,* we also say, "let our lips compensate for the bulls," and we ask Hashem to find the prayers of our lips acceptable and favorable, just as if we had brought the continual offering at its set time and had stood at its station.

The Talmud (*Sotah* 8b) says that Hashem deals with man measure for measure. The priest's blessing in *Bemidbar* (6:25), "The Lord shall make His face shine upon you," is granted to those who "shine their faces" upon their fellowmen.

"Good morning!" Greeting people properly is an act of *chesed* that is guaranteed to rebound back to us. The Mishnah advises us to "greet every man with a pleasant expression" (*Avos* 1:5), to "receive everyone cheerfully" (ibid. 3:16), and to "take the initiative in greeting any person you meet" (ibid. 4:20). Very often, just a cheery, sincere "good morning" can brighten up the day of a person who feels dejected. When we greet people with a friendly smile, we show that we care about them and that we're happy to see them.

Avos DeRabbi Nasan (13:4) states that if you give a person charity with a sad or sour expression on your face, it is as if you gave him nothing. Conversely, if you just greet your friend with a smile, even if you physically gave him nothing, it is as if you gave him all the beautiful presents, physical blessings, and assistance in the world.

"Here I am about to accept upon myself the positive mitzvah of 'Love your neighbor as yourself,' " is our own "good morning" to ourselves! By verbalizing this great rule, perhaps we can go a long way towards replacing the *korbanos* with actual reality in our lives. As we scurry here and there, much like our *kohanim* on duty performing the *avodah*, our own actions will become even more rewarding, meaningful, and acceptable in the eyes of Hashem and our fellowman.

This will become our *shirayim*, "leftovers," for the sixty or seventy years of our lives, after our visit to the Kosel!

SARAH SHAPIRO

When Grown-Ups Are Helpless

One of the standard hallmarks of childhood is a sense of powerlessness, both in relation to one's family and to the world at large. To be a small person surrounded by giants is an experience all humans share – one which we fully expect to escape one day by turning into adults.

But when, eventually, we do find ourselves disguised as those odd-looking creatures called grown-ups, we discover that "being in control" remains, in fact, a pleasure rarely to be savored. Adulthood offers endless opportunities to feel as helpless as a child.

Thanks to Arab terrorism, life in Israel has never been less than unstintingly generous in this respect. If it's existential truths you're after – insights into the transient nature of our sojourn on the planet and the unpredictability of the universe –

then get on an Egged bus to downtown Jerusalem. Walking along the sidewalk, your mind will of itself be attuned keenly not only to each and every passerby (alert to the possibility that the pregnant woman coming your way in her chador may be large not with child but with an explosive belt, and that the Israeli soldier with a *kippah* on his head may not be an Israeli soldier with a *kippah* on his head) but exquisitely attuned, as well, to the gloriously soft breeze upon your face. That's how it works. The profound emotional recognition that you are unceasingly, helplessly vulnerable to the world around you heightens not only your anxiety but all your other senses, too. The capacity for joy is deepened and broadened — a capacity for pleasure in all things large and small. The sky is bluer than blue. Little girls jumping rope — a sudden vision, sometimes, of unearthly loveliness. Simple kindnesses in the course of normal interactions between strangers can be invested with extraordinary poignancy. A Friday night meal in your home, with Shabbos candles flickering and the people you love safely around your table, can induce such a mighty celebration of the heart as to rival the roaring of a happy crowd.

Since human helplessness is obviously one of the main things that life is designed to teach us, one way or another, before we slide off the mortal coil, then getting a crash course such as this can only be to our ultimate advantage. Although we who are fortunate enough to live here cannot claim a corner on the world market when it comes to suffering — the most cursory reading of any daily newspaper will remind us of tornados in Tennessee, earthquakes in Iran, ongoing brutality against civilians in Sierra Leone, a daughter who disappears in Washington, DC, a daughter kidnapped in Utah — we can indeed boast of being star pupils with front-row seats when it comes to learning about the limits of human power. We're being forcibly indoctrinated.

And since as individuals we'd have to absorb the knowledge of our weakness sooner or later, no matter where we were living, it is a great privilege to get the message in a uniquely meaningful fashion, in this setting, under these circumstances, all together as a people. We watch ourselves up on center stage, as prophesied history unfolds.

♦ ♦ ♦

In a taxi on the way downtown an hour ago, the 4 p.m. news reported that a warning is out in America that terrorists might be planning an attack on nuclear facilities.

"What was that?" I asked the driver sharply from the backseat. Suspiciousness has become second nature. In a most unwelcome fashion, this bulletin had managed in an instant to unearth that ancient childhood sense of being utterly, maddeningly at the mercy of strangers toying dangerously with my world.

The driver, an Ethiopian in his early twenties, said, "Oh, it's America, *geveret*. Nothing here. Don't worry."

"Don't worry? How can I not worry? My relatives are in America! And that would start a whole new era, and besides, any nuclear radiation over there will get here, too! Don't you know that?"

"Here?" His eyes met mine in his rear-view mirror. He seemed skeptical.

"Yes! Of course, here! Radiation goes everywhere!"

"We are in God's hands, *geveret*."

I'm in the quiet upstairs atrium of a café on Ben Yehuda

Street, the pedestrian mall in the center of town where many suicide bombers have detonated themselves over the years, where so many, many Jews have lost their eyes, their hearing, their faces, their hands, their feet, their children, their parents, their friends, their health, their peace of mind.

We thank You for our souls that are entrusted to You.

An hour ago when I emerged from the taxi, it was a toss-up. Should I come here, to my favorite café, or to the other one, with security guards at the entrance? *...in Whose hand is the spirit of every human being.* Given the situation not only on this street but in the world, I'm glad to have opted for the greater pleasure. From this small cozy corner table that I favor, I glance down watchfully from time to time at the door.

Two ambulances flash by, shrill sirens screaming, and instantly, in an admirable demonstration of Jewish unity, all the coffee-drinkers stiffen, alert. Did something happen? *In Your hand are the souls of the living and the dead.*

Will there be more sirens? *Into Your hand I entrust my spirit.*

We wait.

YAEL SUROFSKY

A Mother's Plea

Only one drop
of water to ease
his parched throat,
she prayed,
to quench the scorching thirst
that ravaged his body
in a desert of fire.
And God heard, Yishmael,
He heard the cries of the youth
as he was, now.

He knew even then
that one drop
would not quench
nor rivers of blood flowing
would ever quench
the terrible thirst;

not blood of men
nor women,
not blood of grandmothers
nor mothers,
not blood of children
nor babies.
Has this earth witnessed before
blood-soaked sheets
on a little girl's bed?
And blood-drenched strollers strewn
from Jerusalem to Petach Tikva?
From the city of the dawning of Peace,
to the city of the blossoming of Hope,
Peace lies mutilated and dying,
Hope draws her final, rasping breath
on the roads of Megiddo.

And as she prayed,
she turned away,
not to see the death of the boy,
whose cherished laughter was heard
as he frolicked, bow and arrow drawn,
and aimed at Yitzchak,
his hawk eyes zeroed in
on prey.
Tell me, did she not delight
when he focused his gun sights
in cold-calculated swift motions
on Shalhevet's stroller,
targeting her fragile body
in the cross-hairs

to snuff out with ruthless cruelty
her small, gay flame?
Did she not watch
with morbid interest and glee
scorched body parts scattered
on every hill and valley
of the land.

Yishmael, your thirst
is not a thirst for water
Hagar, your compassion
not a compassion of mercy.
Our Father, when will You hear
our voice, lifted to the Heavens,
and have compassion
on Your nation,
for our thirst
is not a thirst for water
nor our hunger, for bread
but only to hear — *lishmoa* — once more,
Your words.

MALKA KAGANOFF

Yerushalayim

And what city do you live in?" asked the voice on the telephone. "Yerushalayim," I replied, and as I did, the enormity of my words hit me. I was born a New Yorker, and was at times a Baltimorean and a Buffalonian. But now I am a Yerushalmi. I still find it hard to believe that Yerushalayim, the golden city, the holy city, is indeed my home. For thousands of years Jews dreamed of Yerushalayim, longing for a glimpse of the skyline. And now, God, in His great kindness, has opened the doors of His chosen city and allowed us back. No longer do Jews merely face east and daven from distant lands; they can stand at the Kosel itself and daven in close proximity to the site of the Beis HaMikdash, may it be rebuilt speedily in our days.

Alas, we are painfully aware that we have not yet merited to live in Rebuilt Yerushalayim. We have not yet reached the days of Mashiach and the fulfillment of the prophecies of all nations streaming to Yerushalayim to pay homage to Hashem, the King of the entire world. There are clear signs that we are still in *galus*, even in our precious Yerushalayim. But if we merit it, we can enjoy the blessing of the psalmist (*Tehillim* 128:5) and observe the goodness of Yerushalayim. If we open our eyes, we see that Yerushalayim shines. In *Tehillim* (48:3), we read of Yerushalayim as "*yefeh nof, mesos kol ha'aretz*" – beautiful in its scenic view, and the joy of the whole world." Indeed, the Gemara tells us that ten measures of beauty descended to the world, and Yerushalayim acquired nine of them.

Gazing out at the surrounding mountains, one is reminded daily of the Divine protection that the mountains symbolize (*Tehillim* 125:2). We on the east side of the city can begin our day with a view of the sun rising from behind these mountains. Later in the day, our friends on the west side of the city are treated to spectacular displays of color as the sun recedes beyond the far mountains. And at points in between, Jerusalemites savor the beauty of the skyline, in varying shades of Jerusalem stone.

Surpassing the physical beauty of the city is an ethereal, spiritual beauty that one can perceive. One can feel the approaching Shabbos as the stores close and residents young and old scurry to prepare for Shabbos. The excitement of preparing for *yom tov*, or the solemness of Yom Kippur, permeates the air as Yerushalayim moves to the pulse of the Jewish year and its special days.

Shortly after we had moved to Israel, I asked my daughter, who was six years old at the time, whether she was happy about our move. When she answered in the affirmative, I asked her what made her prefer life in Yerushalayim. With the innocence and purity of a child, she replied, "This is the place where Hashem wants us to live, and the parashah seems so much more real because it happened here." With that short statement, she succeeded in crystallizing our attachment to Yerushalayim, the home of our heritage, and the Palace of our King.

A short tour through the Old City of Jerusalem resembles a history lesson. As we look around, we see remnents of the Second Temple era, even of the First Temple, alongside evidence of the Old Yishuv of the last century and of the struggles to reclaim undivided Yerushalayim. Standing at the Kosel, I imagine Rav Yosef Chaim Sonnenfeld might arrive soon, as he was wont to do a century ago. Or perhaps the Ohr HaChaim, a resident of over 250 years ago, or the Ramban of 750 years ago. Standing in the Kosel tunnels, it is hard to believe that I am standing on a sidewalk that my ancestors traversed over 2,000 years ago. Yet for all its history, Yerushalayim is a very current city, a city where thousands upon thousands live their lives as Jews. It is also a future oriented city, waiting to be reelevated to its place as the true pride of its people.

What is it about Yerushalayim that draws me to it? It is difficult to delineate, but I think that it is the Jewishness of the city. There is no need to apologize for being Jewish, for doing mitzvos. A few short vignettes will clarify what I mean.

- One afternoon I found myself at the counter in the post office, writing a check. "What is the date?" I asked the clerk. "Is it August 24?"

  "It is *heh* Elul," the clerk answered with a mild tone of rebuke. Implicit in his voice was the assertion that we do not have to march to the tune of the secular world. We have a different calendar, and it behooves us to date our checks accordingly.

- I searched the Yellow Pages for a notary and picked one practically at random. The address listed was not far from my home, in a neighborhood that is not predominantly religious.

  "Is the lawyer in?" I inquired.

"He will be home after 1:30, *im yirtze Hashem*," was the reply I received.

Later in the day I spoke to the lawyer himself to set up an appointment. "Come any time in the afternoon," he encouraged, "except for davening time." In Yerushalayim, lawyers live with the help of Hashem, and make sure their clients know that they will be attended to after davening.

- I found myself in a store that had been the site of a terrorist bomb several days earlier. A saleswoman in an adjacent store entered and greeted the man who was waiting on me. He diverted his attention to this saleswoman, who was not, upon appearances, religious.

  "Did you *bench gomel*?" she queried, and I understood that the man had been injured by the bomb and this was his first day back.

  "You know me," was the reply. "I am not a religious man, I am a Yom Kippur Jew."

  "What does 'religious' have to do with this?" was the emphatic reply. "God saved you and you have to thank Him."

- "Good day," said my husband to the driver as he entered the taxi.

  "It will be a better day when Mashiach comes," was the automatic reply from the bare-headed driver.

  "Yet another profound taxi driver," I commented when my husband recounted this story. Like the shepherds of yesteryear, today's taxi drivers have ample time to think as they cruise. And if you are lucky, they will treat you to some food for thought as you ride.

  In the right corner of a taxi window, you will find a sign with the name of the taxi company. This information is important, since people like to know which company assumes responsibility for the driver. My eye has caught unusual signs in the windshield of taxis: "Shomer Shabbos" proclaims one taxi in big letters. Yet another taxi has a different sign, "*Shivisi Hashem l'negdi tamid* — I place Hashem before me constantly" (*Tehillim* 16:8). Now we know what responsibilities the drivers assume.

- I was unsure how to fill in the form in front of me. What was I to enter in the the slot that asked me to list my husband's profession? The receptionist saw my hesitation and wanted to help. I tried to explain to her that my husband did not have a job at the moment. He was involved in talmudic research and writing. "Ah, *avrech*," she declared knowingly, as if being a *kollel* fellow was the most common occupation in town.

- A decorated copy of the Shlah's *berachah* for educating children arrived in the mail. Being an American I was quite used to this sort of mail — a *sefer* or religious object sent by a Jewish organization, complete with an envelope. But when I examined the gift more closely, I realized that it was just that — a gift, with no envelope attached, wishing me a good year, from the phone company. The secular phone company is encouraging me to pray for my children. Actually, I should not be too surprised. The society here values children as our greatest natural resource. A woman who has many children is not viewed as saddled with children. She is called *beruchot yeladim*, blessed with children.

- *Tehillim* seems to be the most popular book in the city. Bus travelers spend their time reciting *tehillim*. Groups meet at all hours of the day to complete the whole *sefer Tehillim* together. There was even an ad campaign decorating the buses, "*Omrim tehillim b'ad haneshamah*." Say *tehillim* for your soul.

- "Are the grapes good today?" I asked Eli, my greengrocer.

  "Make a *berachah*," he said, "and taste some."

  Eli is concerned that the grapes are good for my soul as well as my tastebuds. A nut stand in the market has a sign encouraging the consumers to say "*lichvod Shabbos Kodesh* – for the sake of the Holy Shabbos" before they eat the foods that they purchase.

- As an experienced mom, I thought I was well informed about the procedure for birthday parties for little girls. Imagine my surprise when I discovered an added ingredient in a birthday party in Jerusalem kindergartens. Each of the friends of the birthday girls is encouraged to get up and present the little girl with a blessing.

  If they begin in kindergarten, imagine how proficient in blessing others they will become when they are adults.

Since my move to Yerushalayim I have met countless wonderful people. They go out of their way to be helpful, run to classes, and have good priorities. They outdo each other thinking of new ways to create *gemach*s, free loan centers. One can borrow sheets, suitcases, challos, books, medical equipment, and so on. I often wonder whether Yerushalayim attracts wonderful people or whether the air of Yerushalayim makes them so wonderful. And then I wonder if it matters which option is true.

What is of significance is that Yerushalayim is a vibrant city of Torah and *chesed*. May we merit to see the fulfillment of the prayer, that the Builder of Yerushalayim rebuild it speedily in our days as an everlasting city of peace.

ILANA STEIN

One Fine Day in the African Veld

The kosher safari is a relatively new concept in the world of tourism, and educational ones even more so. I joined three other observant game rangers to form African Safari Experience, where taking tourists from all over the world to Africa — and inspiring them with spectacular views of Hashem's creations — is the aim of the game.

It was 4:30 a.m. when I awoke, and my first thought was "No civilized person should be up at this time!" But as I stepped outside into the cool air I realized I was wrong — this is exactly the time to be up. The sky was fading from inky-black to Israeli-blue, Venus hung low on the horizon, and the birds were singing with all the verve of professional sopranos. Finally, and with a sense of awe, I heard it: the morning greeting of the lion. Midway between a roar and a grunt, a drawn-out groan that began deep in his gut, the sound reverberated on the still air. Like the best ventriloquist, though, it was impossible to hear the direction from which the sound emanated.

Pity, because we were hoping to catch sight of a lion today. We had been in the Kruger National Park in South Africa for a couple of days now and had seen some wonderful creatures, from elephants to buffalos, but the sighting that many people consider the ultimate thrill — the lion — had so far eluded us. Mind you, I found the sight of a honey badger — which is strictly nocturnal and almost never seen — to be quite as thrilling, but I understood the pull of the King of Beasts as much as any visitor fresh from England.

There was no time to imagine where the lion was. It was time to get everyone up and out of their chalets despite the hour. In fact, because of it. In the bush, the best time to see animals on the move is early in the morning and late in the afternoon, and so we change our human rhythms to match those of the wilderness. A Scops owl prrrt-ed nearby and crickets still chirped as eight yawning Londoners emerged into the predawn light and made their way to the waiting jeep. Here our two game rangers, Raymond and Tapelo, met us, wide smiles on their dark faces and rifles in their arms.

It was still too early for breakfast, and since we hadn't davened we decided just to have some fruit and coffee before we left. Usually, breakfast (and in fact all meals on safari) is a serious affair, with cereal, bagels and butter, fruit, coffee, tea, and even croissants! Considering that the nearest kosher bakery is 370 miles away, this is no mean feat. So, every two days fresh food arrives at camp all the way from Johannesburg — meat for the barbecue, bread rolls, delicious muffins and buns, fish and salads. My favorite sight is Friday night dinner, when our visitors finish an inspiring shul service under the African stars to find a lavish table, laid with white Shabbos tablecloths, and groaning under fresh challos, wine, and a three-course meal! Who says you need to rough it on Shabbos in the veld?

However, back to our bushwalk. As we drove to a spot some twenty kilometers away from the camp — and hence from any civilized structure such as a building to run into or a fence to hide behind — the light changed to a pearly-pink, but if anything, it got colder. The wind whipped through us like airy ice cubes as we drove down an empty road to the start of our walk.

We had explained to the rangers that we needed time to pray before beginning our trek (we also explained this wasn't because we feared for our lives, but that it was something we did every day). So we spent half an hour simultaneously soaking up the early morning sun and trying to turn the pages of our siddurim with benumbed fingers. But the sunlight slanting through the waving, golden grass and squinting through the branches of the acacia thorn trees warmed us, and never have I read "Who creates light and makes darkness" with more understanding or *kavanah*.

Finally, lacing up our hiking boots, checking our water bottles, single file, one ranger in front and one behind, we stepped intrepidly onto a game path and left our city-selves behind.

To walk in the bush is no ordinary experience. For one thing, you're on the animals' territory now; there is nothing — and I mean nothing, no metal, no jeep door, no cage — between you and any creature you meet. You need to obey the rules of nature, not the other way around. Then there's the exhilaration of walking free in a place almost unchanged since Hashem made it. The sky was a deep blue, brown-headed parrots flitted from one bush to another, and the smell of the rich, red African earth rose up to meet us. Imagine no sound of traffic, no roar of engines. Nothing but the whispering of a gentle breeze through the grass and trees and the cry of a lone bird in the distance.

One problem with walking is that the animals aren't used to

humans on foot. Ironically, they are habituated to the noise of vehicles in the park and many are not all that disturbed even when you drive up to them, but the sound of humans stomping along, snapping twigs and crunching grass underfoot, makes most species a little nervous. So there was no telling what we'd see today. The diehards will tell you that with the bush it is "pure luck" – meaning that there are no hard and fast rules as to where an animal will be. Of course, as *frum* diehards, we knew full well that there's no such thing as luck, but rather whatever Hashem has decided that we should see, we would see.

So far, it had been a wonderful walk. We'd caught sight of a giraffe moving off, lumbering in its beige and brown pyjama skin, long neck bobbing ponderously above the trees. A knocking sound in a nearby leadwood tree turned out to be a woodpecker, enthusiastically trying to find dinner inside the trunk. Raymond showed us how a shallow pan of water is formed, just from buffalo and rhino deciding to have a roll in the mud. Once they've moved on, other animals can come and drink the water – muddy but vital in parched Africa. To see the small details of nature this close makes one realize that everything fits into the most perfect of Divine plans: the type of soil is exactly right for the species of grass to grow, which is just nutritious enough for the zebra, buffalo, and antelope to graze on. These animals are perfectly adapted to their environment, with enough young born so that the species as a whole survives its predators. There's a tremendous sense of the greater picture, of the world of nature working perfectly just as Hashem designed it, down to the last raindrop falling on dry soil.

Then, as we walked along a muddy path, Raymond put up his hand to signal us to stop. There in front of him were the markings of lion, paw prints the size of soup-plates, and something had been dragged. We waited, surrounded by thick bush and grass that towered over us, while he went to check it out. He returned to tell us, with a slight tremor in his voice, that there was a male lion, lying up with an antelope he had killed (the dragging marks were from the prey being hauled across the path earlier that morning).

Um, he asked, did we want to see the lion? Raymond warned us that lions with kills tend to be a touch aggressive and apt to charge anyone in the vicinity. Did we still want to see it? Um, okay, we said (indemnity forms flashing through our minds). So, as quietly as we could, we crept forward toward a low hillock on which the King was lying. As we got closer, we heard another sound over that of our hearts hammering: a continuous, deep, rolling growl that seemed to shake the ground itself. Finally, we saw him: an enormous male, golden-brown with a black mane. His eyes burned yellow, and his tail with its black tuft twitched angrily as he glared at us. On the ground in front of him lay his prey — an impala — and he had not yet begun feeding. At this point he got to his feet, the growl becoming even louder, and, deciding that discretion was the better part of valor, we backed off in a hurry.

For the remainder of the walk, we all moved in a dreamlike state, dazed at our encounter. We stopped in a dry, sandy riverbed to drink much-needed water and share a packet of biscuits, where we relived the experience over and over.

On the way back, we stopped to watch a herd of zebra and impala as they moved through the long golden grass, grazing quietly. The striped faces and large black eyes stared at us, large ears twitched this way and that, and tails swished back and forth, then they moved away. We stared back, contemplating life and death, cycles of life, and Hashem's Divine plan in the bushveld.

RABBI SHAUL DOV FELMAN

A Jew Does Not Get Lost!

While glimpsing through the writings of HaGaon HaTzaddik Rav Shalom Shwadron, *zt"l*, my attention was caught by a discussion on the *pasuk* in *Parashas Vayeira* (21:14), which states that Hagar got lost in the desert of Be'er Sheva. Rashi comments that this teaches us that she returned to the practice of idolatry. Rav Shalom asks the obvious question: How could Rashi possibly determine, from the mere fact that Hagar lost her way, that she went back to idolatry?

Rav Shalom attempts to shed light on this particular Rashi with the aid of a story. It seems that there was once a certain Reb Mordechai Progemansky who was traveling to a distant city together with a companion who was a *shochet* and a *mohel*. They intended to arrive at their destination before Shabbos, which they planned to spend together. To their misfortune, they became deeply involved in conversation and missed their stop. When they realized their predicament, the *shochet* voiced tremendous frustration. "We are lost! What will we do for Shabbos?"

Reb Mordechai comforted him and told him not to worry. "There is no such thing as a Jew being lost! Everything will be fine. Hashem's hand conducts the world and there must be a good reason that this happened."

As it was nearly Shabbos, they proceeded to disembark from the train at the very next station. They got off at a town whose name they did not recognize. There were absolutely no Jews in sight. When they asked as to whether or not there were any Jews residing in the town, they were directed to the house of the sole Jew that lived there.

They were taken aback to see the startled look on the face of the Jew that opened the door, then he burst into tears. They wondered why their arrival had prompted such a reaction. The Jew related to them how his wife had bore him a baby boy one week ago on the previous Shabbos. There were no other Jews in the city, and he was not able to arrange a *bris milah* for the eighth day. He spent the entire week davening and crying to *HaKadosh baruch Hu* to enable him to perform this precious mitzvah. Seeing these two Jews arriving literally out of nowhere, he felt sure that somehow they would be able to help him with his dilemma. When he heard that, indeed, one of the gentlemen was a *mohel*, he was overcome with joy that Hashem had granted him the opportunity to perform this great mitzvah in its time. Reb Mordechai turned to his friend and said, "I told you that there is no such thing as a Jew being lost!"

Rav Shalom, *zt"l*, explains that this was Rashi's proof that Hagar had returned to the idolatry of her father. A Jew does not get lost! If Hagar was indeed lost, it must be that she had returned to the ways of her father and had severed her Jewish ties.

♦ ♦ ♦

I myself am a *mohel,* and I've seen something similar to Rav Shalom's story several times in my own experience. On various occasions I have accompanied *bachurim* on the Nesivos Tours' visits to Eastern Europe. It dawned on me that since the area we intended to visit was a spiritual desert as far as Judaism is concerned, maybe there would be someone that could use my services. Several months in advance of one of our planned trips, we advised our connection in Warsaw, the director of the Lauder Foundation who is responsible for promoting Jewish activity there, that a member of our staff is a *mohel.*

To our great surprise we were immediately informed that our contact's wife was expecting their first child on Shushan Purim, approximately two weeks before our expected arrival. A few weeks before our departure, we were notified by our travel agent that because of certain technicalities we had to depart a day earlier. This happened to be a Tuesday. We then received word that the expectant mother had actually delivered on Tuesday, one week before our arrival. This meant that our group would arrive just in time for the *bris.* But there was more to it. The new mother had attended Lamaze classes where she had met another Jewish woman. Through their encounters the other woman became interested in having a *bris* performed on her own son, even though her husband was a gentile! Guess what? She gave birth that very same Tuesday, and the *bris* of her son was scheduled for the following Tuesday as well.

With a a busy day ahead of me, I took an earlier flight, arriving in time to perform the *bris* of the second child that morning in their home. Later in the afternoon, with much fanfare, the *bris* of our friends from the Lauder Foundation was performed in the Nozyk Shul in Warsaw. No one could remember when the last *bris* had taken place. It was truly an event which attracted much attention. It seemed that anyone that had anything to do with Judaism in Warsaw was there, including the Israeli Ambassador to Poland. We merited two opportunities to perform the great mitzvah of *bris milah* in Poland — of all places. What *hashgachah pratis.*

The next year I traveled to Poland once again. We notified our contact of our impending arrival, but there did not seem to be any need for a *mohel* on this occasion. Nevertheless, I took my equipment with me. After all, you never know! Actually, in Krakow a Jewish man came over to me and begged me to perform a circumcision on his son. I refused due to the fact that the mother was not Jewish. As the visit continued it seemed that I had brought the equipment for nothing.

A day before our departure from Poland, we were informed by the travel agent that our flight was overbooked and there was no way to send us back directly to Eretz Yisrael. We would have to go to Budapest for a day, from where we would be able to catch a flight the following evening. It sounded great. A free trip to Budapest! What a bargain! However, it was a few days before Pesach. My wife was at home expecting our tenth child, taking care of the other children, and preparing for Pesach alone. How would I tell her I'd be away for another day? Perhaps I could promise her a new recipe for Hungarian goulash? However, there wasn't much that I could do about it, and off to Budapest we went.

I can't say that it was the most thrilling experience: a statue here and a lake over there. As lunchtime approached. I went to speak to the practicing rabbi to find out about the *hechsher* of the restaurant where we were to dine. He was quite helpful, and I asked him if he would be kind enough to come and tell our group about the Hungarian Jewish community, the largest in Eastern Europe. In the midst of the discussion, I asked, "What do you do about *mohalim* here?" He told me it was truly a problem. Indeed the head of the Neolog (Reform) community had contacted him about a family member who needed a *bris* tomorrow!

My jaw dropped. The *bachurim* from my group promptly informed the rabbi that I was a *mohel*, and he asked me if I would be willing to stay the extra day. He promised to take care of any ticketing and accommodation expenses. How would I face my wife? On the other hand, how could I turn him down? Arrangements were made, and a few boys stayed on with me to see this special event. Imagine: The whole group had been sent to Budapest without really understanding why. Hashem, though, knew the answer very well. There was a little boy that needed a *bris*, and he was destined to have it done properly on the eighth day.

Indeed, a Jew does not get lost!

DR. MEIR WIKLER

A Unique Travelers' Insurance

"What's that red light flashing on the dashboard?"

"Oh, that's just the temperature light," I answer with false reassurance. "But I think I'd better pull off the highway for a minute, anyway."

Steam billows from the hood. Quickly, off onto the shoulder. Grab the kids from the car. Open the hood. Steam coming from everywhere.

"I think we're going to be here for a while." The steam dies down. The culprit is found. A leak in the water hose.

"What does that mean?"

"It means we either have to walk five miles in this heat back to the last gas station or walk who knows how far ahead. But even once we get to a gas station, we'll never find a mechanic on duty on a Sunday!"

"Funny how we just finished saying *Tefillas HaDerech* (Traveler's Prayer)."

"Well, I suppose this could have happened ten miles away from that gas station, too."

We sit down to contemplate alternatives and ruminate over what we should have or could have done differently.

"Do you think anyone will stop to help us?"

"Would we stop for anyone? Nowadays everyone is so scared of strangers that they don't even pause to consider stopping."

"We would stop if we saw frum people in trouble."

"Yes. I suppose we would."

"Look! Someone's stopping to help us!"

It practically goes without saying that the two *yeshivah bachurim* who stopped thoroughly examined the difficulty. They agreed that a mechanic was needed and offered to push the car along the highway to the nearest exit. It is also probably no surprise that they continued to push us through many side streets looking for an open gas station and finally succeeded only in finding an open body shop. There we got some tape for the hose and water for the radiator.

"How far do you think I'll be able to get like this?" I asked, trying to hide my apprehensions.

"Don't worry, we'll drive behind you until you get to a mechanic."

About ten miles later, I pulled into an open gas station with a mechanic on duty.

"I don't know how to thank you both!"

"Forget it," one of the *bachurim* said, looking away with embarrassment. Although the setting sun and cloud of smoke were missing, they drove away before we could find out anything about them. All in all, they gave us about two hours of their time and saved us more than twice as much time, a good deal of money, and immeasurable *agmas nefesh* (anguish). In some ways their generosity was incredible. In other ways, it was almost expected.

"You know," I said once we were safely back on the highway, "we religious Jews belong to a pretty exclusive club. We have members all over the world, in every major city. Most members wear an easily recognizable uniform and can be spotted even from a speeding car.

"Of course, if you happen to be traveling through an area in which club members are not favorably received by the local residents, wearing the uniform can be a disadvantage. I, for one, have received entirely unsolicited verbal and, at times, physical abuse from the more uninhibited nonmembers. It was obvious that I was the target of this abuse for no other reason than my having worn the club uniform.

"In spite of these liabilities, wearing the uniform provides club members with numerous advantages, such as a unique form of travelers' insurance. If your car breaks down or if you have any other kind of travel problem, for that matter, just stand in clear view and do not hide your distress. If you are wearing the club uniform, the first club member who passes will offer you advice, directions, or assistance of food, lodging, and at times even monetary loans. Although I'm not in the insurance business, I don't imagine you could ever buy that kind of worldwide travelers' insurance coverage. We're really very fortunate to be members."

"Meir, look, I think I saw frum people in that car we just passed. Maybe we should stop and try to help them."

"*Shalom aleichem*."

"*Aleichem shalom*."

"What seems to be the trouble?"

"I think the radiator overheated."

"Funny, the same thing happened to me a few hours ago. This weather has been overheating a lot of cars today. Wait until your radiator cools off. I'll give you some water and we'll see if that gets you going..."

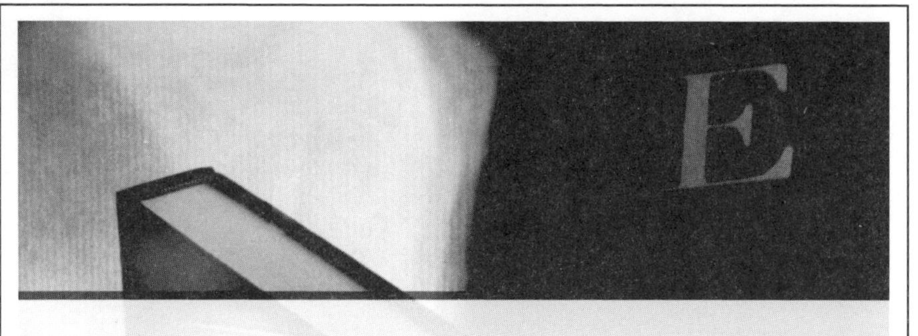

The Jewish Family

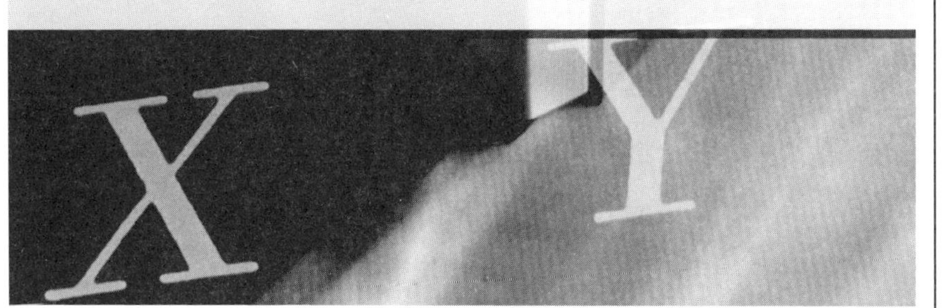

REBBETZIN TZIPORAH HELLER

Wanting to Want

Guilt has one major advantage: it's free. One of parents' most guilt-provoking and uncomfortable moments is hearing that the example we set (i.e., who we are) will affect our children's lives forever. Of course it doesn't end there. God willing, our children will have children who in turn will have children. We don't know how far-reaching our imperfections will be.

The Nesivos Shalom left us many gifts. My personal favorite is his book on *chinuch,* called *Nesivos Chinuch.* Don't be deceived by its brevity. Its contents should be transformational. He offers us tools that allow us to face reality with hope and optimism rather than with denial or guilt. The comfort he offers those of us who are imperfect is that we can still "want to want."

Our children see us with emotional lucidity that we have long since lost. They see the authenticity of our desire to move beyond our current limitations as vividly as they see the limitations themselves.

The Maharal (in *Nesiv HaTznius*) tells us that of all the traits that compose our character, the one that is most "hereditary" is our relationship to *tznius*. It is there that we choose to define ourselves spiritually, rather than superficially. Sometimes we are imperfect; the profound authenticity and integration of *tznius* in us may never reach that of Shaul, Esther or Rachel, who are presented in the Talmud as exemplifying this virtue. Yet we do have the ability to "want to want" this level of integration. Our children will observe this and the effect upon them can be profound.

It is far more difficult to achieve true integration with this virtue, because we can't help being affected by living in a society in which *tznius* is perceived as a drawback. One aspect of *tznius* that is difficult for many people to integrate internally is hair covering. There are far more women today who cover their hair than there were as recently as fifty years ago. Yet deep emotional and spiritual integration is sometimes another issue entirely.

The girls I face in Neve Yerhushalyim's beginners program have never known anyone who covered her hair for religious reasons. They have been groomed for moral independence. Autonomy is a value that they absorbed through the kind of education that stresses individuality more than morality.

It is for this very reason that the basic assumptions underlying the laws of modesty are consistently appealing to them. The young women, especially those who have been to university or begun their careers, have seen the consequences of surrendering their choice of personal style to faceless others. Women pay an appalling price for yielding, time and time again, to whatever image the media projects as being "cool." In many cases they're sick of paying the price; they no longer want to hate who and what they are.

Self-esteem and dignity are closely entwined, and human

beings experience an enormous thirst for both. Thus, the laws of modesty – while they may at first appear somewhat extreme to those who are looking from the outside – sell themselves. Yet the issue of hair covering is still hard to accept. We live in a society in which "no one" covers her hair.

Psychologists tell us that our sense of normalcy is pretty well frozen somewhere between the ages of three and seven. Hair covering is, therefore, unlikely to feel "normal" to women who never saw it practiced until they found themselves in Yerushalayim.

What is hair-covering all about? Why do we treat it with such bizarre ambiguity?

The *Mishnah Berurah* presents the laws of hair covering with an interesting addition. It quotes the *Zohar* in *Parashas Naso*, which gives us a deeper perspective on what is actually taking place, not only on the surface, but within the soul of the woman who covers her hair. Perhaps in the interest of brevity, the Chafetz Chaim quotes only the heart of the message. Let us look at both this and the context in which it is presented.

The discourse begins with a citation from Rabbi Chizkiya. He questions the meaning of the famous quote from Tehillim, which describes the goodness of the life of a God-fearing man: "Your wife is like a fruitful vine in the corners of your house." In what way is the comparison apt? In what sense is a woman like a vine?

He answers by pointing out that it is impossible to graft a grape with any other fruit and get a new fruit (grapelope? granana?). The Jewish woman is fruitful, particularly in terms of her own essential human blossoming – her desire for self-expression in the deepest and most self-definitive sense – within the walls of her home. Her self-definition must not be externalized through blossoming in the "marketplace."

The Chafetz Chaim here touches a raw nerve. The conflict between work and home is more real in our times than ever before. The problem is not only technical; the difficulty of fitting a thirty-hour day into twenty-four hours is a genuine cause of stress.

Yet there is another cause of internal stress that is often swept under the carpet. The workplace provides many women with a sense of adequacy, social bonding, and validation — the "blossoming" for which we all yearn — in a way that is intoxicating and addictive. However, its address is the marketplace and not the home, and a woman who grows in the setting of the marketplace and not the home has lost her inner self, for this setting is ultimately an external, relatively shallow, impermanent (and often commercial) one. What she loses, to return to the words of the *Zohar*, is a covenant, a bond that is eternal.

Which home is more impoverished than one in which eternal bonding is trivial? What message does this give to children? How are they affected by this message? The message that they receive is, of course, that they are not important enough to be the mother's real focus.

Children are far more advanced than we are when it comes to emotional intelligence. They know where they fit into the scheme of things. Does their mother really value the need to bond with them? Is it to them that she shows her best self? Or are the children mere inconveniences and obstacles on the course she is running? And if they are not important to her, can they possibly feel important in their own eyes? Will they believe in themselves enough to commit themselves to goals that have eternal value?

Rav Chizkiya says that they won't. The self-esteem that is the foundation of their ambitions will be undernourished. How many children and adolescents do we encounter who are ravenous for meaning and approval? In the society in which we live, children far too often see the picture as it is: they are not important, and may never be important.

This is not what we want, neither for ourselves nor for our families.

Rav Chizkiya tells us how the opposite behavior affects a mother and her family. When she presents her deepest self to her family, she blossoms. Her children are compared to olive trees. Unlike other fruit trees, olive trees don't shed their leaves or become brown in the winter; they are always fresh and green. This symbolizes that ultimately they are fully aware of who they are. They are eternal; regardless of what the rest of the world tells them about themselves, they will always know that they have value. The self-esteem that this produces is the greatest blessing a mother can give her children.

We want eternity, and to this end we make trade-offs constantly when our lifestyle is in direct conflict with societal values. We eat kosher, we pay tuition, and we dress modestly. We are, nonetheless, affected by the subtle messages that we breathe in the air. Not only are we involved with work, we have also bought into the fantasy that real accomplishment must be visible and receive compensation, and that it is more fun to bond with adults than it is to bond with kids. We can take more and give less.

When we cover our hair the message that we give others and ourselves is different. We don't offer our deepest capacity to bond to the marketplace. Our identity is bonded only with that of our husbands. We must rethink not what we do, but how we do it. We can rise above superficiality in the realm of *tznius*, as in other areas. We can cover our hair with the pride and dignity that the mitzvah deserves. We can begin to do this by wanting to want.

Reprinted with permission from *Hamodia* English newspaper.

SARAH CHANA RADCLIFFE

Why Modern Parenting Fails

Modern parenting fails. It fails at producing caring, giving, self-sacrificing human beings — the kind of human beings the world depends upon for working on great causes and moving us forward. Hard work, duty, and obligation — these words do not exist in the modern vocabulary. Indeed, they represent the antithesis of current values, which stress fun, self-fulfillment, and instant gratification. Today's children know how to get what they want. What they don't know is how to give others what they need.

And it is our fault. We have misled them. From the time they were infants, we worked hard to give them everything, to gratify their every need and wish. Past toddlerhood, when the first stirrings of independent striving occur, we did for them and did some more. Into the school years, and into the teen years, our only concern was to make them happy and provide them with every opportunity, gift, and service that would enable them to flourish and prosper. Not that it was so wrong for us to give in this way. What was wrong was that we did not, in our process of diligent giving, teach them to give back, nor even to show gratitude!

The result: the "Me" generation, or in *heimish* circles, the "*es kumt mir*" generation. This is a generation of children who feel that they are entitled to every good thing. When denied, their self-righteous anger knows no bounds. As young adults they are still demanding of their parents, "You owe me. Your money is mine. Buy me... Give me..." Where did children ever learn that the world exists for them? From their parents. We taught them this by our endless giving, never asking for anything in return, never teaching them that, in fact, it is *us* who is owed and not them.

Yes, children owe their parents. They owe them gratitude for bringing them into this world, for providing for them, taking care of them, educating them, and raising them to adulthood. They owe them honor and respect for being their teachers and leaders, their spiritual, emotional, and physical protectors, defenders, and guides. They owe them service in return for all the service that was provided. And, if children can't recognize that they do, in fact, owe all of this to their parents — and more — then how will they recognize the good that *anyone* does for them — even Hashem? How will they develop the feelings of wanting to give in return?

Indeed, instead of wanting to do for their children what their parents did for them, children like these are more likely to see their own offspring as impediments to their freedom and enjoyment of life! People who have been taught only to take and never to give find it difficult and cumbersome to give, to give up, and to put themselves out.

Are these the children who will gladly bring their aging parents into their homes to return the caring and giving they once received? No. These children know little about serving Hashem with *mesiras nefesh* – putting their own interests aside. These children can barely bring themselves to be civil to their in-laws if they don't "like" them! These children, used to having it all their way, cannot extend themselves beyond their comfort zones. Lacking all sense of responsibility or obligation, they do what feels good to them and nothing else. To "suffer" by having to act pleasantly can be too much for them. What have we done?

What can we do? Parenting must take a new direction. An old direction, really. Parenting must once again take on the shape and form of Torah. Torah parenting demands that a child learn, from his earliest years, to give. The commandment to honor our parents is laden with responsibilities of the child toward the parent. Hashem, knowing the loving heart he instilled within parents, does not command us to do for our children. He knows that we can't help ourselves – we will do everything we can do. However, in His wisdom, Hashem knows that children do not automatically feel the desire to do for others, not even their parents. This must be trained and instilled in them. Therefore He commands children to do for their parents. This mitzvah, this obligation, benefits only the child; through giving, the child comes to feel the sort of love for his parents that his parents feel naturally toward him. Love is generated by the very act of giving (Rabbi Dessler in *Strive for Truth*). It is up to parents to see to it that children learn to fulfill this mitzvah.

If we will teach our children to accept responsibilities toward us they will learn that the world is not "a free ride." We must repay those who do good for us. Indeed, "the wicked one borrows and does not repay" (*Avos* 2:14). We must fulfill our own missions by putting out, rather than taking in. We are to be givers, rather than takers — we are to produce, not passively receive. In this way, we become dynamic achievers, people who can offer the world something, rather than demand their due from it.

Parents need a new (old) map in parenting in order to achieve the goal of raising children capable of such giving. We have been told enough how to raise our children's self-esteem — so much, in fact, that all our children have is *self*-esteem. Now we must teach them how to have esteem for others by thinking about the feelings, needs, and wishes of others and striving to fulfill them. We must raise them with the yoke of giving, of taking responsibility, so that this will be the only way for them to live. As soon as the child can talk he must learn to say "thank you." As soon as he can walk, he must learn to bring his parents what they need. We cannot wait until the child is a teenager to begin to make demands upon him, for then it is far too late. He has already learned by that time that we are there to serve him, and not the other way around. No, we parents must start these lessons early and persevere throughout the parenting process.

Can it be done? Can we really raise children in today's world who will be comfortable with fulfilling their duties to man and Hashem? Yes. However, we must support each other. Books, articles, parenting courses — all must move away from the philosophy of endless giving and begin to address the need of the parent to *teach* giving in accordance with Torah values. Then, with Hashem's help, we will raise a new generation of children faithful to the values of their forefathers and ready to change today's world.

SHOSHANA SCHWARTZ

Reflections

The baby was crawling around on the floor. It was Pesach time, and the baby's mother was sweeping up yet another pile of smashed matzo crumbs and little balls of chocolate brownie cake. The cake was particularly moist, as Pesach cakes tend to be, and did not permit itself to be swept up with ease. As the mother swept, little dust bunnies formed on the end of the broom. She finally managed to make a pile, of sorts, in the middle of the kitchen. She reached into the broom closet for the dustpan. In the split second it took to open the door of the broom closet, the baby moved, making a beeline toward the pile.

"No!" the mother screeched. "Not the pile! It took me ten minutes to sweep that stuff together. Can't you go find some toys or something to play with?"

The baby, not liking his mother's tone of voice, began to fuss.

I stood nearby, taking in this scene. And I began to comment to myself. "Why should he go find a toy? Can't she see that that dirt pile is by far the most interesting thing in the kitchen at this time?"

"Shoo," the mother said. "Go play."

The baby didn't move.

"She's being very hard on that poor little baby," I commented wordlessly. "He's just a year old, and he doesn't understand what she wants from him, not at all. She just keeps using this harsh tone of voice and a barely hidden scowl."

The baby spotted a piece of onionskin, which had somehow escaped the broom. Temporarily distracted, he moved away from the dirt pile, and his mother quickly scooped it up.

I softened. This mother has surely had a hard day. The baby had decided to shorten his nap by some hour-and-a-half, occupying much of the time she had planned to make both lunch and supper. And her reaction is just a knee-jerk reaction. When she was a little girl, *chinuch banim* was not a hot topic. People treated their kids more or less the way they felt like it — not because they didn't care, but because that was the way things were done then. No child-raising books, no "how-to" seminars, no dial-a-parenting lectures. People did what they thought was right, even if they did, at times, miss the boat. So this woman is just falling back on tried-and-true parenting techniques, namely, winging it. Judge her favorably. Right now she is falling back on the non-techniques she learned growing up.

And then the thought struck me. Maybe I should say something to her? Maybe I should point out what she's doing?

My stomach did a flip-flop. Me? Who am I to say something to her? Okay, once upon a time, when she had only one kid, the two of you used to be close. You used to make the time to talk to each other and really get down to the serious issues. You'd talk about self-improvement and the direction you'd like to take in life. You'd talk about keeping strong in difficult times. And yes, you'd talk a lot about raising children. But that was long ago. She's been so busy lately, this mother of five, she barely has time to tie her own shoes!

You've seen how over the past few years she's made less and less time for you. No, I don't take it personally. It's not just me, it's all her friends, even her husband. She just became so wrapped up in her kids, and trying to keep entropy at bay, that she just hasn't made time for you, or any form of serious discussion or introspection. And no, I can't say I blame her. But since we haven't had a really good *shmeuss* in so long, well, I'm not sure I'm going to be able to get anywhere by talking to her. She won't even notice. She'll probably go do the laundry in the middle or something.

But I began to feel guilty. If I don't say something, so who will?

So I gathered my courage and thought of a plan. I thought, I'll catch her at a good time, like when the kids are off to school and the baby is napping. I'll start small. I won't remind her that she used to read parenting books, and go to *shiurim,* and be very careful how she spoke to her kids and all that. No, I don't want her to feel guilty. I'll just tell her that I think it's important to make time for me, her old friend. That's it! Then, once she agrees, I can, here and there, instill some good solid values back into her life. I can remind her about the things she used to do to get herself moving, out of a rut. I'll remind her about the time she kept her cool when her oldest broke her grandmother's heirloom vase, and the time she said nothing when the same child turned off the air conditioner on Shabbos in the middle of a heat wave. I have lots and lots of nice stories like that.

Once she makes the time for me, once I can get a foot in the door, then I know I can start to talk to her about the things that really matter. Her *hashkafos* are in the right place, she just, well, got distracted. So it's up to me to help her remember.

Oh, wait, here's a good chance! She just put the kids to bed, and her husband is out with a *chavrusa*. Quick, before she goes to sleep. Right...now!

As I passed the mirror, I caught myself, and looked myself in the eye, and I said, "Hello, stranger. Remember me?"

RACHEL GREENBLATT

Give Thanks

Give thanks,
though the fledglings' demands seem incessant, and their shrill chirps threaten to ruffle your feathers for the thousandth time.

Give thanks,
though the chattering and squabbling never seem to end, and the nest is so crowded and unkempt that at times the very straw and fabric seem to be coming apart.

Give thanks,
as they take their first cautious steps, and test their wingspan against your better knowledge, and then take flight, and soar so high and swift that you gasp for breath.

Give thanks,

while you wait their return, by day, by night – and wait, and wonder until...from afar you hear their familiar sound, and your chest swells with pride.

Give thanks,

for who knows what time may bring, when the fledglings finally leave the nest forever and the sounds of their songs are but echoes on the wind, and their piercing cries will have turned into distant calls.

Give thanks,

for who can know what the winds of change might bring that blow around the warm and cozy nest which now vibrates with life and love.

Give thanks,

for the silence would surely be worse.

JENNIFER HALL

No Tefillah Is in Vain –A Granny's Viewpoint

"You don't have to daven for him anymore."

I was stunned. I couldn't speak. I had been so optimistic. What exactly did my daughter mean? I was too frightened to ask.

"Will you phone people and tell them?" I heard her say.

I wondered what I would tell our friends all over the world. Friends who had spent the whole of one week storming the gates of Heaven. I would have to choose my words carefully. They would have to be words that would convey just how we, as a family, were facing this reality.

"Chizkiyahu has accomplished his mission in life," I told them. Every one, without exception, understood.

A good friend gently asked my daughter, "What good has come out of this?"

* Written after the *petirah* of her one-week-old grandson, Chizkiyahu ben Shoshana Ruth

Tehillim groups formed community and worldwide. In Ramot, Telshstone, Johannesburg, Vienna, Paris, Australia. The whole family was enveloped in the *achdus* (unity) of caring communities.

The women of Ramot took care of my daughter's children. Members of N'shei Telshestone offered to make me meals. One friend drove me to the hospital twice. The first time to enable me to see the baby (I never got another chance) and the second to take my granddaughter Esther Leah to see her mother. This *chesed* was my friend's personal *gemach* in memory of a child she lost similarly twenty-two years earlier.

A friend in London donated the book *A Living Torah* in Chizkiyahu's name, another gave *tzedakah*. Friends in Manchester said they would try to daven at the *kever* (gravesite) of the late Manchester *rosh yeshivah*, Rav Yehuda Zev Segal. Local friends went to daven in Hevron at the *Ma'arat HaMachpeilah*, the burial place of the Patriarchs. Yet others went to the Kosel.

What good has come out of this?

We have had the opportunity to experience that sometimes the answer is "no." We have to understand that sometimes one must accept the unacceptable. We have to find the strength and the courage to cope with this situation, not only within the family, but also in our relationship with other people. We have been privileged to receive the enormous outpouring of *chesed* in our respective communities.

Now we understand that it is in tragedy, as well as in *simchah*, that a community gathers together, bringing *tefillah* to the world for those who need their prayers.

Esther Leah never saw the baby, but in the manner of a four year old, was happy to draw him a picture. "This is for our baby," she declared.

"Which baby?" her mother asked (after all Shaina Brocha at age two was no longer a baby).

"Chizkiyahu," she replied, simply.

"When are you going to give it to him? Because he is in *Shamayim.*"

"When Mashiach comes," replied Esther Leah without looking up.

What good has come out of this?

My daughter has opened a crib *gemach* named "Chasdei Chizkiyahu" lending cribs for newborn babies in Ramot. We have all grown from the experience.

We will never know what Chizkiyahu's mission in life was, but the family accepts that he was a gift, to be in our possession for only one short week.

During the *shalom zachor,* my son-in-law noticed that the candle that was lit for Chizkiyahu burnt brightest — then it went out before the others.

Chizkiyahu lived. He was, and still is, part of our family.

Post Script:

My daughter was expecting again. During the entire pregnancy she couldn't get the name out of her head.

Nechoma. Nechoma Lieba.

Convinced that she was carrying a boy — she was equally convinced that it wasn't a name she would be using.

Nechoma Lieba was born on Tuesday. She was named on Thursday.

On Shabbos morning I went to my usual Shabbos morning *shiur*. The *shiurim* were on the Haftaros of the seven weeks of comfort — the *zayin de'nechemta.*

This particular Shabbos the rabbi would be giving the *shiur* he should have given the Shabbos before, which was postponed due to his ill health.

At 9:30 a.m. the rabbi strode punctually and swiftly into the room and sat down.

"Ladies," he began, "I am going to tell you the meaning of the word *nechamah.*

"Ladies, listen carefully.

"The word *nechamah* does not mean comfort.

"The word *nechamah* means:

" 'Hashem, please replace my loss.' "

BAYLA GIMMEL

On Marriages and Picket Fences

When we lived in the States, my children had a delightful picture book about an endearing pair of grandparents who decided to sell their house.

This older couple had gone to visit friends who lived in a pretty, colorful cottage with white shutters, a picket fence, and a lovely garden. It was when they returned to their own rather drab house that they made the decision to put their home on the market and move to an attractive cottage similar to that of their friends.

The first prospective buyer rejected the house because of its dull color. In his enthusiasm to sell the house, the old man immediately got to work and painted the outside walls a cheerful color. The next people who came along said, no, they were only interested in a house with shutters. The old man added those.

Again and again, people looked at the house and voiced their complaints. In response, the old man put up a picket fence, planted rose bushes, and spruced up the interior.

Finally, the house was beautiful. At that point, the old woman said, "Now we can sell our house and move to one that has..." and went on to reel off all of the features of their friends' cottage, which of course their present abode now had.

The old man pointed out this seemingly obvious fact, and, as in all storybooks, they lived happily ever after in their newly renovated house.

Years ago, divorce was very rare in the Jewish world. Unfortunately, this is no longer the case.

I know quite a few people who are divorced. Among them are several who have remarried. Most of the time, when I meet the new spouse, I have a feeling of déjà vu. In so many of these cases, the new wife or husband is very similar to the old one.

I can't help but think of the story of the old couple and their house. If only the first spouse had changed in some minor way, (s)he would look or act or be exactly like the replacement.

If you ask any *bachur* who is in *shidduchim* what he is looking for, he will tell you that he wants a kind girl with good *middos* who will be devoted to him and raise their children in the Torah *derech*. Every seminary or post-seminary girl will tell you she wants a husband who will learn Torah, be a responsible person, and care for her and their children.

Of course, just as one attractive house has a tile roof and another has a nice shade tree, there will be small details about the prospective *shidduchim* that may differ. Some are looking for a person who wants to live in the city where they grew up and others want to move to Eretz Yisrael. Some want a partner with job skills. A boy may request a girl who is on the thin side or one with a particular coloring. A girl may say that she has always admired *bachurim* who have learned at a certain yeshivah.

Things are narrowed down, a good *shidduch* is suggested, everyone is checked out, and both sides agree.

The couple meet, date a few times, and become engaged. What follows, often in rapid succession, are a splendid *chasanah*, a cute new apartment, some delightful babies, and a bunch of responsibilities for both husband and wife.

In the early stages of marriage, everything is whizzing by so quickly that the newlyweds don't really get to know each other. During *shanah rishonah*, they do spend every evening together, but more often than not, she is on the phone with her girlfriends or busy writing thank-you letters for the *chasanah* gifts, while he is copying his notes or preparing tomorrow's *blatt*.

Every Friday, they pack up a little suitcase, roll it out to the bus stop, and go off to be Shabbos guests.

As soon as the first child arrives, baby takes center stage with all of the wonderful "firsts." Around the time the firstborn is showing off her walking skills, along comes a new brother or sister, and then more of the same.

Then comes the inevitable day when Totty rushes home to grab a quick supper before running off to meet his night *seder chavrusa*. He finds the apartment a total mess, nothing edible in the fridge or on the stove — let alone on the table — a whining three-year-old refusing to go to bed, a two-year-old throwing a temper fit on the floor, and a cranky baby draped over the arm of his exhausted wife.

This is the moment of truth. Does he comfort his wife and run down to the market for a dozen eggs and a loaf of bread, or does he start yelling that he is supposed to be at night *seder* in half an hour? Does his wife apologize for the unexpected turn of events, or does she berate him, screaming back that he never helps in the house?

It is inevitable that there will be days in a marriage where things just don't go well. However, it is not inevitable that the partners blame each other or that they hurl insults at each other. Even if only one of them can keep a cool head and refuse to be pulled into a fight, then things can be salvaged. It is when minor irritations provoke hurtful words, and then retorts, and then round after round of escalation, that marriages end up turning sour.

If things continue in a downward spiral and the bad days start to outnumber the good ones, divorce may look like the only way out. However, in most cases, that is not the best solution.

The old man in the story kept improving his house with the intention that he was going to sell it and buy one that was better. Either partner in a shaky marriage can make some important self-improvements. He can cool his temper. She can get organized. He can help more. She can show appreciation. At any point, they can turn their marriage into the one they really want.

There is only one other detail that is necessary. In the story, it is obvious that the improved old house is just great and that the little old man and the little old woman do not have to sell it in order to live in the house of their dreams. However, on the last page, just before "the end," the little old man has to reveal this great insight to his spouse!

Once a marriage becomes shaky and there has been talk of divorce, even after husband, wife, or both have made maximum effort to put things right, it still may be necessary for outsiders to convince one or both that improvements have been made and that they are married to the partner of their dreams.

Then, hopefully, all will go well, both partners will be willing and able to continue the marriage, and they will solidify the relationship. A true *bayis ne'eman b'Yisrael* will be built — with or without shutters, picket fence, and rose garden — and the story will end "happily ever after."

YITTI BISK

Dialing the Sunshine

The shame. The thought of her mother's immaculate home. She and her three siblings were always well nourished and taken care of.

Whenever her mother called she tried to sound happy. "Everything is great, Ma. Yes, the baby is feeling fine. Well, gotta go. I have a ton of things to do in town today." Yeah, sure – town. What a joke. The last time she got on a bus to go to the doctor's office in town, she began to feel claustrophobic. All those people, packed together like sardines. Panic rose in her chest. She couldn't breath. She got off at the next stop and walked home. She never did see the doctor.

She couldn't tell anyone but sometimes she felt she might be going crazy. Often she had repetitive and frightening thoughts. She slept fitfully between the nighttime feeding schedule, her

* A compilation of NITZA case histories has been utilized to create this story.

mind filled with a strange foreboding... She'd even stooped to keeping her husband home with lame excuses about not feeling up to the day. In truth, she didn't want to be alone.

Yesterday she thought she'd loose her mind altogether if that baby cried one more time. Oh, that crying! It grated on her nerves. Made her feel jumpy and agitated. She hated it when he cried. She hated him when he cried. She had even contemplated hurting him. But she was tired, you know. She couldn't fall back to sleep when the baby woke up at night, and then, when she finally dozed off, that baby's shrill screams would wake her up again, demanding attention. How could a mother hate her own baby? She fantasized that they had given her the wrong baby at the hospital. Crazy. She must be crazy.

She recalled those days after the baby had been born. The labor had gone reasonably well. Her baby was thankfully whole and healthy. Everyone wished her congratulations. They showered her with gifts. They told her what an adorable little boy she has. How he looks just like his father...his father, he was so happy with her, with the baby. His son. He took over the household chores: cooking, cleaning, shopping. He even made her breakfast for the first week. He jumped out of bed in the middle of the night at the mere whimper, to pick up his newborn. He sang to him as he changed his diaper and powdered him, savoring the few moments of precious nurturing before handing him over to his mother to suckle.

So tired. Yesterday her husband ran out of clean socks. She didn't even listen when he mentioned it to her, ever so hesitantly. She didn't really care. "You learn how to use the washing machine," she had replied tensely. Can't he see how tired I am? She barely changed her robe lately. Why bother? They'd have Cornflakes for supper...again. Those meals brought in by well-meaning neighbors were now a memory. Before the baby was born she had cooked, baked and packaged dozens of carefully labeled meals and stored them neatly in the freezer. Now, they were all gone.

What's wrong with me? she asked herself. Abigail next door seems so put together. We gave birth the same week, for goodness sake! Why is she having guests for Shabbos while I can't even get off the couch?

The guilt. The fear of being found out. She had even contemplated ending it all — who needed her anyway?

This morning, she looked through the mail. Three bills, an assortment of junk mail, and a brochure. She scrutinized the front panel of the brochure. A picture of a woman standing by a window, crying. She read the brochure carefully, and then she read it again.

Slowly, she lifted the phone receiver. Carefully, she dialed the number printed on the bottom of the brochure.

Momentarily, she heard a pleasant voice answer, "Nitza. Good morning, may I help you?' "

A small ray of sunlight filtered into the room.

NITZA, The Jerusalem Postpartum Support Network, fills a crucial gap, providing support to women and their families suffering from the often devastating effects of postpartum depression and its related syndromes. For more information call (02) 533-2810 in Israel, or 972-2-533-2810 from any country in the world.

TAMAR FIX

Pink Pretties

When I was a little girl my mother would always walk me to the bus stop where I would wait for my school van. On the way we would smell all the flowers we saw and give them silly names like "pink pretty." On sunny days, we would tilt our heads towards the sun to see if we could look at it without squinting. My mother had a soft voice. She'd always sing me the song "You Are My Sunshine," and I wondered if I'd ever have a sunshine too.

And then I did.

One day, I noticed another little girl across the street waiting for her school van. Everyday she sat in a magic chair that had all these buttons that would make her spin and twirl. "What a fun ride," I'd think to myself. Her school van looked like just as much fun. When the doors opened there was this big slide that would come down and she would go up the slide in her magic chair. She laughed a lot with her mother too. But sometimes, when it was time for her to go, I would look at her mother and see the sadness in her eyes. The look in her mother's eyes stayed with me long after my own school van came to pick me up.

One morning, when I got to the bus stop, I didn't see her. I asked my mother where was the little girl in the magic chair, but she said she didn't know. It was cold out now and there weren't any more flowers to smell and talk about. Instead my mother would hold me close to keep me warm, and together we would turn the clouds into all kinds of shapes and animals.

A few weeks passed and still the little girl wasn't there. I asked my mother if we could try and find her. She smiled and nodded. The next day was rainy, and as we walked across the street to ask the other *kinderlach* about her I stomped my feet in all the puddles I could find. "Excuse me," I said when we got to her bus stop, "do you know the little girl in the magic chair?"

By the time I got home from school that day, the rain had turned to snow and I couldn't wait to build a snowman and make snow angels. But first, I wanted to see her. I raced into my house ready to race right back out, but my parents were talking quietly to each other and I didn't disturb them. I sat on a chair in the kitchen and waited, watching the snowflakes outside melt as soon as they hit the window. After what seemed to me like forever, my mother walked into the kitchen. She stooped down to talk to me and I could see her eyes were red and puffy. I took a piece of hair out from under her tichel and twirled it around my fingers. Then one tear trickled down the side of her cheek. I watched it fall. She told me that the little girl was very sick and asked if I would still like to go see her. "I do," I said, and that was that.

My mother reminded me of my Uncle Moishy tape and that we were doing the same thing the *bikur cholim* song teaches us. She said I was doing a big mitzvah, and I remember feeling proud.

We got to her house, and then it happened. I saw the most beautiful thing in the world! In the middle of the snow covered street, through the wind, the cold, and the rain, there it was. One single, beautiful pink pretty sticking out of the snow for all to see. My mother was already on the porch and knocking on the door. I smelled it and then quickly snatched it up. I stuck it in my pocket, and I remember my hand carefully holding it in my pocket like a secret treasure that's in need of protection.

I was thankful to come in from the freezing cold to the warmth of the hallway. Her mother led us to the very last door and knocked gently. Then, slowly, she opened the door and poked her head in, whispering something I couldn't hear. I tried to peek in between her mother and the door but I couldn't see. I had to wait only a second more, for at that moment the door opened wide and I finally saw the little girl in the magic chair once again. Only this time, she was lying down in bed, and her magic chair was next to it. When our mothers stepped into the hallway to talk, I walked over to her bedside and asked her to open her hand. Then, ever so lovingly, I placed the pink pretty in her hand, sat in her magic chair and sang her "You Are My Sunshine."

That was the last time I ever saw the little girl with the magic chair but it was certainly not the last time I ever thought of her.

Little girl,

Wherever you are, know that even when the snow is falling and the sun is hiding,

There will always be pink pretties, and you will always be...my sunshine.

For my nephew, Aharon Yehuda. We went on a walk one day and discovered a pink pretty. Thank you for always showing me the flowers. I love you Huda. Tante.

CHANA KLEIN

Step-Letters

Letter to a Stepmother

Dear Savta,

Thank you for your calls and offer to come and help with Rachelli. I know my father thinks it's a good idea for you to come and help me with my first baby, but especially now, I don't. I know how hard you worked to help make my wedding as wonderful as it was, and I do appreciate that. But after your offer, I called the Rebbetzin and we had a long chat. She agreed with me that sharing one's first child with a mother is different from trying to do that with a stepmother. She said I should let you know how I feel about your offer, and other things that have been on my mind these past five years.

I feel it would put too much pressure on both of us to try to pretend that this is a normal situation and that you would feel

* The author is using a pseudonym.

comfortable here with me and be able to share the joy of the *simchah*. You won't, and I won't, and a mother is a mother. My mother's absence now is more painful than at the time of the wedding, because all the excitement and buying and running around we were doing then didn't allow me the time to think about the past, or what could have been...should have been.

Now I have time to think, too much time. It's not easy to make friends in a new place, and we are sometimes with Menachem's family, but everything is so different here. Baby Rachelli is adorable, and very good. She sleeps a lot, so between feedings I do a small amount of housekeeping — laundry for her mainly. Menachem is working hard and learning mornings and evenings, and he loves to hold her when he's home. But he's afraid he'll drop her so he sits down! He helps with the cooking and cleaning for Shabbos so that I can rest between feedings. And with the money you gave us for a helper, we have someone come in to do the heavy cleaning and ironing. So I have time to think, and the Rebbetzin says it's time I share these thoughts with you.

You may not know this, but even though we all suffered from the tragedy of my mother's sudden, unexpected leaving us, and even though the older of us children tried to keep the family together and succeeded, we knew my father needed to remarry. He tried hard to keep things going and make things good for us. His job kept him busy, both at the office and on his business trips, which kept his mind off his loss and his grief; but we felt, and saw, that he wasn't himself, and couldn't be without someone like my mother. So we urged him to remarry. We felt sure he would find someone from amongst our friends, who knew us and would understand us. He almost did, but he married you. In no way were you like our mother. It was a big shock and disappointment. Especially since you brought with you your younger children and your way of life, which was very different from ours. And you took him away from us! How could you have expected us to call you "Mother"? Even if he thought that was a way to bring the families together, you should have known better.

For the younger children, I was the mother. I wondered, what would be with them? They depended on me so much from the time my mother left us. I know you and my father tried to change this by sending me away to seminary so that I wouldn't have to be responsible for them. It helped that I knew someone else would help them; but all those years I was the one they came to when they needed something. It was important for them to rely on me, and maybe even more important for me.

It's hard for me to think they don't really need me anymore. Especially since I am so far away from them, I worry. I know you try, but you really don't know them! And it's natural for your kids to come first; you understand them. So I feel caught between my knowing that you two are the parents and that I shouldn't encourage their depending on me, and my concern that you both really don't understand them and the confusion they are suffering from trying to adjust to all the changes in the family. I know I won't want anyone interfering with how I raise my children! So this is a dilemma.

Thank you for explaining to me that I could call you by your first name. Now when we're together I can call you Savta! That will be easier for me and for the children. I really do want Rachelli to know you as Savta, and I will try to let you both be the parents to the children. After all, it is five years now since you married my father, and by this time I'm sure you do know them and are fair in how you treat them. I was very pleased that my father helped me choose the carriage; it's great and converts to a stroller later. In this cold weather, it will keep Rachelli warm and it has rain covers for the stroller when she's older. Your Elisheva told us that it was the best one to buy, as it lasted her through three children; but it is not the most expensive one, so I hope it will last.

That reminds me how different things used to be in the family. We always got the best because it lasted the longest and it had to go down the line in the family. Like the bicycle: we had only one in the family, but it was the best! You don't want the kids to fight, so you get them both one, but it won't last. You made a big deal about birthdays, but we got lots of new clothes and toys whenever my father went away on a trip. Then you persuaded him not to "overindulge" us, but to buy things for our birthdays and bring us little things when he traveled.

Then you took trips with him overnight and had someone else stay with the kids. That wasn't fair! It doesn't matter that he said he was too tired after teaching to drive back. It doesn't matter that you said parents are people also and need some time to be together by themselves. It just wasn't right that you should leave them with Elisheva, even though she said she didn't mind. She didn't know them either! It was very hard for me, because I was away at seminary and couldn't come home to take care of them. I still worry about them and hope you will let them call me whenever they want and come to visit as soon as school is out.

I know that Bracha is very excited at being an Auntie at ten! Your Ruthie is younger, so she wouldn't enjoy being here at all and I really couldn't take care of two kids. I hope we can work that out during the summer holidays. I miss Bracha very much and hate to be so far from her when I know she needs me.

Thank you for hearing me out. I'm old enough to know that

this is not only a personal but also a family situation. I hope you understand I appreciate what you have done for my father; but I feel it has been at our expense. I want to believe that you both will be parents to all of the children equally; but should Bracha need me, I am here for her.

Give my love to my father and the children.

Yours,
Leah

Letter to a Stepdaughter

Dear Leah,

It is so good to hear that Rachelli is such a good baby. Of course it's lonely for you being away from home and all your friends. We are very pleased you spoke to the Rebbitzen, and although I am disappointed not to be able to help you as I helped Elisheva, I do understand. Babies are very sensitive to tension in a family, and get very fussy when they feel their mother is under stress, and it is best this way as you say.

I am happy Daddy was with you to pick out the carriage. You may remember he was also with you when you were on *shidduchim*, even if it meant he had to take time away from work when you were at seminary. He was also with you when you were first married for the few days he could spare during his travels, and he was able to fill your freezer with all the special dishes you enjoyed and wanted to share with Menachem but couldn't cook well enough then. (You were luckier than I was. I had to learn to cook from a book, as I hadn't done any cooking until I was married!) He came specially for Rachelli's kiddush over Shabbos, which was a great effort on his part. (Unfortunately we couldn't be there, as Ruthie was quite ill.)

All families are different, especially if they are from different backgrounds. We try very hard to celebrate all occasions possible in the family, because Daddy believes there are so many sad things that have happened. That's why he made special benchers when you got married, and also for the boys bar mitzvahs. That's why he took time to get things whenever he traveled. When you children stopped welcoming him, and just asked what he brought you, we decided it was because you were getting too much. Everyone needs thanks and appreciation, even fathers. Too much candy spoils your stomach, and too many things spoil your ability to appreciate them. Daddy didn't have to show he loved you by buying all those extravagant toys, which other children here didn't have. He was always here for you when you needed him, and still is.

Five years is a long time. It takes a long time to get to know other people, but when you live with them and respect them and try to understand them, you can. Although our families did not know each other, our values are the same. We want our children to be the best they can be and learn and live Torah. We try to help each child achieve what is possible for them, whether it is my children or your brothers and sisters. All parents want the best for all of their children. That was our goal when we decided to marry: to help all of our children become the best they could be.

We hope your brothers will continue in their learning, and marry and start a family as you have. The younger children seem to do very well when you older children are not trying to remind them that they are really a separate family. They were, but now we are together. If you older children keep insisting on keeping your family separate from our new family, you will create serious problems. I hope we can avoid that. It can only be avoided if you can release yourself from being overprotective and respecting that your father and I are capable and loving parents. Otherwise, you may find yourself forever Bracha's mother.

I know how confusing it must have been for all of you to meet me instead of the friend your father had been seeing. No one can ever replace a parent, especially a mother for a teenage daughter. You did remarkably well in keeping the family together and the household in order and in taking care of the younger children. They show the effects of your good care. We appreciate all that you have done, and have tried to show you that by freeing you from the burdens of their care and allowing you to be their older sister.

You and your brothers were clever and considerate of your father in realizing his need for companionship. No one can replace your mother, and I am not trying to. That your father thought you should call me "Mother" was his effort to mend the family, not to be disloyal or disrespectful to your mother. The closeness they had is why he needed to remarry. Those who have been well married, remarry quickly (if their children allow them to). My children also lost their father, and they suffer from that loss. It is required that single Jewish parents remarry, especially men. Children need two parents.

The younger children didn't know their mother very well, so they don't have your close bond nor feel your great grief. Their world has changed, and that is disturbing and difficult for them. They may be able to form a bond with your father and myself as part of a new family because they need a family and parents to love and rely on. Please give that to them. Release them.

Thank you for following the Rebbitzen's advice and telling me what has been bothering you. I hope we can continue this discussion, and that I can eventually become the friend that I shall continue to try to be. Enjoy the baby, and I hope soon you will make friends in your new home.

Yours,

Savta

TZVIA EHRLICH-KLEIN

The Single Mothers Among Us: How We Can Help

We all know that the home is the mainstay of the Jewish family, and that the family is one of the pillars of Jewish life. Yet somehow, in today's world, it unfortunately seems that some families are not able to stay all together.

In addition to being a tragedy for the Jewish people, it is also a tragedy for those involved, even if it is necessary. Because, though it may be difficult to raise a family of happy, well-adjusted, Torah-loving children in today's world, it is even harder to do so when you are a single parent.

I would like to propose a few ideas on how we, as members of a caring community, can help the single mother and her children, and how we can all become more sensitive to and aware of the special needs they have.

It is a tremendous mitzvah to offer to help put up a *sukkah* if a divorcée or widow has children. Even if the single parent doesn't have any boys, she may want to have a *sukkah* for the educational value for her girls, or simply so that her children will not have an additional reason to feel even more left out or different from their friends than they already do.

Simchas Torah is another holiday which is particularly difficult for single mothers. Don't wait for a single-parent mother to have to ask you if your husband would pick up her little boy or (or two- or three-year-old little girl) during the dancing in shul. Can you imagine what it is like to go to shul on Simchas Torah and stand there in the women's section with your little boy or girl, watching as most of the other little children are twirled around high on their fathers' shoulders, laughing and happy, while you and your children just stand there and watch, alone?

Can you imagine how much it hurts to realize that not one person in your entire circle of acquaintances thought of you and your children's pain on this *chag*?

On Shavuos, it is easy to forget that the single mother doesn't have anyone to sit up late learning with her little boy, or willing to go with him early to shul. These are all things which it is very hard to ask neighbors to do for you, and yet, if offered, demonstrate real *chesed*, as well as being an excellent lesson for one's whole family in true thoughtfulness, consideration, and concern for other people.

Chol HaMoed is often a particularly long and lonely time. Few single parents are going to cook an entire *seudah* for one or two people. Luncheon invitations are particularly important and appreciated as there are many long hours of daylight and, as people eat their meals at different times, singles are hesitant to barge in on families and visit without a specific invitation.

Don't be afraid of not knowing at precisely what time you will be starting the *seudah*. Simply say, "Probably around X o'clock, but call first to be sure we're back." Everyone understands that you may be out visiting.

During a Pesach Seder, please do not forget to get the guest-children involved in the Torah talk at the table. It is hard and embarrassing for them to participate without your active help. If you can get them to join in the conversations, you will have made a wonderful, memorable evening for them as well as for their parent.

Simply sitting as a noninvolved observer when all family members are happily participating can make even the most well-adjusted guest feel very "outsiderish" and left out of the close family gathering. Be particularly sensitive to encourage any young guest-children to ask the Four Questions (just being asked will make the single-parent family feel good).

The younger the children, the more the single parent will appreciate Shabbos and holiday invitations. Pay attention to inviting them before your Shabbos table fills up. Don't assume that someone else has probably invited the single parent: it is not necessarily so.

Be aware that, though many single-parent families are forgotten during the year, there is often an upsurge in remembrance the week or two before major holidays. Therefore, if, by the time you get around to inviting that single-parent family, they have already accepted an invitation, invite them at that time for a few weeks hence. Don't assume that because they are booked for the next week or two, they must therefore always have lots of invitations. They probably don't.

Though Shabbos and holiday invitations are very important

to single-parent families with young children, by the time the kids are older it becomes less vital, since by then everyone in the single-parent family has probably gotten used to eating Shabbos and holiday meals alone. Also, older children will often invite their own guests to their home, so their own Shabbos table will not feel so empty.

If a single mother with young sons lives nearby, realize that she probably needs someone to take her boys to shul each Shabbos. If your family cannot help each week, at least offer to take the children once or twice a month. You can also ask around among your friends in the neighborhood, or ask your husband to keep his eyes out in shul for an appropriate person, perhaps an older, retired man who might even become a surrogate grandfather.

It is very difficult emotionally for a single mother to have to explain her whole situation to everyone, asking different people to do the *chesed* of taking her child to shul and sitting with him, showing him when to stand, what to do, etc. It is embarrassing to ask strangers, and depressing to be forced to ask friends who haven't offered on their own volition.

Since you are not emotionally involved, asking around on behalf of the single mother will be much easier for you. Ask the single mother if she would like some help (i.e., you) to organize this. You can't imagine how many single mothers desperately need this kindness, but find it too difficult and embarrassing to ask, and so just don't.

Havdalah is a lonely time, and most single mothers (as well as single women and girls) try to hear it said by a man. An invitation, open or otherwise, to come over for Havdalah is particularly kind and appreciated. If you really want to be sensitive to the feelings of the single parent, an invitation to come early "so we can have some time to visit together" will probably make her glow with happiness.

It is a tremendously big *chesed* to try to find opportunities to compliment the single parent in front of his or her children. This is a particularly important point because there is very little positive reinforcement or compliments being addressed to the parent within the child's hearing, from outsiders.

Remember, the child from a single-parent home has probably never heard — or at least very, very rarely heard — his parent being told, "It was so nice the way you said X," or "What a lovely dinner you made tonight. You really do a lot to make everything nice." (If the thought, "Boy, my spouse never tells me that either" even flitters through your mind, perhaps you should sit down and really try to think through and imagine what truly being completely without any adult reinforcement, ever, means. It may even help you to appreciate what you do have a little more!)

Though this sounds like an unnecessary point to make, please be aware that, if even one parent dies, a child is called an "orphan" and everyone feels sympathy for that orphan. Yet a child from a divorced home is usually referred to as coming from a "broken home," no matter how well-adjusted the child may remain. Your child will overhear such phrases if you use them, and perhaps use them as well. But for you to use that expression within the hearing of a divorcée will make her feel as if her heart is being torn apart inside.

Even doing homework can be a problem for a single mother who doesn't have a huge *sefarim* library in her home, or the knowledge of how and where to find what piece of learning the child needs. It is a rare ex-husband who will leave his Mishnah, *Mishnah Berurah*, etc., for his ex-wife, and, even if he did, not all women have a thorough yeshivah education to be able to help the child.

A considerate neighbor will periodically "remind" the single mother that she is always welcome to send her boys or girls over to borrow whichever *sefarim* they need for homework, or to get help from the neighbor's husband or older children. Though this might sound simple or elementary, realize that virtually no one offers this, though almost every single parent truly needs this help.

A list of special single-parent-family needs can go on and on, from offering suggestions for good bar mitzvah teachers to the need for someone to hold pre-puberty "man-to-man" talks.

The point is for each of us to think of the other person, to remember the neighbor or friend who doesn't have everything that we have.

SHAINA MEDWED

Ketzi Lulu

In this physical world of illusion, things are often not what they appear to be. Sometimes God gives us a deeper glimpse into His design. Although our Sages warn us not to delve too deeply into life's mysteries, when they jump up onto our dining room table how can we not help but stand back flabbergasted and awed? The following story happened in the home of Rabbi and Rebbetzin Berman, respected Torah educators for over thirty-five years.

The Bermans had a cat, and as all cat owners know, cats can be very human, to such a degree that it bothers you sometimes. You look at a cat, you look into its eyes, you look into its face, and you wonder, "Does this thing understand people completely?"

Well, the Bermans' cat, which they had for seven years, was such that there were many times when Rebbetzin Berman used to wonder if it really was a cat or not. But she always told herself, "Of course it's a cat. What else could it be?"

Their cat was a house cat. When he went out into the street, the alley cats, who were very jealous of him, used to fight with him. As a pampered house cat, he certainly wasn't a fighter. They easily bested him, and he used to come home bruised, torn, and ripped. The Bermans had a lot of *rachmanus* for him because he was such a beautiful, good cat. To give you an example, this cat never, ever meowed in the house. Whenever he had to go out at night, he would jump up on the bed and tap Rebbetzin Berman with his paws until she woke up. Then, when he saw her wake up, he'd jump off the bed quietly, without a sound, and run to the door, looking back to see if she was following him. After she opened the door, he'd walk right out, in absolute silence.

In the morning, when he wanted to come back into the house, he'd just sit patiently outside the front door. He never meowed, he never scratched the door or acted in any of the usual cat ways, he just sat there waiting. When neighbors on their way up the stairs would see him sitting outside the door, they would ring the bell. Rebbetzin Berman would go to the door and in would walk the cat. When he got bigger, he would try to turn the handle of the door with his paws, but with no success. He just couldn't reach it. So the neighbors continued to ring the bell.

This was their Ketzi Lulu, as they called him, a very phenomenal cat.

When Rebbetzin Berman baked challah for Shabbos, Ketzi Lulu would always run to the oven. That's when he would meow to let them know he wanted challah. He loved challah. She said to him once, "Silly goose, don't you see they are in the oven? I can't give them to you now. Come back tonight after Kiddush and you'll get challah." Sure enough, that Friday night they were all at the table waiting to hear the Rabbi make Kiddush when all of a sudden they heard a noise outside the front door. They opened the door and the cat came strolling into the house, went straight over to the Rabbi, and sat down next to his right foot, waiting for his challah. This was too much. But again, they thought it was just coincidence.

Another Friday night Ketzi was in the house when the challahs were on the table. They went crazy that Friday night trying to keep him from jumping on the table. Don't forget, a cat is *muktzeh* on Shabbos. They fed him and talked to him and tried to coax him, but all he wanted was the challah, and he was very upset about having to wait for it. They kept telling him, "When Abba comes home from shul you'll get challah." Finally the Rabbi came home from shul, but instead of going straight over to the table to make Kiddush, he first went to look something up in a *sefer*. He stopped at the bookshelf on the way to his place. Well, the cat took one look at him and they could see he was very disturbed. He jumped off the couch, went right up to the Rabbi and rubbed up against his leg, meowing plaintively.

The Rabbi looked up in surprise. What could the cat possibly want from him? The cat again rubbed and meowed. "What does the cat want?" he asked.

His wife answered, "He's hoping you'll make Kiddush so he can get some challah." The family was hysterical, but the Rabbi calmly continued looking in the *sefer*. The cat, seeing his message wasn't getting across, walked over to the place by the table where he sat every Friday night, picked up his paw, banged on the floor and meowed more insistently. They almost went through the floor. This was a scene of scenes.

The Rabbi looked up and said, "Okay, let's go, Ketzi wants challah." He made Kiddush, they all went out to wash. Ketzi just sat there, waiting for his challah.

He got his challah that Shabbos and every Shabbos after that. No matter how hard they tried to get him out of the dining room onto the kitchen porch, he always managed to stick to his post by the Rabbi's side when it came to Friday night, Shabbos, or *yom tov*. He refused to eat outside of the dining room. Rebbetzin Berman would try to coax him away with food. She would take the food towards the kitchen to lure him to come after her, but he refused to budge. He looked at her as if she were crazy and stamped his foot on the floor. She would have to take the food back to him.

When all these things happened Rebbetzin Berman would think, that's how cats are. She made a big mistake. He wasn't a cat. He was a *gilgul*.

Even when the veterinarian came to the house to treat his infected neck, she still didn't realize it. Ketzi smelled dog all over the doctor and ran panic stricken from the room, trying to escape. He was jumping on the windowsills and under and over the beds while she drove herself crazy trying to catch him. She finally caught him in the study and held him tightly. The doctor took a look at the cat's neck and said he would need a shot of antibiotics. The Rebbetzin stood with her back up against the *sefarim*, the cat held tightly in her hands. The doctor took out a long needle to inject the medicine right into the cat's stomach.

Years ago, Rebbetzin Berman's father had taught her how to treat animals. When she was a child there was a cat in the house. She once took a glass of milk to drink while the cat sat there watching and meowing pitifully. She was only about ten or so, and she remembers thinking, "What does he want of me — I'm dying of thirst! First I'll drink my glass of milk and then I'll give the cat some milk in a dish."

Did her father give it to her! He said, "What do you think you are doing? You have to feed the cat first!" She wanted her father to know that she was not ignoring the cat, so she said, "I'll give him his milk when I have finished mine."

"That's *tzar ba'alei chaim*. He has *tzar* every second that you are not giving it to him. He doesn't know that you are going to give it to him later. He only knows the now. Now he sees that you are drinking and he's not. The poor thing is in pain."

That's how she first learned about *tzar ba'alei chaim* and now here she was, years later, married and the mother of teenagers, holding this cat in her hands, holding his neck and his paws so that he couldn't bite her or scratch her or the doctor while the needle was going into his stomach. Suddenly, in one horrible moment, the cat's mouth somehow got free and in an instant her finger was trapped between his teeth. She felt sharp needles all over her finger. Her first reaction was that she must let go of the cat to save her finger. Then she realized she couldn't because the needle was still in its stomach, and the doctor was right near the cat's paws. If she let go of the cat, he would scratch the doctor in the face.

The doctor looked her straight in the eyes. She looked back at him. They both knew the score. It was a dreadful moment, but she kept her cool and didn't let go of the cat. The doctor removed the needle and the cat released her finger.

There wasn't one piece of broken skin.

This is the part she doesn't understand. The vet and Rebbetzin Berman were both amazed. The cat's first reaction should have been to scratch or bite, to get rid of her, to get rid of the doctor, and to get rid of that pain in his stomach. Yet it seemed as if he never really meant to bite her finger, but just bit down for security. It was an unbelievable experience. But she still said it was only a cat.

Then came that eventful day when what happened proved that he wasn't a cat, but a *gilgul*.

Rabbi Berman had just obtained for the first time a tape of

Rav Aharon Kotler, *zt"l*, and he was listening to it in the dining room. The Rebbetzin walked into the dining room and got a shock. There was the cat. He had been asleep in the children's room, when all of a sudden, upon hearing the tape, he ran out of the room and jumped onto the dining room chairs. When they were around, he never went up on the chairs. Now, in front of both of them, there he was, an intent look on his face, standing on his hind legs on the chair. His left foreleg was on the dining room table, and his front right paw was swinging in a semicircle in front of the tape recorder, in constant motion to the voice of the speaker, Rav Aharon. He seemed mesmerized by the voice coming from the tape. He did not respond to her husband's presence or to her sudden entrance into the room.

The Rabbi looked at her, and she looked back at him and shivered. Then he said, "Maybe he is doing this because he hears voices."

She replied, "He hears tapes — Torah tapes, children's tapes, and the radio — all the time. The only thing he is afraid of is the hissing of insect repellent and musical instruments."

"What does this mean?" the Rabbi mused.

His wife answered, "Well, you have two choices. One, the *gilgul* inside him was a *talmid* of Rav Aharon, *zt"l;* or two, he learned that *gemara* some place before. Take your choice. I would never know, unless the cat told me himself."

That's when they realized they had a *gilgul* in the house. He went on living his normal daily cat routine, but they never felt the same towards him. That was their Ketzi Lulu.

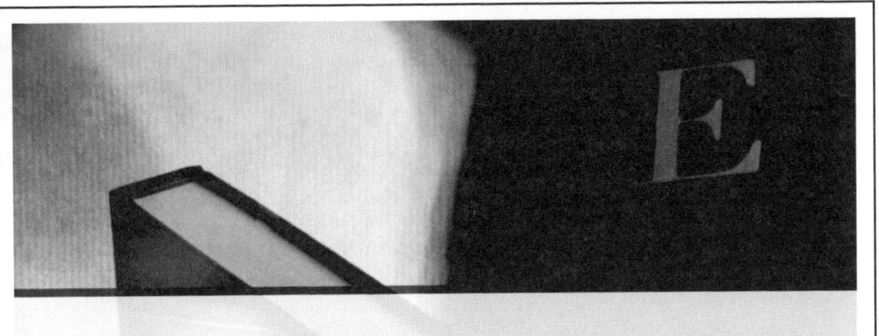

History and Biography

DR. MEIR TAMARI

Safe at Last, in Kiryat Ye'arim

"And the men of Kiryat Ye'arim came and brought up the ark of the Lord."

(*Shmuel* I 6:21–7:2)

This book finds its beginnings in the picturesque village of Kiryat Ye'arim. Locally known as Telshestone after the Telshe Yeshiva, and Irving Stone, who provided much of its financing. The Kiryah nestles in the Judean Hills close to Jerusalem and hosts a community of approximately 450 families, 300 of whom are English speakers. Modern-day Telshestone also boasts one of the largest English-language Torah libraries in Israel, containing an astounding array of over 4,000 books. It is against this backdrop that this book finds its way to its readers.

There is only one way from the coastal plain through the mountains of Judea, and it has always been through Sha'ar Hagai up to Kiryat Ye'arim and then over the hills to Jerusalem. From there, one can go along the crest of the mountains either north to Shechem, south to Beer Sheva, or down to Jericho and across Jordan to Iraq. Ever since the dawn of history, merchants, warriors, pilgrims, and common travelers — Canaanites, Israelites, Philistines, Greeks, Romans, and Crusaders — have come along this road.

Along this road, too, some 3,000 years ago, came the *aron hakodesh*, ark of the covenant, from the towns of the Philistines. It journeyed through Beit Shemesh in the foothills, to Kiryat Ye'arim on the crest of the hills of Judea, and there it rested for twenty years, before being taken by David to Jerusalem. Kiryat Ye'arim, the City of Forests, was a Gibeonite town before the conquest of the Israelites. It lies on this ancient highway, straddling the borders of the tribal territories of Yehudah and Binyamin.

At its spring, the physical reason for its establishment, there remains to this day the dam created by the Romans. On the wall of the building they built to protect it, one can see the signature of one of the officers of the Tenth Legion, which destroyed the Second Beis HaMikdash. They encamped there on their way to Jerusalem.

Israel, having just suffered a defeat at the hands of the Philistines, decided that in order to assure victory they would take the *aron hakodesh* with them into battle. This they did, with much fanfare and joy, together with the two sons of Eli the *kohen gadol*. However, once again they were defeated; 30,000 of them were killed in battle and the *aron* was taken into captivity. "The glory of Israel has departed," mourned the daughter-in-law of Eli, and, dying in childbirth, called her newly born son Ichavod, loosely translated as "lacking honor."

Naturally, the Philistines saw not only a military victory but also a spiritual one. They placed the aron in the temple of their god, Dagon, in Ashdod, then the most important city of their five city-states. Then "the hand of the God of Israel was heavy on them" and they found the body and head of Dagon shattered on the floor, while they themselves suffered painful illness.

Assuming that God was angry at their city, they sent the *aron* first to Gat and then to Ekron, hoping that there He would be satisfied with them. However, the same story of suffering was repeated. So they decided to send it back to Israel, treating it with great honor, building a special cart for it and loading it with gold. As a sign of respect, the cart was yoked to two cows who had never been yoked for work before, and whose calves were kept behind so that they should not distract from the ceremonial dignity by running after the cart.

Relying on Divine intervention, they let the cows make their own way to whatever destination God would lead them. Thus they came to Beit Shemesh on the banks of Nahal Sorek, formerly a Canaanite city, which after Yehoshua's conquest became one of the cities of the *kohanim* in the territory of the tribe of Yehudah (*Yehoshua* 21:16). It was the time of the harvest and all of Beit Shemesh were busy in the fields when the *aron hakodesh* arrived, filling them with thanksgiving for its return. They placed it on the high rock at which the cows had stopped of their own accord and offered sacrifices and prayers to Hashem. However, they were unable to restrain their ecstasy and joy, so that they touched and opened the *aron*, which was forbidden. Punishment was not slow in coming, killing seventy of them. Seeing the Divine anger and sorrow that came to them for their disrespectful behavior, and cognizant of what had happened to the Philistine cities, they sent a message to the people of Kiryat

Ye'arim to come and take the *aron hakodesh* up to their city.

"And they brought up the ark of the Lord to the house of Avinadav that was on the hill, and they sanctified Elazar, his son to guard the ark of the Lord" (*Shmuel* I 7:1). Avinadav was a *kohen* or, according to Josephus, a *levi*. Strictly speaking, the name Avinadav means "my Father is generous," but it is possible that his name was an acronym of the names of the two sons of Aharon, Nadav and Avihu, symbols of religious ecstasy and the outpouring of religiosity. It is interesting in this respect that Avinadav's son bears the same name as another son of Aharon HaKohen, Elazar, who succeeded his father as the high priest.

The new site of the *aron hakodesh*, on the hill overlooking Kiryat Ye'arim, actually lies within the portion of the tribe of Binyamin. In the blessing of Binyamin by Moshe Rabbeinu, we read, "The beloved of the Lord shall dwell in safety by Him; and the Lord shall cover [protect] all the day long, and He shall dwell between his shoulders" (*Devarim* 33:12). Perhaps it was in fulfillment of this vision that there was no attempt to return the ark to the Tabernacle at Givon or at Nov, after the destruction of Shiloh. Rather it remained there in Kiryat Ye'arim until David brought it to Jerusalem.

The spiritual greatness of Avinadav, Elazar, and the people of Kiryat Ye'arim, and their devotion to the sanctity of the *aron hakodesh*, is to be seen at the conclusion of the story. There, the last verse tells us that the *aron* was brought to Kiryat Ye'arim and remained there for twenty years, during which time the whole House of Israel followed Hashem.

Many, many centuries later, today's Kiryat Ye'arim still bears the badge of honor given it for accommodating the ark in its holy environs.

HANOCH TELLER

The Seed That Germinated in Telshe

The yeshivah career of the father of contemporary yeshivos, Rabbi Yosef Shlomo Kahaneman — better known as The Ponevizher Rav — commenced in Telshe. Yet the chances of this boy ever being admitted to this prestigious yeshivah were virtually zero.

Many promising students wished to learn in Telshe and the yeshivah could neither accommodate nor award the education that it deemed appropriate to more than a certain number. Accordingly, the yeshivah placed a quota on each city and town, limiting the number of students eligible for admittance from each region. The allotment from Kuhl, Yosef Shlomo's hometown, was already filled, so attempts were made to circumvent this injunction. The plan was intricate, elaborate, and clever, but ultimately it failed.

But that wasn't the only problem preventing this boy from

gaining admission to the academy of his dreams. Notwithstanding his superior intellect and exceedingly kind nature, Yosef Shlomo was simply too young to be considered. According to the Telshe rules only senior students were eligible for admission, and he was firmly told that the faculty made no exceptions. Yosef Shlomo was even denied the opportunity for an interview.

There seemed to be no way in, when the young boy fortuitously encountered one of Telshe's senior *roshei yeshivah*, Rabbi Shimon Shkop. Rabbi Shkop, accompanied by numerous students, was vacationing in the resort town of Polangen. Yosef Shlomo approached Reb Shimon and asked permission to attend the *shiur* to be delivered during the upcoming Shabbos.

"Why?" asked a puzzled Reb Shimon. A youngster requesting to attend his *shiur* was akin to a second-grader asking to study organic chemistry.

Yosef Shlomo confidently responded that he would be able to comprehend the lecture; as proof, he would relay it in its entirety on Sunday. Reb Shimon found this very hard to believe, but Yosef Shlomo persisted, begging and even crying, thereby convincing Reb Shimon to acquiesce.

On Sunday, Yosef Shlomo kept his word, recapitulating the entire *shiur*, detail for detail, displaying profound understanding. Reb Shimon was highly impressed. Realizing that he finally had the *rosh yeshivah*'s attention, Yosef Shlomo articulated his desire to be admitted to Telshe. A few days later a letter of acceptance arrived in the mail. Rabbi Yosef Shlomo Kahaneman would always say that this was one of the happiest days of his life.

Thus began the questing youth's spiritual and intellectual apprenticeship to some of the greatest teachers and rabbinic minds of the day. In the Telshe yeshivah, Yosef Shlomo fell under the dynamic influence of the Telsher Rav, Rabbi Elazar Gordon. From there he would travel on to Novardhok, staying only briefly, and then on to the yeshivah of the Chafetz Chaim in Radin.

But even after he had become the *rosh yeshivah* of the rapidly expanding yeshivah in Ponevizh, Lithuania, and traveled throughout Europe raising funds and interviewing prospective students, he often referred young men anxious to attend *his* yeshivah to go to Telshe, where he had acquired his beginning.

DEVORAH TAMARI

Tribute to Rebbe and Rebbetzin Wasserman

God smiled on me
And showered me with years
Filled
With joy,
And tears.

He let me feel
Their love,
So wide and deep;
But now,
I feel overwhelming
Grief.

I spoke today
With children born
Who wouldn't have been;
Who saw the dawn
Because of them.

They left behind
Their worldly wares;
Their outworn mantles.
But we have still their essence –
Gentle strength
And loving care.

The author is one of their rescued *tinokim shenisbu bein hagoyim.*

RABBI YISROEL SHAW

The Rav of Shanghai, Rav Meir Ashkenazi, zt"l

While God is the ultimate Judge of the degree to which an individual fulfills the unique purpose for which he was created, He seems, on occasion, to allow us a glimpse of one who discerned his life's purpose and made every effort to fulfill it. Knowing such a person, or at least knowing about such a person, can provide us with profound lessons for fulfilling our unique mission in life.

Rav Meir Ashkenazi, the "Shanghai'er Rav," was such a person. He was the leader of the community that served as a haven for thousands of Jews during a time of unprecedented tragedy. When the doors of almost all civilized (and uncivilized) countries were shut and locked in the face of European Jewry,

Divine providence arranged that a far-flung city should leave its doors open. When almost every country refused admittance to those without a life-saving visa, Shanghai's International Settlement permitted entry without one.

Deteriorating conditions in Europe in the 1930s led to a slow stream of German, Austrian, and Russian Jews relocating in the Far East, which increased considerably at the outbreak of the Second World War. By the end of 1941, there were 18,000 Jewish refugees in Shanghai, ten times the number of Jews in Shanghai just ten years earlier. The story of the miraculous escape of 2,000 Polish refugees through Siberia to Kobe, Japan, and then the relocation of 1,000 of them – including the entire Mirrer Yeshiva – to Shanghai is well known. Less well known is who laid the foundations in Shanghai to provide them with the spiritual and material support that literally enabled them to survive, and who was at the forefront of every humanitarian activity on behalf of all of the Jewish refugees?

From Tcherikov to Manchuria to Vladivostok

Rav Meir Ashkenazi was born in 1891 in Tcherikov, in Russia's Pale of Settlement. His parents, Reb Shneur Zalman and Kayla Ashkenazi, were devout and learned Lubavitcher Chassidim, who recognized and nurtured their son's intellectual aptitude, his caring heart, and his motivation to dedicate himself to the service of God. He studied at Yeshiva Tomchei Temimim, where he became one of the most distinguished students.

At the outbreak of the First World War, his family – together with many others, Jews and gentiles alike – fled Russia to the neighboring region of Manchuria (under Chinese rule at the time). It was there, in the city of Harbin, that Rav Meir and

Toiba Liba were married. Rebbetzin Toiba Liba's father, a member of the esteemed Soloveitchik family, had been the chief Rav of the town of Tcherikov and, in fact, was Rav Meir's first teacher and mentor.

For unknown reasons, Rav Ashkenazi, his parents, and family returned to Russia, to the port-city of Vladivostok on the far-eastern coast of Russia. Not long afterwards, in 1918, the community there appointed Rav Ashkenazi as their rabbi. He served them with dedication and love, as is reflected in the community's letter to him upon his departure in 1926:

> For seven consecutive years...he guided our community upon the proper path with his wisdom and his Torah...he drew after him the hearts of all of his community, who...accepted upon themselves willingly all of the enactments that were necessary for a Jewish community. Besides all of this, with his good nature he shared in the pain of every person... His home was always open to every needy and downtrodden person.

From Vladivostok to Shanghai

After serving as the spiritual leader of Vladivostok's Jews for seven years, Rav Ashkenazi received clear signs that it was time to leave. The Communist fever that raged throughout Russia after the Bolshevik Revolution sought to strangle any expression of Jewishness, especially a flourishing synagogue with a scholarly, dynamic, and beloved rabbi. By the time the Communist regime had caused the dissolution of his synagogue, the Rav had received an offer to lead an established community in New York. The Rav and his wife were already preparing for the journey when a registered letter from the small Russian Jewish community in Shanghai arrived, beseeching him to become their rabbi. He was now faced with a monumental decision, one which would have implications far greater than he ever could have imagined.

America had everything that his family could dream of — a growing Jewish community with synagogues, study halls, and Torah scholars, an educational infrastructure for his children, kosher food and religious items, a good income, and liberty and justice for all. There was one thing, however, that America did not have — Jews who needed him more than they needed him in Shanghai.

With a small community maintaining tenuous ties to their *Yiddishkeit* at best, virtually no Torah educational infrastructure, and only a few old Jews still observing Shabbos and kashrus while the young were assimilating rapidly, Shanghai's Jews were starving for guidance, and Rav Ashkenazi could not refuse their plea. The only factor that he would consider was where he was needed most. Thus, in 1926, he and his wife were Shanghai-bound, to lead the small community of Russian Jews.

It seems to be have been the Divine plan, perhaps laying the foundations for the role that the community would serve in the coming years, that Shanghai receive as their rabbi such an eminent *talmid chacham* whose immense Torah scholarship was complemented by a profound concern for others. This legendary compassion for his fellow Jews was demonstrated by an incident that occurred just before the Bolshevik Revolution.

Czar Nicholas II, heavily involved in a World War, was also struggling against internal insurgent movements. Among his staunchest opponents was the Bolshevik Party, which would eventually take over the country. Many assimilated, "enlightened" Jewish youths were caught up in the fervor of the movement. Some of these Jewish revolutionaries came to Vladivostok to garner support for their cause. Many of the residents resented and opposed them, and informed the authorities of their presence. Aware that they were being pursued — and if caught, would likely be punished with death — they sought refuge at the home of the only man who might let them in; who, they had heard, never closed his door to any Jew.

They begged Rav Ashkenazi to let them in, to hide them, to save their lives. Rav Ashkenazi paid no heed to the immense chasm which separated these wayward Jews from himself; he saw beyond their bare heads and shaven faces. In front of him he saw only Jews in dire need. When his wife voiced her concerns, gripped by the fear of the mortal reprisal of such a crime — harboring traitors to the czar — Rav Ashkenazi calmed her fears and said, "The halachah obligates us to save Jews who are being pursued. It is our obligation to do this according to the law of the Torah, and all other concerns are null and void to the law of the Torah." The young Jews hid in his home until they were able to flee from Vladivostok.

This act of kindness, or, as Rav Ashkenazi put it, simply following halachah, would suffice in itself as an example of the selfless dedication that he had for his fellow Jews. There is, however, the rest of the story.

Not long afterwards, the Bolsheviks took control of Russia, and they began to fashion the Communist "paradise." The creation of this "paradise" included the repression of counterrevolutionary movements and anything perceived as such. Hence, throughout the Soviet Union, Jews — and especially Jewish leaders — were persecuted. One Pesach night, in the middle of the Seder, Russian police officers stormed into Rav Ashkenazi's home and took him away for an "interrogation."

Although he was allowed to return home after the interrogation, the incident proved that their future in Russia was bleak.

Leaving the Soviet paradise, however, was easier dreamed of than said or done, for the two latter actions carried severe punishment. Applying for permission to leave meant labeling oneself as a traitor to the country. While mulling over their predicament, the Rebbetzin recalled that one of the Jewish revolutionaries whom they had harbored in their home now held an important government position. She urged her husband to appeal to that Jew for help in procuring permission to leave.

Rav Ashkenazi listened to his wife's idea, the plan that might save their lives. He considered the plan in the only light that he considered anything — the light of the Torah. He chose not to ask the Jew to intervene. "We did what we did," he said, "because that is what the halachah required of us, and not in order to reap any personal benefit. When a Jew does what Heaven wants him to do, it is not proper to seek personal benefit from the mitzvah that he fulfilled."

The Rebbetzin, however, frightened by the danger facing them, decided to travel to the former revolutionary and request his assistance in obtaining permission to leave, but he refused. This iron-willed woman confronted the representative of the Iron Curtain with her pleas and then with her tears, and a spark of gratitude flickered in the Jew's heart. However, since it was impossible to legally permit a rabbi to leave, the former revolutionaries "smuggled" Rav Ashkenazi out of Russia, alone. The Rebbetzin stayed behind with two young children, and joined her husband a few weeks later when the young communists were able to procure some sort of "legal" documentation for her and her children.

Rav of Shanghai

The Rav and his wife arrived in Shanghai in 1926. His parents and siblings (two sisters and two brothers) also settled there. Immediately upon arriving, Rav Ashkenazi set to work at building a viable Jewish community. At the time, the Jewish community in Shanghai consisted of two distinct groups: the Sephardim, who had come to Shanghai from Iraq and India as early as the 1850s, and the Russians, who came at first to escape the pogroms, and then to escape the Bolsheviks. (Only after 1933, when Hitler came to power, did the influx of German Jews begin. He forged strong ties with the established Sephardic community, and he served throughout his years in Shanghai as the unifying bridge between the Ashkenazim and Sephardim. (One member of a prominent Sephardic family told this writer, "Everybody respected the Rav. He was a true *tzaddik* and a tremendous *talmid chacham*. All of our big *she'eilot* went to him, even though he was the Rav of the Ashkenazim.")

One of Rav Ashkenazi's first activities in Shanghai was the building of a synagogue for his community. The *kehillah* was originally established in 1902 by the twenty-five Russian families who lived in the city at that time. For the Russians' small congregation, the Sephardic Jews rented rooms to them in the Sephardic synagogue, She'erith Israel. By the mid-1920s, when their numbers grew to about 250 families (or 1,000 people), the rented quarters had become inadequate. Thus, in 1927, Rav Ashkenazi established the Oheil Moishe Synagogue in the Hongkew section of the city.

This was the center of religious and communal activities for the *kehillah* until the start of the Sino-Japanese War of 1937, when the Japanese devastated Hongkew with their bombardment, and the Chinese with their "scorched earth policy." At that time, most of the members of the *kehillah* who had lived and worked in Hongkew moved to the French Concession (or Frenchtown), a residential area. There Rav Ashkenazi coordinated the building of the large New Synagogue in 1941. A number of Jews remained at the original synagogue in Hongkew, and later it served the large number of Polish Jews who arrived. Rav Ashkenazi continued to oversee activities at both branches of Oheil Moishe.

When the numbers of German Jewish refugees increased, they sought permission to form their own congregation. Permission was granted by the leaders of the Sephardic and Ashkenazic communities, under the general leadership of Rav Ashkenazi, who stipulated only that the services be conducted according to Torah law and tradition.

In 1931, more Jews began to pour into Shanghai. This time, they were from Harbin, Manchuria. In that year, Japan occupied Manchuria and unofficially sanctioned a reign of terror, encouraging the White Russians living there to fulfill their anti-Semitic desires. Three quarters of the Jewish population of Harbin fled, many to Shanghai. By the late 1930s, Shanghai's Russian Jewish population had increased to over 4,000 people. Rav Ashkenazi and his wife continued to serve them with devotion. One woman, born in Shanghai, told this writer that "the Rabbi and Rebbetzin were like our parents' counselors, and their home was always open."

After the Nazis ascended to power in Germany in 1933, a new wave of Jews made their way to Shanghai. As the Nazi plans for the Jews became manifest, German Jews began to emigrate. By 1939, the number of German and Austrian Jews to emigrate to Shanghai approached 14,000. Despite the fact that many of these were assimilated Jews, the Ashkenazi family made every effort to welcome them to the city and to help them adjust to the strange, new culture. Without hesitation, Rav Ashkenazi appealed to the wealthy members of the Russian and Sephardic communities to assist the refugees. Giving away sizable amounts of his own limited income, he served as an example of generosity. His heart was greatly pained by the suffering of his brethren, and he made every effort to alleviate their distress.

Under the general auspices of the American Joint Distribution Committee, relief agencies were formed to raise money for housing and food. Eventually, communal refugee shelters, or "Heime," were formed. In cooperation with the relief organizations, Rav Ashkenazi was able to establish religious services and kosher kitchen facilities in these shelters. Rav Ashkenazi frequently visited the shelters, speaking with the refugees and taking an interest in their lives, despite their apathy towards religion. Many of them began, for the first time in their lives, to attend prayer services and Torah lectures that Rav Ashkenazi organized, and some of the assimilated Jews eventually experienced a religious revival. In the involuntary ghetto that the Japanese formed for the refugees after Japan entered the war and occupied Shanghai, half of the shops were closed on Shabbos (despite the great economic privation that already existed), even though only a small percentage of the refugee population was Torah-observant.

This rekindled spirit for Shabbos observance was spawned by a special campaign launched by Rav Ashkenazi together with the Amshenover Rebbe, Rav Shimon Kalish, in 1941. Together, these two great Torah personalities visited stores, families, and individuals, teaching them in loving tones about the importance of Shabbos. In addition, they gave lectures, distributed leaflets, and wrote newspaper articles on the subject, and their efforts were very successful. Rav Ashkenazi also helped to arrange special Shabbos meals every Friday night and Shabbos day, in a unique Shabbos setting, at one of the refugee Heime.

Rav Ashkenazi established a *beis din* which issued rulings in monetary disputes and handled rabbinical functions, such as marriage and divorce. His *beis din* was also responsible for making kosher provisions available, and it even set up stands in the Chinese and Japanese food markets which the refugees frequented, where kosher meat and poultry could be purchased. Rav Ashkenazi's *beis din* maintained total jurisdiction for as long as it existed. Rav Ashkenazi saw to it that the *beis din* had representatives from every group — the Sephardim, German refugees, and Eastern European (Polish and Lithuanian) refugees.

Establishing Schools

In response to the growing need for a more solid Jewish education, Rav Ashkenazi, together with a committee of his Russian and Sephardic supporters, founded a Talmud Torah, which opened its doors in December 1939 with thirty-five students. By 1941, it had an enrollment of 120 students. It eventually grew to nearly 300 students, with two branches, one in Hongkew (the ghetto) and one in Frenchtown. The Talmud Torah also arranged special classes and activities for the children on Shabbos and Sundays, and it provided food and periodic distributions of clothing for the many poor refugee children.

The Talmud Torah was so successful, especially after the arrival of the Eastern European refugees at the end of 1941, that a more advanced school was needed to provide for its graduates. Rav Ashkenazi was again instrumental in helping to found a full-day *yeshivah ketanah,* headed by an outstanding young *talmid chacham,* his son-in-law, Rav Hershel Milner. Rav Milner headed a staff of four, who were students of the Mirrer Yeshiva. This *yeshivah ketanah* grew to about forty students, and its graduates in turn joined the higher *yeshivos* in Shanghai, such as the Mirrer Yeshiva.

These schools were established only after the Jewish population of Shanghai surged due to the influx of refugees. There was no yeshivah, though, for Rav Ashkenazi's own son, Moshe, when he turned thirteen. In 1934, in a great act of sacrifice for Torah, the Rabbi and Rebbetzin sent their only son (one of three children) to Eretz Yisrael with Rav Ashkenazi's parents, to be raised in the holy atmosphere of Jerusalem. They did not see their son for fourteen years.

While Rav Ashkenazi had to deal with the initial opposition to the opening of a Talmud Torah and *yeshivah ketanah* in Shanghai, Rebbetzin Ashkenazi's task was even more daunting – to deal with the even greater opposition to the opening of a Beis Yaakov school for girls. Through their dedicated and unwavering efforts, a few strong-willed women (such as Rebbetzins Ashkenazi, Mannes, and Shafran) succeeded in bringing about a favorable attitude towards the establishment of such a school. Eventually, the Beis Yaakov served over one hundred girls in two branches, one in Hongkew and one in Frenchtown.

Unfounded Criticism

Some of the liberal elements among the refugees accused Rav Ashkenazi of having a negative attitude toward the German refugees in general. For example, in July of 1945, when United States bombers attacked Hongkew, thirty-one Jews were tragically killed. Rav Ashkenazi ruled – in accordance with Jewish law – that the ritual of *taharah* was not to be performed on the mutilated bodies of the victims. The German refugees regarded this as a personal insult. They were, of course, wrong. Rav Ashkenazi's attitude and decisions were forged by a love for God, His Torah, and His people. Unfortunately, the liberal Jews' own prejudices blinded them to the true caring that Rav Ashkenazi had for them.

His caring was evidenced by his "open-door policy." Anyone who came at any time received the most cordial hospitality in the Ashkenazis' humble apartment of four small rooms. Indeed, into this small apartment he and his wife took a total stranger, a poor refugee girl from an assimilated German family, to live with his two daughters of the same age. She attests that she was always treated as one of the family, and she personally emphasizes the fact that Rav Ashkenazi, known for his strict adherence to Torah law, nevertheless took into his own household a girl from a totally assimilated German Jewish family.

The Arrival of the Mirrer Yeshiva in Shanghai

As noted above, the arrival of thousands of refugees opened an entirely new chapter in the Shanghai'er Rav's life. The arrival of the Mirrer Yeshiva — the only yeshivah to survive the war completely intact — had a similar effect. While the great Torah centers of Europe were being decimated, the spiritually starved metropolis of Shanghai, China, was suddenly transformed into one of the most important Torah centers in the world. Nearly 1,000 refugees from Poland and Eastern Europe arrived, via Kobe, Japan, in August of 1941, including over 400 yeshivah students (250 in the Mirrer Yeshiva alone), and some of the greatest Torah personalities of Europe. Before their arrival, this group of Torah scholars contacted Rav Ashkenazi and asked him to form a separate relief organization for them, so that they would not be subject to the conditions in which the other refugees had to live, which were unsuitable for Torah-observant Jews. Rav Ashkenazi spent day and night making arrangements for them (such as where to sleep, what to eat, and where to set up their study halls), and he endured much personal abuse in his efforts to secure assistance for them.

It is well known that the Mirrer Yeshiva occupied the Beit Aharon synagogue — whose seating capacity exactly matched the number of yeshivah students — when they arrived in Shanghai, and there they continued their holy studies uninterrupted. It is not widely known that it was Rav Ashkenazi — with his influence in the Sephardic community — who had contacted various figures of authority and successfully persuaded them to let the Mirrer Yeshiva have use of the facility as their *beis midrash*. With the dedicated assistance of D. J. Abraham, the leader of the Sephardic community, Rav Ashkenazi enabled the Mirrer Yeshiva to use the large and comfortable building for over three years (from their arrival in August 1941 to September 1944), until the Japanese forced them to stay in the Hongkew ghetto.

It was also Rav Ashkenazi who was responsible for obtaining permission from the Japanese authorities for Rav Chaim Shmuelevitz and the Amshenover Rebbe to live outside of the ghetto for the entire duration of the war.

Even before the arrival of the yeshivah students, Rav Ashkenazi concerned himself with the needs of each and every student. He worked tirelessly, like a father for his own son, in order to ensure that the students, and their *roshei yeshivah*, including Rav Chaim Shmuelevitz, would be able to dedicate their time and energy to uninterrupted Torah study.

His help went beyond providing them with the basic necessities. Rav Ashkenazi headed a committee of Russian Jews who financed the first part of the reprinting of books for the yeshivah students. The first offset volume was tractate *Gittin*, of which 250 copies were printed in May 1942. The printing became a cause of public celebration in Shanghai. As one non-observant Polish journalist wrote upon witnessing the scene, "One who did not witness the Amshenover Rebbe and yeshivah students dance at receiving this marvelous gift has never seen true Jewish joy and felt the secret of the Jew's eternity." The project eventually reached close to one hundred titles, including all the tractates of Gemara, the *Chumash* and commentaries, *Rambam*, and other halachic and ethical works, and even original Torah journals written by the yeshivah students themselves.

When the Japanese forced all of the refugees into the Hongkew ghetto, Rav Ashkenazi saved the lives of a number of students who had refused the orders of the Japanese gestapo to relocate to a certain building in Hongkew. The building was occupied by gentile drunkards, ex-convicts, and other derelicts, and the yeshivah students adamantly refused to reside with the dregs of Shanghai society. After a violent demonstration at the offices of the committee in charge of relocating the refugees, thirty-three students were arrested and jailed. It was only through the intervention of Rav Ashkenazi that they were set free and saved from severe punishment. The students' revolt ultimately saved their lives in another way. The building in which they were to be located was later hit by a bomb in an air raid and completely demolished.

The Rebbetzin, too, toiled to help the yeshivah students to such an extent that they called her "the mother of all the refugees." Like a devoted mother, she perceived and tended to the students' needs. For the students of marriageable age, she endeavored to find matches among the worthy daughters of the refugees. She was in charge of a charitable fund designated for young brides and grooms, and she personally cooked the meals for the weddings of the yeshivah students, with the assistance of her sister-in-law (Rav Ashkenazi's sister).

When the Rav and Rebbetzin learned that the *kallah* of an eminent *rosh yeshivah*'s son (who himself would later become one of the most prominent *roshei yeshivah* in America) had arrived, they brought her into their home and cared for her like their own daughter for the duration of her stay in Shanghai. (This woman's son and Rebbetzin Ashkenazi's great-granddaughter married each other nearly fifty years later.)

In addition to the students of the Mirrer Yeshiva, there were individuals and small groups of students from other Polish and Lithuanian yeshivos, including Kaminetz, Baranovich, Pinsk, Lublin, Kletsk, and Lubavitch. Upon their arrival, Rav Ashkenazi established a yeshivah for them so that they could continue their studies, and he served as their *rosh yeshivah*, despite his many other responsibilities. The yeshivah was named Yeshivas Mizrach HaRachok, and it published a number of original Torah journals, which included some of Rav Ashkenazi's own Talmudic lectures and ethical discourses.

Whence Will Come My Help

Basic sustenance in Shanghai was the primary challenge for the refugees during the war years, and Rav Ashkenazi rose to this challenge with all of his might. In reference to this, one eminent *rosh yeshivah* who had been a refugee in Shanghai told a grandchild of Rav Ashkenazi, "Your grandfather, that *tzaddik*, saved an entire world of Torah when it stood at the verge of destruction."

As mentioned earlier, he did not hesitate to call upon the established Sephardic and Russian Jews to contribute their resources to help their brethren. However, much of the internal support ceased when Japan entered the war and occupied Shanghai in December 1941, just after Pearl Harbor. At that time, all enemy nationals – including the wealthiest Sephardic Jews of Shanghai who held British citizenship – were interred in detainment camps, their bank accounts frozen, and their businesses taken over by the Japanese. The 4,000 Russian Jews of Shanghai were left alone by the Japanese because they held citizenship in a nation recognized by Japan, and because of a mutual neutrality pact signed with Russia in mid-1941. However, the war took a heavy toll on their income, and virtually all businesses suffered.

The primary source of support for most of the refugees, especially when internal support was curtailed after Pearl Harbor, was the American Joint Distribution Committee (JDC). However, in May of 1942, in a move that dumbfounded even the Japanese, the JDC in New York declared that it would no longer send any money to, or even communicate with, its representative in Shanghai, in compliance with America's "Trading with the Enemy Act." The main source of relief for the refugees was cut off.

Through the ceaseless efforts of a number of individuals around the globe, the refugees in Shanghai were spared starvation. Rav Avraham Kalmanowitz, *zt"l,* and other leaders of Va'ad Hatzalah in America, managed to circumvent the law for the sake of saving Jewish lives and sent money to Shanghai via neutral countries, with the help of such selfless individuals as the Sternbuch family in Switzerland and Rav Wolbe and Rav Jacobson in Sweden. Illicit means were used to transfer the money.

Eventually, largely due to the efforts of Rav Kalmanowitz,

the United States redefined its Trading with the Enemy Act, and in March of 1944 the JDC resumed its major role in providing financial support to the refugees in Shanghai. During this entire period, throughout the war years, it was Rav Ashkenazi — who held an officially recognized position in Shanghai and was not a citizen of an enemy nation — who received the transferred funds and assumed responsibility for distributing them. He did this at great personal risk, for if the source of the money (i.e., an enemy nation, the United States) had been discovered, the repercussions would have been catastrophic.

Rav Ashkenazi was indeed brought to jail for interrogation by the Japanese gestapo on a number of occasions; knowing well that he might not return, he always brought his tallis and tefillin with him. He ignored pleas that he stop endangering his life, for he knew that the money he was receiving was saving the lives of hundreds of Torah scholars, and he was prepared to risk imprisonment, torture, and death in order to fulfill his role as God's emissary to save his fellow Jews. He conducted himself in this way from mid-1942 until the war ended in August 1945.

Opening their Home, Caring for the Ill

To open one's home to a single family in need for a week, a month, or six months would certainly be considered a great act of *hachnasas orchim*. It is beyond our scope of experience to imagine the extent to which the Ashkenazis fulfilled this mitzvah. For many years, from the beginning of the influx of refugees into Shanghai until the end of the war in 1945, the Ashkenazis' home was host to hundreds of families and individuals.

Another significant challenge in Shanghai, especially during the war years, was the sanitary conditions. Amoebic dysentery, typhoid fever, beri-beri, cholera, and other tropical diseases plagued the refugee community. In this area, it was Rebbetzin Ashkenazi who rose to the challenge. Every day she visited the sick and helped provide them with their needs. Often her home became a clinic for deathly ill residents, where she waited on them without rest. She trusted in her Creator to protect her from the highly contagious diseases as she involved herself in this important mitzvah. The lives of many ill refugees were saved due to her care. One of the many yeshivah students helped by the Rebbetzin when deathly ill is today a renowned *rosh yeshivah* in New York. At the Rebbetzin's funeral, he expressed to her family his profound appreciation for the Rebbetzin.

A Pure Soul Returns to Its Maker

In 1949, shortly before the Communists came to power, and after the thousands of refugees had left and most of the original Jewish residents of Shanghai dispersed to other places around the globe, Rav Meir Ashkenazi and his wife left Shanghai. They came to New York, where their two daughters and their families lived, and settled in Crown Heights. There they were accorded much homage and esteem, and Rav Ashkenazi spent his final years learning Torah and serving God in holiness and purity. On the 26th of Av (August 25), 1954, the life that had been totally dedicated to God's service came to an end.

Yisroel Shaw studies in and writes for Kollel Iyun Hadaf (daf@dafyomi.co.il) in Jerusalem. His wife is a great-granddaughter of Rav Meir and Toiba Ashkenazi.

REFERENCES

Bernstein, A., Y. Porges, and Y. Naveh. *HaZerichah b'Pa'atei Kedem* (Hebrew). Bnei Brak: Merkaz Prager – Machon l'Moreshet Yisrael, 2001. Ch. 46.

Kirzner-Weiss, F. *For My Fathers, For My Children*. Jerusalem: 2000.

Kranzler, D. *Japanese, Nazis, and Jews: The Refugee Community of Shanghai, 1938–1945*. New York: Yeshiva University Press, 1976; personal conversation with author.

Tokayer, M., and M. Swartz. *Desperate Voyagers*. New York: Dell Publishing Co., 1979.

RABBI PHILIP GREENBERG

Jewish Survival

One of the most emotive stories I ever read took place after the Holocaust, when a group of Holocaust survivors returned to their former village in Poland, hoping to rebuild their shattered lives.

The story took place on Simchas Torah only a few days after their return. With broken hearts they assembled in their once beautiful shul and began to dance in honor of *yom tov* and the *hakafos*. Tears and sadness filled their hearts instead of joy. How can one dance *hakafos* without a *sefer Torah*? At that moment the doors opened and a young couple, themselves survivors from the concentration camps, entered with a young baby, miraculously born in the camps, who had survived together with its parents.

After a moment's reflection, one of the older men asked permission to dance, holding the baby. With a new-found sense of joy and happiness, he sang aloud, "This is our Torah, this is our future, this is the new generation: *am Yisrael, am Yisrael chai.*"

It is a wonderful sight to see our children singing "*Am Yisrael Chai*," the Nation of Israel lives. Throughout Jewish history, whenever the spiritual future of Israel has appeared to be in doubt, Divine protection has ensured that a spiritual revival would take place

What has been the single outstanding cause of this spiritual revival?

There is an interesting thought developed by Rabbi Elchanan Wasserman, *zt"l*, who himself died as a martyr during the Holocaust. He refers to the struggle of Yaakov with the angel of Eisav, and he asks, if the angel wanted to destroy the people of Israel, why did he not attack Avraham or Yitzchak, why wait for Yaakov? Rabbi Wasserman said that the three forefathers represent different qualities and characteristics. Avraham represents *chesed*, while Yitzchak represents *avodah*. Only a Yaakov who insisted on teaching to all his children unadulterated Torah, could guarantee the future righteous tribes of Israel. The angel of Eisav realized that wrestling with Yaakov was his last chance to destroy the children of Israel.

The Talmud (*Bava Metzia* 85b) says, "The Torah returns to its original home." This is the literal meaning, but it is also a promise. If there are three generations in one family in which each individual has himself become a *talmid chacham*, then that family is promised that the knowledge of Torah will always remain within that family. Future generations will take their place amongst the *talmidei chachamim* yet to be born.

This promise is also a promise to the Jewish nation that no matter how deeply their family is affected by assimilation, no matter how great may be the spiritual losses of one generation, or even two, Hashem promises His nation that events will occur that will act as a spiritual catalyst and the third generation will return to the faith of its forefathers.

The late chief rabbi of Great Britain, Chief Rabbi Lord Jacobovits, *zt"l*, once told me the following: If you take a globe of the world and insert a red pin into every thriving or revitalized Jewish community throughout the world, then insert a blue pin into every dying Jewish community, then make a list of all the vibrant communities worldwide, you will discover that, without exception, they all share a common denominator. They all have either a Jewish senior school, or a yeshivah, or a *kollel*, or a girls' seminary, or some other major Jewish Torah educational academy in the community, which has acted as a catalyst for Jewish revival.

Our losses have been manifold, history has been cruel to us, our enemies have been only too successful, yet God's promise is being and will be fulfilled. *Am Yisrael chai*.

EDITED BY RACHEL GREENBLATT

Along the Telshe Derech

Events one would think of as coincidences occurred frequently in my life and should be understood as *hashgachah pratis* (Divine providence). This certainly must have been the case with my miraculous recovery after a drop through the window at the age of one and a half years. Later, too, with a *meshulach* from abroad, who "happened" to come to Copenhagen (my home) from time to time. This particular individual helped shape my spiritual and mental development and was surely a messenger from Heaven. It was this *meshulach*, who encouraged my father to send me to the Telshe Yeshiva in Poland.

In 1929, upon being accepted to join the hundreds of other *bachurim* studying at Telshe, I discovered that the Polish passport with which I had already traveled earlier had expired. (My parents had moved from Poland to Denmark soon after their marriage, and when I was born in 1910, my parents were still Polish citizens, and so I automatically received Polish citizenship.)

I applied for an extension to my Polish passport, but to this day, I have no idea why I received instead a "Nansen passport." At that time, after the First World War, there were a huge number of refugees and displaced persons. Of course these unfortunate individuals had little or no hope of returning to their country of origin. An international organization under the leadership of a Norwegian, Mr. Nansen, introduced the idea of a stateless identification certificate known as the Nansen passport. Suddenly, I was no longer a Polish citizen, but a displaced person without a homeland.

Little did I know at that time that this occurrence was *mamash min haShamayim* (truly Heaven sent). We Jews believe and know that the so-called "by chance happenings" are not by chance at all, but are guided from Above.

A point in case is that of my passport. If I would have attempted to enter Lithuania on a Polish passport, I would most likely have been sent directly back to my last "stop," or worse still, faced immediate arrest. I later learned what neither my father nor I had previously been aware of, namely, that Lithuania and Poland were in a state of war. It was a war without battlefields, but, lacking diplomatic relations, the borders between them were hermetically sealed. I learned further that boys who came to Telshe from Poland could not travel directly back to their homes, and that correspondence too, had to be delivered via other countries, such as Germany or the USA, where it would be readdressed to Telshe.

Landing thankfully at my destination port, Memel, I somehow discovered a Jewish restaurant, and, having identified myself as a German from Konigsberg (I had stopped there last), the kind owner ordered me a horse-drawn carriage to take me the last thirty kilometers to my destination — Telshe Yeshiva. The road was no more than a dirt-track, uneven and full of holes. Lying on the bottom of the carriage (I felt sea-sick again) and with half-closed eyes, I dozed as we passed through a series of small villages. I had not the slightest idea that in these simple dilapidated wooden houses, Jewish families lived, nearly all of them dedicated to the teachings and guidance of the giants of our nation, the luminaries on the firmament of our people's history. Here lived many of the Lithuanian *gedolim* who have formed and molded *klal Yisrael* through the generations. All this I only learned later on.

The wooden building of the yeshivah did not differ much from the other houses I had seen, other than being a little larger and longer. The first room I entered, the cloakroom, was sparsely furnished with a few long tables and benches. In front of me was the big entrance door to the yeshivah hall. Hesitating, and a little frightened, I opened the door, though I did not know what to do next.

What I saw was a huge *beis midrash* with hundreds and hundreds of *bachurim* sitting with their Gemaras on their *shtenders*, learning by themselves, or together with another fellow, or in groups. Such a view (by now so familiar) left me quite overwhelmed and bewildered but also touched and excited.

I was taken under the wing of Shimon Asher, who headed a group of boys from abroad. He himself was the son of Rabbi Asher of Aix-les-Bains, the principal of a well-known exclusive seminary for girls. I was placed in a local "hotel" — a house similar to all the others where I felt thoroughly grateful for a clean bed and a warm shower.

On the day after my arrival, I was ushered in to see Rav Chaim Rabinowitz, *zt"l,* known in the yeshivah world as Reb Chaim Telzer. Here I received my first *farher* (examination on Torah learning). The *bachurim* were divided into four classes according to their level. I had to be introduced into the very unique learning method known as the Telshe *derech* (way) usually described as one of deep understanding and logical analysis. I spent half my day learning in *chavrusa* together with a young man from my *shiur* and the rest of the day with some of the higher classes. We also learned a daily *mussar* lesson by ourselves. I had the *zechus* of being a yeshivah man in this world famous yeshivah for only five *zemanim* (learning periods).

The first Shabbos after my arrival, I heard a *schmues* by the *menahel* of the yeshivah, the Telzer Rav, Reb Yosef Leib Bloch. About half a year after my arrival, Reb Yosef Leib passed away. On Yom Kippur he had a sudden severe nosebleed. Several specialists were called in from the bigger towns in the country, but in vain. Reb Yosef Leib never recovered and passed away at the beginning of Cheshvan. Rabbanim and *roshei yeshivah* from all over Lithuania joined the funeral, which started in the morning and culminated in the burial that night, illuminated by torches in the pitch black cemetery. It had been delayed due to the volume of *hespeidim.*

In addition to this tragic even, Reb Chaim also passed away half a year later. As he was very ill, he was hospitalized in Kovno, the capital. The president of Lithuania, Mr. Smetana, had put his private railway carriage at the disposal of the *rosh yeshivah,* to ease his traveling! The *levayah* took place in Slabodka, a suburb of Kovno; most of the Telshe *bachurim,* including myself, participated.

♦ ♦ ♦

Feeling uncomfortable at being the only boy in a hotel, I soon joined my fellow *bachurim* in the unending search for accommodation and meals. The majority of the students lived in rooms rented from the various families in the village, approximately 1,500 families. This numbered about half the population of Telshe. Lodging never quite seemed to be ideal, and circumstances seemed to force one to move quite frequently. Bed bugs were a constant torture. In one particular lodging, my roommate (Yaakov Rotenberg, *z"l,* who later became the Rav of Machsike Hadas in Paris) and I cleverly placed the legs of our beds in jars of water. The bed bugs outsmarted us, dropping on their prey from the ceiling above.

For a while I rented a two-room flat together with another *bachur*. Our room contained nothing but two wooden frames for beds, boasting straw-filled sacks for mattresses. There was no heating, and despite the harsh Russian winter we had to make do with thin blankets to keep ourselves warm. Sanitary facilities were extremely primitive. We, like many of the yeshivah community, were both struck with an epidemic disease known as *Kopfgrippe,* similar to a mild form of meningitis. Although we both survived the illness, the problem of food chased all the *bachurim* relentlessly. Although I personally had an arrangement with the local butcher, some boys had to be content with bread and tea the entire week. On Shabbos they would be invited to a local Jewish family to eat, and this would often be their only real meal of the week.

Most of the students received "*chalukah*" in the form of coupons accepted in all shops in Telshe. This funding came from good Jews around the world, mainly South Africa, and in many cases, it helped the *bachurim* survive.

My stay at the yeshivah was all too short, although when I left Telshe for Copenhagen, I had every intention of returning. I did not even say a proper farewell to those I had become close to, such as Rav Rogosnitzky, *z"l*, later to become the Rav of Cardiff, Wales; Rav Ordman from the Bridge Lane Shul, London; Rav Chaim Stein, *shlita*, father of Zippora Weinberg, later *rosh yeshivah* in Telshe, Cleveland; and Rav Paperman, later of Kiryat Ye'arim Telshestone, outside Jerusalem.

Unbeknownst to me, this decision to leave was to be a fateful one for me once again. My departure took place at the beginning of the 1930s as Hitler gained power in Germany. I remained in Copenhagen and completed my degree in medicine. Even at the end of the summer of 1943, I was totally ignorant of the fact that the majority of the European Jewish population had been annihilated by the "enlightened" Nazis.

On August 29, 1943, the Germans crossed the "red line," putting us in a similarly precarious position. We were protected, initially, by Dr. Christiansen, a fellow practitioner, who welcomed us into his home. He had about thirty or forty other Jews already hiding there. We had no place to sleep but we were relatively safe. As a doctor, I had taken over Dr. Christiansen's practice, as he was fully occupied collecting people from their various hiding places and assisting them to join in an escape plan. Eventually, we ourselves benefited from his immense kindness, joining others in Sweden, where I met up with a childhood friend whom I soon married.

According to my father's sister, my Auntie Esther Leah, there were at least thirty-six members of our family who perished in Poland.

In this light, I have much again to be thankful for, and am

grateful to the *Ribbono shel Olam* for allowing and assisting me to follow the Telshe *derech.*

> The late author's daughter has kindly given us permission to extract details of her father's experiences as a young man during the war years. We gratefully acknowledge her kind contribution.

RABBI YISROEL REISMAN

The Old Man Counted to Nine

Every week the visitor came. And every week he expounded on another spiritual facet of the number nine...passing through the *galus-geulah* cycle...passing from the pangs of birth, through the trials of life, to death.

The Old Man sometimes visited our home. We knew very little about him — not where he lived nor where he was headed. He appeared at our door before a Shabbos meal and was quickly welcomed to the Shabbos table. Purportedly, he came to eat. Actually, he did most of the feeding.

The Old Man rarely talked about himself. Scraps of conversation revealed years of fleeing the Nazis and decades of defying the Russians; even a pitiful attempt at battling the bureaucratic secular government in Eretz Yisrael. Somehow, these experiences left our guest with a wisdom and insight I've never experienced in yeshivah...a wisdom he was quick to share at the Shabbos table.

Often, we — actually he — talked about the *churban*:

> It seems obvious that the *churban* should have taken place in the month of Shevat, for the meaning of Shevat is "stick," a word related to destruction. But instead Hashem brought about the *churban* in the month of Av, which means "father." For His rebuke — like that of a father — is wholesome and good, and never destructive.

Tishah B'Av — a day of sad memories for a nation that has long grown weary of remembering. A day of *kinnos* that seem to go on forever, in recollection of one tragedy after another. And a day of somber and dazed reflection over the lost world of our parents and grandparents, shattered and destroyed by a decade of hate and hopelessness.

But there exists another dimension to Tishah B'Av. A world of hope and joy, of laughter and glee. This is a faraway world rarely visited or understood, and then only by the greatest of men. Rabbi Akiva lived in this world. The sight of the desolation of the Beis HaMikdash brought laughter to his lips, an eerie laughter in the ears of his fellow Tannaim, a laughter which rings hollow in our poor ears and minds. Yet, Rabbi Akiva's laughter was genuine; in his sphere of existence, these heart-rending sights caused no tears. Someday, perhaps, we'll understand. We're taught that Mashiach will uncover the portal to this curious dimension of Tishah B'Av. On that day, we will learn to sing and dance with Rabbi Akiva, and Tishah B'Av will become a holiday, surpassing all others. But until then, we sit on the ground and weep...adding our tears to the millions of others — mere mortals like us — who understood Tishah B'Av by its simple meaning. Unless, of course, you have an old visitor who can peek through the curtains and reveal some of the secrets....

Did you ever wonder why the *churban* took place on the ninth day of the month, rather than on another day? The Old Man knew.

> Look at the letter *tes*, the ninth letter of the *alef-beis*. The letter is shaped like a circle, which, instead of closing, points toward its own center. Do you know why it has such a peculiar shape? [Know?! I'd never even noticed.]
>
> *Tes* symbolizes *tov*, goodness — and the letter tells us never to judge anything from its outer circumference. The *tes* points to its center, for the good in events is to be found deep in the hidden recesses and secret chambers of Hashem's plans. Tishah B'Av certainly represents a cycle of calamities. But somehow, somewhere the *tov* of Tishah B'Av will be penetrated...
>
> Appropriately, the ninth plague in Egypt was the Plague of Darkness. *Tes* is always enveloped in a cloak of darkness; the *tov* hidden until the light of Mashiach. So, too, the ninth of the Ten levels of redemption is "and there was light" — a light of wisdom which will pierce all veils and reveal the goodness of our history.

Herded out of boxcars, a group of Chassidim huddled around their Rebbe, in what they knew were their final moments. Suddenly, one remembered: "Today is Simchas Torah — we must dance and rejoice with the Torah!"

"But, Rebbe, we have no *sefer Torah* to dance with."

"Then we will dance with each other."

And dance they did, with a joy that is incomprehensible, in honor of Simchas Torah. How they could sing and rejoice to such a degree under those circumstances is beyond us. But perhaps, just perhaps, in their final moments, these Yidden were privileged to experience that joyful dimension of Tishah B'Av that lies way beyond our grasp; to somehow comprehend a blinding light of goodness, even in their situation; and to sing and dance in the realm of Rabbi Akiva.

♦ ♦ ♦

Our Old Man loved children. Young or old, he relished singing with them and getting them to dance around the Shabbos table. And, often, he would tell a story of another time and another place, where children sang and danced…

In 1946, most of the remnants of European Jewry were squeezed into DP camps awaiting a chance to go someplace — anyplace — to begin rebuilding their lives. In one such camp, clandestine preparations were being made.

Somehow, by combining their meager resources, a group of Yidden had gotten together to buy an old merchant ship, the *Queen*. And crammed with poor, tired, but excited refugees, she prepared to set sail for Eretz Yisrael. One section had been set aside for children, but at boarding time that section had overflowed. A quick decision was made: those children with parents on board would go. All others were made to disembark. Thirty-five children, orphans of the war, left the ship — knocked, in a single moment, from the heights of expectation to the depths of depression. Our remarkable Old Man left with them, to guide and protect children who were left all alone.

Shabbos was coming and the mood of despair was stifling. Our Old Man looked around the Shabbos table at thirty-five faces of defeat. Then, he decided to speak. He spoke of hope and joy, of a little lamb among the wolves, and of a shepherd who hides, but never sleeps. He spoke a little about the past and a lot about the future; of the children who happily tossed themselves into the sea to avoid the Roman slave market; and of the morrows when they would finally get their chance, certainly a better chance, to start again. And he told them of a lesson Rabbi Akiva had taught 2,000 years earlier: "*Kol d'avid Rachmana l'tav avid,*" All that Hashem causes to happen is — in some secret, mysterious way — for the best.

And, miraculously, the children understood. Soon thirty-five children, so fearfully alone, felt alone no longer. Somehow, they were singing: "*Kol d'avid Rachmana...*" And, certainly, Rabbi Akiva — from high above — was singing along.

It was many months later that I chanced upon the history of the *Queen*. She had arrived in Palestine, only to be turned back and wander from one European port to another. Ultimately its passengers returned to the very country from which they had set sail months earlier.

But my discovery had no real effect on the Old Man. "Mine is a belief in intrinsic goodness. Focusing on an obvious good serves only to cloak the infinite, still secret *tov* that our eyes are too dull to see. No, yours is not an ending to my tale; my story is more truthful without it."

♦ ♦ ♦

Nines. The Old Man loved nines. Whenever the *mesorah* used the number nine, the Old Man saw a message for Tishah B'Av — his message of hope and joy. He ridiculed the idea of coincidence, and showed us (when we could keep up with him) that the message of *tes* — of ultimate goodness — was there to be seen by those acute enough to see it. His eyes glowed as they focused on some faraway place, and plucked nines from *mesorah* onto our Shabbos table, nines that all had the same basic message. Various insights into Ibn Ezra's nonagon and Maharal's exposition of 9 = 32 became regular staples of our Shabbos diet. The fact that the *churban* takes place at the end of the ninth *sefer* of *Tanach* was just another message of hope. "Do you know how many years it was from the building of the First Temple until the final *churban*, destruction of the Second Temple?" he asked. I didn't have to bother figuring it out: nine hundred years ("exactly!"). It just had to be that way.

On Shabbos *Parashas Vayeishev*, our Old Man barely had time to eat. The selling of Yosef — the first step of the first *galus* of *klal Yisrael* — surely had his lesson of hope. And it does. The sale of Yosef by his brothers was a seemingly tragic event at the time it occurred. But in the end, the *shevatim*, the brothers, are told, "You thought to do bad, but Hashem planned it for good!"

"*Parashas Vayeishev*," the Old Man smiled, "the ninth parashah of the Torah."

The ninth mitzvah of the Torah, too, symbolizes a similar hope. *Hashbasas sior* — the burning of *chametz* on *erev Pesach* — is kabbalistically symbolic of the destroying of evil on the *erev*, the eve, of the final redemption. "The son of David will not come until the (spiritual) leaven is expunged from the dough." This is symbolized, too, in the ninth *masechta* of *Shas*, *Masechta Challah*, which deals with the elevating of dough to a level of holiness.

The Old Man's intensity overpowered me. The content of his remarks was good, sometimes unbelievably so, but his enthusiasm was the core of his power. He didn't just believe that there is joy in everything; he knew it. He didn't search for the good in events; the good was only-too-obviously there. Even in Siberia…

The Russians jailed him for fifteen years for teaching Hebrew. One morning, he was summoned to the office of the commandant, and a deal was offered. If he would sign a letter of "repentance" recanting his belief in God, he would be set free.

The Old Man was overjoyed. "Commandant, I've wasted fifteen years of the best years of my life rotting in your prison – and for what? For teaching an illegal language. How much better is it that my suffering be for my belief in God."

The commandant was unimpressed. The Old Man was sent back to his cell to serve out his sentence, singing his praise of Hashem for this most wonderful turn of events.

Chazal teach us that there are eight levels of existence – a world and seven heavens. Sometimes, I think our Old Man has a level all to himself...a ninth world that is all his own.

♦ ♦ ♦

One Pesach, our guest made arrangements to eat Seder with us. That's not really accurate. The Old Man never came to eat – he came to share his wealth with us. We invited him into our home, but he invited us into his world. On Pesach this was especially so. In a realm where *Eichah* is a book of hope and redemption, the Haggadah is pure ecstasy.

While preparing for the Seder, I hit upon a plan: on this Night of Questions, I would catch our Old Man – who always had an answer – without one.

At the *eser makkos,* the ten plagues, the Old Man spoke – as I had expected – of darkness, the ninth *makkah,* and of the plague of darkness we still suffer when we refuse to see the *tov* around us. Other nines sprouted up and blended neatly into his message of joy. I asked him, "Do you mean that nines always represent the same idea?" Without hesitation, he said that it was certainly so. I had baited my trap.

It was way past *chatzos*, and the seven pairs of bleary eyes around our Seder table inched towards *Chad Gadya*. Together we chanted, "*Echad mi yode'a... Shnayim mi yode'a,*" and soon, "*Tishah mi yode'a, tishah ani yode'a, tishah yarchei leidah*" — and I spoke up. "Nine months of pregnancy — Why nine? Certainly, it bears no connection to Tishah B'Av!" I could see no possible connection, and when the Old Man hesitated, I was sure that I had him stumped.

But I had underestimated our guest. He had hesitated just a second — to settle back onto his *hesebah* pillows, and to assume that familiar faraway look.

> It's late and I wasn't going to keep you, but since you've asked — yes, Rav Yisrael Salanter explained that the nine months it takes a baby to form are very central to our theme.
>
> For two and a half years, the schools of Shammai and Hillel argued. Some said that man would be better off had he not been created at all, while the others argued that man's existence was the best for him. Finally, they agreed. It would be better for man had he not been created, but, once created, let him carefully examine his actions.
>
> How puzzling! We, also have a *mesorah* that "all Hashem does is for the best," are told that the very Creation was not for the best?
>
> But, Rav Yisrael Salanter explained, this is not the point at all. It is indisputable that Creation was an absolute good; the Schools of Shammai and Hillel argued about man's capacity to appreciate the goodness of Creation, to see his own good fortune in being born. This is something worthy of two and a half years of argument!
>
> And in the end all agreed. Man's birth, while

> inherently good, is not apparently good. When we try to analyze the pros and cons of existence, the raison d'etre of our birth, we'll inevitably fall short. As in the *churban*, the true *tov* is hidden — and the nine is there to remind us that it exists.

"We know that Hashem created the world with *asarah ma'amaros*, ten utterances. Take a *Chumash*," he beckoned to me. "What is the ninth *ma'amar*?"

Carefully, I counted to the ninth *amirah* of Creation: "And Hashem said, 'Let us create man...' "

A nine at Creation, and a nine at birth. Soon I was to learn of the nine at death.

♦ ♦ ♦

Spring arrived, Shavuos passed, and before we knew it, summer was approaching. And no sign of our Old Man. On Friday evenings our eyes would scan the deserted block, searching desperately for that slow, familiar walk. But it was not to be, for the Old Man — our strong invulnerable teacher — had contracted a dreaded disease from which he would never recover.

Apparently he did not want to worry us, for it wasn't until mid-July that we heard from him. I rushed to Mt. Sinai hospital to pay him a visit, hoping that somehow everything was all right. But it wasn't.

Propped up on pillows, the Old Man was even skinnier than I had remembered him. Pipes and tubes ran to his arms and nose. Somehow he seemed thin but not weak, pale but not frightened. His eyes still shone with a living brightness as I walked through the doorway. In a barely audible voice, he told me: "Everything is all right. I have my *Tehillim*" — he tapped the faded brown *sefer* in his hands — "and that's more than I've had for most of my life." He could barely speak — or even smile — but the satisfaction he felt as his eyes read through the lines of his *Tehillim* was apparent.

Like the *talmidim* of Rabbi Akiva, so many years before, I felt like asking him, "But, Rebbe, to such an extent..."

Just two days later, I arrived at his room to find that the Old Man had lapsed into a coma. Gently, I held his hand and whispered to him, but there was no response.

His *Tehillim* was open on the patient-table beside him. Curious, I glanced inside...and I gasped.

The *Tehillim* was opened to the ninth chapter: "A song on the death of a son...I will be joyful and happy with you, I will sing your song from on High."

Time passes and memories dim. But lessons remain. Whenever I'm upset by one of life's minor travails, I remember: the tip of the *tes* points inward, to the ineffable joy within.

Reprinted with permission from the *Jewish Observer*.

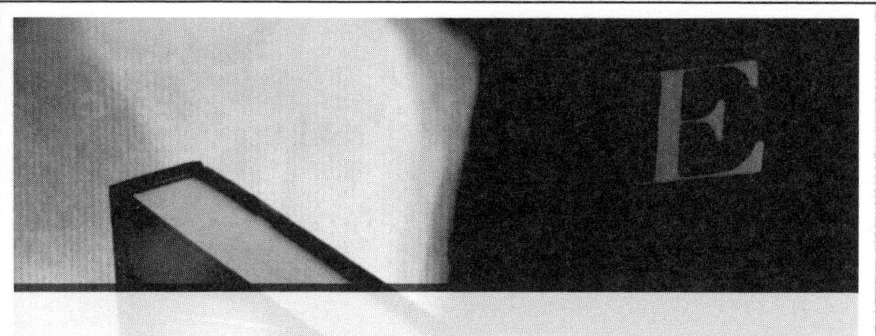

Science and Torah

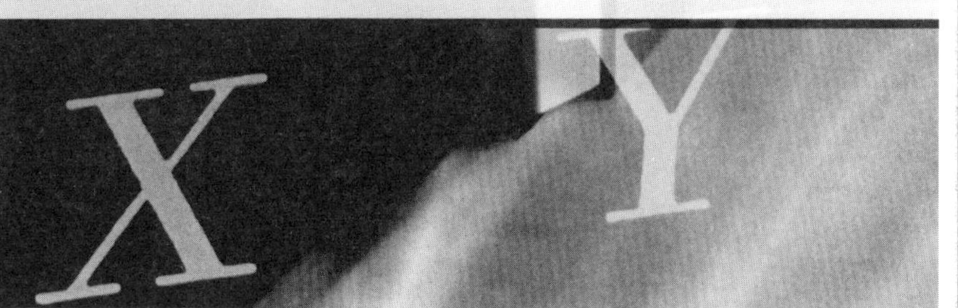

DR. JULIAN SCHAMROTH

The Solar Year in the Judaic Calendar

The Judaic calendar is based on both the solar and lunar year and thus has a very complex structure. This article deals with the first aspect of the Hebrew calendar: that of the solar year and its associated events.

The solar year (or more correctly, the tropical year) is the time taken by the sun to complete one circuit of the celestial sphere, from its position at one vernal (spring) equinox to the next. The current value is

365 days, 5 hours, 48 minutes, 45 seconds
= 365.24219 days

The Judaic calendar, however, uses two different measurements for the tropical year. These are the "Mar Shmuel" year and the "Rav Adda" year.

The Mar Shmuel Year

According to Mar Shmuel, each season lasts 91 days and 7½ hours (*Eruvin* 56a). The duration of a tropical year is thus

4 x (91d 7h 30m) = 365.25000 days

Mar Shmuel, also known as Shmuel Yarchinai, was a prominent Talmudic scholar, physician, and astronomer who lived in the third century (165–250 CE). Although he was no doubt aware of the more accurate duration of a tropical year, he used the less accurate figure of 365¼ days since:

a) The figure of 365¼ days was already being used at that time by the Romans.

b) The figure of 365¼ days was much easier to work with, especially for the general populace who were not proficient in mathematics. (Even Ptolemy, the famous astronomer, acknowledged that he too used multiples of 60 in order to avoid dealing with fractions.) Similarly, we find that the Talmud gives a value of 3 instead of pi (3.141592...) for the relation between the diameter and the circumference of a circle (*Eruvin* 13b).

It is clear that Mar Shmuel's duration of the year, the value of pi, and other values in the Talmud (such as the relation of the area of a circle to its circumscribed square) [*Sukkah* 8a]) were accurately known, but were rounded off to enable easier computations for the performance of the necessary religious precept.

The Mar Shmuel year is currently only used for determining when to say the Blessing on the Sun (*Birkat HaChamah*) and the Prayer for Dew and Rain (*Tal 'matar*).

The Rav Adda Year

According to Rav Adda bar Ahava, the tropical year is defined as one-nineteenth of a 19-year solar cycle. Its duration is given as

365d 5h 55m 25.4s = 365.24682 days

The Rav Adda year is about 5 minutes less than the Mar Shmuel year and is the more accurate of the two systems. It is used for all civil and religious calculations, apart from the two prayers mentioned above.

According to Piniles (*Darko Shel Torah*, Vienna 1861, pp. 147–150), the source of the Rav Adda year is unknown, but may be based on a statement of Rabbi Yochanan in the Jerusalem Talmud (*Avodah Zarah* 1:2).

Let us now compare some aspects of the secular calendar with the Judaic calendar.

The Julian Calendar

The Julian calendar was introduced by Julius Caesar in 46 BCE and, like that of Mar Shmuel, was based on a year of 365¼ days.

To correct previous inaccuracies, the year 46 BCE was made to last 445 days...the so-called *annus confusionis*. That year ran from October 13, 47 BCE to December 31, 46 BCE.

The Julian calendar compares with the tropical year as follows:

In each 1,000-year period, there are

250 leap years = 250 x 366 = 91,500 days
750 normal years = 750 x 365 = 273,750 days

There are thus a total of 365,250 days every 1,000 Julian years compared with 365,242.19 days every 1,000 tropical years. The Julian year (as does the year of Mar Shmuel) thus gains on the tropical year by

$$365{,}250 - 365{,}242.19 = 7.81 \text{ days every } 1{,}000 \text{ years}$$

The Gregorian Calendar

By the year 1582, the Julian calendar was about 10 days ahead of the tropical year, and an adjustment was again necessary. With the help of the astronomer Christopher Clavius, Pope Gregory XIII consequently introduced two adjustments, and the Gregorian calendar — which is still in use today — was established. (Interestingly, the calendar adjustments, which were promulgated by the Council of Nicaea, were deliberately made so that the date of Easter would not coincide with the Jewish Passover.)

These two calendar adjustments were as follows:

> a) Ten days were removed from the calendar in 1582. This was immediately accepted in Spain, Portugal, and Italy. October 5 of that year was thus followed by October 15. Riots actually broke out in several European cities since people believed their lives were being shortened by ten days! Germany, Sweden, and Denmark accepted the changes in 1700, whereas the Gregorian calendar system was only accepted in England in 1752. By that time, the Julian calendar was 12 days ahead of the tropical year, so September 2 of that year was thus followed by September 14. In Russia, the Gregorian calendar was finally accepted on February 14, 1918, by which time 13 days had to be dropped. The Russian Orthodox Church still keeps its

ecclesiastical calendar according to the Julian calendar. These points should be borne in mind when consulting very old calendars or dated documents. For example, an Eastern European document dated, say, 1904, may be 13 days off.

b) A centenary year not divisible by 400 is not a leap year. The years 1700, 1800, and 1900 are therefore not leap years, whereas the years 1600 and 2000 are.

It follows that the Gregorian calendar is currently 13 days ahead of the Julian calendar (10 days for the initial correction, plus 1 day each for the three "skipped" leap years in 1700, 1800, and 1900). Thus January 1 in the Julian (or Mar Shmuel) calendar corresponds to January 14 in the current Gregorian calendar.

Just how accurate is the Gregorian calendar? In each 1,000 year period there are:

242 leap years = 242 x 366= 88,572 days
758 normal years = 758 x 365 = 276,670 days

There are thus a total of 365,242 days every 1,000 Gregorian years compared with 365,242.19 days every 1,000 tropical years. The Gregorian year thus differs from the true tropical year by only

365,242 - 365,242.19 = .19 days every 1,000 years

Compare this with 7.81 days every 1,000 years for the Julian year.

Comparison of the Mar Shmuel and Gregorian Calendars

According to the Judaic calendar, the vernal equinox currently falls on April 8 (or April 7 in a leap year), whereas according to the Gregorian calendar it falls on March 21...some 18 days earlier! The 18-day difference arises from:

a) The current 13-day difference between the Gregorian and the Julian (or Mar Shmuel) calendar (see above).

b) The 5-day difference due to Caesar having established the vernal equinox as occurring on March 26 instead of March 21.

A second way of looking at this 18-day difference is to consider that the Mar Shmuel year gains on the Rav Adda year by

$$365.25000 - 365.24682 = 0.00318 \text{ days per year}$$

According to Mar Shmuel, the Hebrew year 5760 is thus ahead of the Rav Adda year by

$$0.00318 \times 5{,}760 = 18.32 \text{ days.}$$

(In the year 2100, this difference will increase by 1 day to 19.32 days.)

At this point, it is appropriate to briefly consider the Blessing on the Sun and the Prayer for Dew and Rain, both of which are based on the Mar Shmuel year.

Blessing on the Sun (Birkat HaChamah)

This prayer is said every 28th year:

The Rabbis taught: Anyone seeing the sun at its turning

> point...should say, "Blessed is He who made the Creation." And when is this? Abaya said: every 28th year.

On what is this 28-year cycle based?

According to Hebrew tradition, the sun was placed at the vernal equinox at the beginning of the fourth day of Creation (Tuesday at 6:00 p.m.), as derived from the passage (*Bereishis* 1:16): "And God made the two great luminaries, the great luminary to rule the day..."

Since the Mar Shmuel year lasts 365¼ days — or 52 weeks plus a remainder of 1¼ days — it follows that after one tropical year, the sun will return to the vernal equinox, but this will fall 1¼ days later in the week, or Wednesday at midnight. After a second year, the sun will return to the vernal equinox, but it will be 2 x 1¼ days later in the week, or Thursday at 6:00 a.m. Only after 28 years will the sun return to the vernal equinox again at the beginning of the fourth day of the week.

The Sages thus used this opportunity to institute a special prayer acknowledging God's might and His creation of the world. This 28-year cycle is called the great cycle (*machzor gadol*).

The Blessing of the Sun was last said on the 8th of Nissan 5741 (April 8, 1981). This was the 205th 28-year cycle of the sun. It will be said again on April 8 in the years 2009, 2037, 2065, and 2093. In the 22nd century, the date will advance to April 9 for the years 2121, 2149, and 2177. (A detailed analysis, in English, of the Blessing of the Sun may be found in the book *Bircas Hachammah* [NY: Mesorah Pub., Inc., 1980].)

Prayer for Dew and Rain (Tal U'matar)

The Prayer for Dew and Rain is said from the 60th day of the autumnal equinox:

> (*Taanis* 10a): Chanania says: In the Diaspora the prayer for rain is said after sixty days in the season.

According to the Gregorian calendar, the autumnal equinox falls on September 23. As explained above, the corresponding Mar Shmuel date falls 18 days later on October 11, and the Prayer for Dew and Rain should thus commence 60 days later on December 9. The prayer, however, is recited some 4 days earlier, from December 5 (or December 6 in leap years). Why, then, the 4-day discrepancy?

According to Mar Shmuel, each season lasts an average of 91 days and 7½ hours (or 91.31 days). However, the elliptical orbit of the Earth results in seasons of differing lengths: summer being about 3½ days longer than winter — a point noted by early Talmudic scholars.

(The Persian calendar takes these seasonal variations into account so that the first day of the 1st, 4th, 7th, and 10th months coincide with the day of the equinoxes and solstices.)

Season Length: Actual vs. Mar Shmuel			
Season	Actual Duration (days)	Cumulated Duration (days)	Cumulated Duration (Mar Shmuel)
Spring (Mar 21 – Jun 20)	92.84	92.84	91.31
Summer (Jun 21– Sep 22)	93.60	186.44	182.62
Autumn (Sep 23 – Dec 21)	89.80	276.24	273.93
Winter (Dec 22 – Mar 20)	89.02	365.26	365.25

From the above table, it is evident that by the time of the autumnal equinox – on the 23rd of September – the true season is almost 4 days ahead of the Mar Shmuel season (186.44 days - 182.62 days). The Prayer for Dew and Rain is thus not recited on December 9, but 4 days earlier on December 5.

Blessings for Other Astronomical Events

In addition to the Blessing on the Sun and the Prayer for Dew and Rain, a blessing may be said on sighting comets (*cochvah d'shavit*) or shooting stars. Comets and their periodicity (i.e., their cyclical reappearance) were known in Talmudic times. The Talmud relates how Rabbi Yehoshua took extra provisions on a sea voyage because once every seventy years a star appears that leads ships astray (*Horayos* 10a).

(Historically, this event does not appear to relate to Halley's comet, which has a periodicity of 76.03 years, and could not have appeared at the time when Rabbi Yehoshua undertook his voyage.)

> (*Berachos* 58b): Shmuel related: I am as familiar with the paths of heaven as with the streets of Nehardea, except for the comet, about which I am ignorant.

The Talmud says that a blessing should be said whenever "*zikin*" are seen (*Berachos* 54a). These could be meteors, or "shooting stars," since *zikin* are defined as "a kind of star that shoots across the sky like an arrow, from one point to another, and whose light is drawn out in a rod-like line" (*Shulchan Aruch, Orach Chaim* 227). An alternative definition of *zikin* could be comets, or "a star with a tail and a rod of light" (*Mishnah Berurah* 227).

Besides the Blessing on the Sun, the Prayer for Dew and

Rain, and blessings on comets and shootings stars, all other events in the Judaic calendar are based on the more complex lunar year.

Dr. Schamroth's article is based on chapter 6 in his book, *A Glimpse of Light* (Targum Press, 1998).

AVRAHAM SUTTON

The Spiritual Significance of the Ketoret

In March 1988, Vendyl Jones and his team of Noahide volunteers found a clay juglet measuring approximately five inches high in a cave at Qumran, just west of the northern end of the Dead Sea.* The juglet contained a most unusual oil. It is believed to be the only surviving sample of the balsam oil that

* Vendyl Jones is a biblical archeologist who has been digging in Qumran, near the Dead Sea, for over twenty years. To date, Vendyl has been successful in identifying the ancient site of Gilgal (the Plymouth Rock of Israel), and the threshing floor of Nachon where Uzza was smitten when he touched the Ark of the Covenant (*Shmuel* II 6:6). These places were hitherto undiscovered until Prof. Jones located them using aerial photography and satellite remote sensing. Vendyl Jones' excavations are based on the Copper Scroll discovered in 1952 in Qumran, as well as other rabbinic sources. These sources indicate where the ancient Mishkan and all the artifacts related to it were hidden during both the First and Second Temple periods.

was prescribed in the Torah for anointing the Mishkan (Tabernacle) and its vessels, as well as the priests (*kohanim*), prophets, and kings of Israel. The oil was still viscous, but because of its age it had solidified into a gelatin-like substance that resembled molasses. The juglet that contained the oil was wrapped in palm leaves and carefully concealed in a three-foot-deep pit that preserved it from looting and the extreme climatological extremes of the area.

Four years later, in April 1992, Vendyl and his team made another discovery. In a cave not far from where the juglet of oil was found, they uncovered 600 kilos of a "reddish-brown organic substance" in a rock silo that had been deliberately concealed. The silo had been constructed in such a way as to protect its contents from the surrounding environment. Subsequent palynological analysis determined that the substance contained traces of all eleven spices that were used in the manufacture of the incense mixture that was burned in the Temple (*pitum haketoret*). In addition to the *ketoret* compound, Sodom salt and Karshina lye, two inorganic ingredients used to prepare the *ketoret*, were also found at the site, in a refined state.

In 1994, a sample of the incense spices was presented to Rabbi Yehudah Getz of blessed memory, late Chief Rabbi of the Western Wall and Holy Places in Israel. A sample was also given to Rabbi Ovadiah Yosef, who had his own chemist analyze the mixture to confirm its organic nature. Both rabbis agreed that Vendyl could "burn" some of the incense for scientific purposes (not with fire but with hydrochloric acid).

The results of the tests were astonishing. Although the spice mixture had lost some of its potency over the two millennia since its burial, it was still powerful. The residue of its fragrance lingered in the vicinity for several days following the experiment. Several people who were present when the test was conducted reported that their hair and clothing retained the aroma. Even more amazing, the area in which the spices were burned had somehow changed. Before the test, it was infested with the usual variety of flies, ants, moths and other insects. But after the *ketoret* was burned, no sign of these pests could be found. The phenomenon was remarkably consistent with the description of the effect of the incense found in *mishnah Avot* (5:5), where it says there were no flies in the area of the Temple, nor was a snake or scorpion ever able to harm anyone anywhere in the vicinity as long as the Temple stood.

The power and long-range effect of the *ketoret*'s aroma was no less astonishing, as brought out in the Talmud (*Yoma* 39b): The goats in Jericho (just north of Qumran) would sneeze from the aroma of the *ketoret*. Women in Jericho never needed to perfume themselves due to the ubiquitous aroma of the *ketoret*. A bride in Jerusalem never needed to wear a perfume pendant (a small packet of herbs worn near the body) due to the ubiquitous aroma of the *ketoret*.

In 1995, I met Vendyl Jones and began working with him. The following year, I met Avraham Sand of Tiferet International Aromatherapy. Avraham isn't an archeologist, but he is a master perfumer. For the last decade he and Reuven Prager of Beged Ivri have been trying to unravel the secret of exactly which ingredients and processes were used to formulate the finely ground *ketoret*. Their work was performed in close association with and under the rabbinical guidance of Rabbi Menachem Burstein, the foremost Jewish authority on the botany and chemistry of Temple artifacts. In order to sidestep the strict prohibition against experimentation with the various plant materials in their original form, Rabbi Burstein advised them that there is no prohibition whatsoever against enjoying the essential oil extracts of these same botanicals. At last report, Avraham and Reuven were able to authenticate and obtain ten of the original eleven incense spices, and produce them in the form of essential oils. In essence, their work and findings parallel Vendyl's discoveries of both the anointing oil and the *ketoret* in Qumran.

The Talmud (*Arachin* 16a) indicates that the Holy Temple (Beit HaMikdash) and the Desert Tabernacle (Mishkan), as well as all their sacred vessels — the holy ark (*aron hakodesh*), candelabra (*menorah*), incense altar (*mizbe'ach haketoret*), showbread table (*shulchan lechem hapanim*), garments of the high priest (*bigdei kohen gadol*), ashes of the red heifer (*efer parah adumah*), etc. — were not just physical artifacts. They represented spiritual levels of closeness to God. The same is true of the anointing oil (*shemen hamishchah*) and the incense (*ketoret*).

What, then, are the implications of these and other finds? Might they be a signal to us, portents of good things to come, parts of a larger drama that is unfolding here in the Land of Israel — not only all around us, but deep down at the root of our very souls? Remember when the juglet of oil (***shemen***) was found in the Temple by the Cha**shm**o**n**aim? Remember what it signified? It was the power of eight (***shemonah***) that calls us to see miracles in the subtle order of nature, in the confusing events of our individual and collective lives, in the hidden pathways of Divine providence that guides Israel and all mankind from behind the scenes of history. Eight is the power that can arouse the souls of men from their collective slumber. By reminding us of those times when God did indeed overtly "interfere with" and "alter" the "natural" course of history, it can arouse us in anticipation of the powerful revelation of His salvation that we await in our own time.

Perhaps more important, by getting back in touch with the

mystery of the *ketoret,* by unearthing its ancient secrets, we can awaken something else within ourselves that is sorely needed at this time. Come let us explore the deeper meaning of the *ketoret* in our time.

Proportions

The table on the following page, taken from Vendyl Jones' *Report on the Excavations at Qumran,* is based on the work of Dr. Marvin Antelmen, Chemical Advisor at Weizzman Institute, Rechovot. In his report, Dr. Antelman writes: "The following table gives the Hebrew terminology of the ingredient followed by a translation culled from various sources by the author of this report, together with the units found in the Talmud and a percentage composition based on approximations. The problem arising in the approximations are that the *maneh* measurement of the Talmud is a weight measure and the *seah* and *kab* are liquid and dry volumetric measures. Approximations of those materials whose amounts are not known are educated guesses. Accordingly, Cypress wine and Karshina lye have been 'guesstimated.' "

Teshuvah

Details are never meant to obscure essence, but rather to give us vessels within which to receive essence. After seeing how much is involved in the *ketoret* (all of which is a necessary preparation to get to the essence), we might tend to lose sight of the fact that a single thread runs throughout this entire discussion from beginning to end. In the siddur, in the section of the *Ketoret* that begins "*Tanu Rabbanan,*" we learn that it is universally agreed upon that a *maneh* of incense mixture was to be of-

The Eleven Ketoret Spices as listed in the Talmud and Siddur:		
Ingredient	Amount in Maneh	%Comp.
1) *ha'tzori*-balsam	70 *maneh*	13.0%
2) *ha'tziporen*-onycha	70 *maneh*	13.0%
3) *ha'chelbenah*-galbanum	70 *maneh*	13.0%
4) *ha'levonah*-frankincense	70 *maneh*	13.0%
5) *mor*-myrrh	16 *maneh*	3.0%
6) *ketzia*-cassia	16 *maneh*	3.0%
7) *shibolet nerd*-spikenard	16 *maneh*	3.0%
8) *kharkom*-saffron	16 *maneh*	3.0%
9) *ha'kosht*-costus	12 *maneh*	2.2%
10) *k'lufah*-aromatic bark	3 *maneh*	0.6%
11) *kinnamon*-cinnamon	9 *maneh*	1.7%
A) *borit* — Karshina-lye	9 *kab*	14.3%
B) *yein Kafrisin* — Cypress wine	3 *se'in*/3 *kabin*	16.8%
C) *melach Sedomit* — Sodom salt	0.25 *kab*	0.3%
D) *maaleh ashan* — smoke producer	*Kol shehu*	0.1%
E) *kipat haYarden* — Jordan amber	*Kol shehu*	0.1%

Technical Note: According to Rabbi Avraham Chayim Naeh, a Mishnaic *maneh* equals 480 grams (slightly less than half a kilogram and slightly more than one pound). A second opinion is that of Rabbi Aryeh Kaplan (*The Living Torah*, Exodus 30:34, p. 445; *The Torah Anthology*, volume 11, p. 43), according to which a *maneh* equals 100 biblical shekels, or five pounds. Thus, according to the first opinion, 368 *maneh*, one year's supply of *ketoret*, amounted to 368+ pounds. According to the second opinion, 368 *maneh* amounted to 2,840 pounds.

Other ingredients used to prepare the eleven primary spices were: nine *kabin* (nine quarts according to Kaplan) of Karshina-vetch lye, three *se'in* and three *kabin* (21 quarts) of Cyprus-caper wine or aged white wine, ¼ *kab* (1 cup) of Sodom salt-nitrate, as well as small amounts of *maaleh ashan* ("smoke-producing herb," probably leptadenia pyrotechnica, which contains nitric acid), and Jordan amber (probably cyclomen).

fered each day of the year. The "dispute" seemed to center around how much incense had to be made at once (368 *maneh*, one for each day of the solar year, plus three extra for Yom Kippur), on the one hand, or how little could be made at once (half a *maneh* for the morning or the evening *ketoret* offering), on the other hand. [See Rabbi Sutton's original essay for a fuller treatment of this subject.]

The truth is that these are just two ways of looking at our lives. Should we see our lives on a "large" annual scale, or should we see them on a relatively "tiny" daily scale. Obviously, both have advantages and both are important. The essence is to live each day to the fullest, paying attention to all the ingredients that go into making them up. This includes seeing the ingredients that don't smell so good as an important part of life. And then, when we get to Rosh HaShanah or Yom Kippur, we can look back on a year full of "full" days. On Yom Kippur, our *ketoret* will already have been ground. With our extra *teshuvah*, we will just grind it finer yet, thus making sure that there is no admixture of evil that hasn't been processed and elevated back to its source.

For this is the essence, isn't it? *Teshuvah* is the ability to restructure a new life and a new personality out of the raw material (and even the broken pieces) we were given to work with. With *teshuvah*, we can transform the greatest darkness into light, the most bitter experience into something sweet.

We saw above how powerful and far-reaching the aroma of the *ketoret* was. It is also taught that the incredible aroma of the *ketoret* was especially conducive to doing *teshuvah*. It is taught that whoever smelled the fragrance of the *ketoret* when it was being burned on the golden altar would have thoughts of *teshuvah*. His heart would be purified of all evil thoughts and saved from the defilement of the evil urge (*Zohar* 2:218b; *Torah Anthology*, volume 9, p. 307).

Vendyl Jones, in *Report on the Excavations at Qumran*, quotes Dr. Terry Hutter (*Palynological Assessment of the Qumran Spices*, May 5, 1994):

> The aroma released from the spice compound during its processing was profuse and almost immediate. It initially saturated my hands as well as the clothes that I was wearing. Within a matter of minutes my laboratory and the surrounding area (for an area of several meters) was affected by the scent released from the spices... On the first day of processing, the aroma was so intense that I could almost taste it... Upon my return home that evening, the scent that had attached itself on my body and clothes was readily apparent to both my wife and daughter. During the course of the week, the odor lessened slightly but was still noticeable in and around my lab. Within a few weeks the distinct aroma of the spices diminished to a freshness or cleanness of the air in my lab and the surrounding area. This aroma was in evidence, if even so slightly, for approximately two months.

The *ketoret* was so powerful because the nature and amount of its ingredients were commanded to Moses by God. This explains something else we see in the text of the siddur, namely, that any admixture of fruit or bee honey into the *ketoret* was forbidden. The first reason given is that nobody would have been able to stand the sweetness of its smell. If the aroma of the *ketoret* was powerful without honey, how much more would it have been with it! But this reason is then followed by a scriptural verse in which it is explicitly stated that honey may not be offered as incense. The question is why say that it is too powerful? Why not just bring the verse? In other words, even if it wasn't so powerful, the verse would prohibit it, so again, why bring a verse?

I asked this question to one of my first teachers, Rabbi Ephraim Asher Rottenberg, of blessed memory. He told me to pay attention to the words used in the text in the siddur. First Bar Kappara says, "Had even a minuscule amount of honey been added (*natan*, from the verb "to place") to the *ketoret*, no one could have resisted its fragrance." The question is then asked, "Why was no honey blended (*me'arvim*, from the verb "to mix") into it?" The questioner understood that it is prohibited to "add" honey to the *ketoret* in a way that would be visible. He was merely asking why it couldn't be "blended in" unnoticeably. For this we need the verse, "You may not burn any leaven or honey as a fire-offering to God" (*Vayikra* 2:11). Leaven and honey both allude to pride. Leaven "puffs" our bread up with hot air. Honey, as well, if cooked on a fire, bubbles and rises more than any other liquid. More than any other quality, puffed-up pride prevents a person from recognizing his or her faults and returning in true and sincere *teshuvah*. This is antithetical to what the *ketoret* stands for.

There are other allusions in the *ketoret*. Rabbi Moshe Sofer (*Chatam Sofer, derashot* 18, quoted in *Siddur Chatam Sofer* ad loc.) explains the symbolic meaning of the names of the four main incense spices, as well as the Karshina lye and Cyprus wine:

> The four spices that are written explicitly in the Torah are *tzori*-balsam, *tziporen*-onycha, *chelbenah*-galbanum, and *levonah zakah*-pure frankincense. *Tzori* alludes to the Torah, which is a *tzori*-balm and healing for the entire body. *Levonah zakah* alludes to God's love for His people through

> which He *melaven* — whitens and bleaches — their sins. Between these two are placed the *tziporen* and *chelbenah*. As known, *chelbenah* alludes to complete sinners. The *tziporen*, on the other hand, alludes to the majority of the Jewish people. Like a *tziporen*-fingernail, they are smooth and unblemished on the inside, and only darkened on the outside... It is for this reason that we are required to rub the *tziporen* with Karshina lye, to beautify it and remove its external blackness. This alludes to *teshuvah* and good deeds... Soaking the *tziporen* in Cyprus wine to make it *azah* [pungent or strong] alludes to the wine [secret teachings] of the Torah which imbues Israel with the ability to remain firm and unyielding in their faith when they walk among the nations.

Momentous Revelations in Our Days

As we have mentioned, according to ancient tradition, the Beit HaMikdash and the Mishkan, as well as all their sacred vessels, were more than just physical artifacts. They represented spiritual levels of closeness to God — the return to the level of Adam and Eve in the Garden of Eden, the return to the level of Unity that existed before the Shattering of the Vessels.

The discovery of a juglet of anointing oil and 600 kilograms of *ketoret* in our time in a cave in Qumran is a tiny hint of things to come. When the actual artifacts of the ancient Temple will be unearthed, this will be a sign that their accompanying spiritual levels are about to be revealed as well.

According to the Midrash (*Tanchuma, Tetzaveh* 14), the letters of the word "*ketoret*" can be read as an acronym: *kedushah, taharah, rachamim, tikvah* (holiness, purity, mercy, and hope).

May we merit to see the great holiness, purity, and mercy of the Blessed Holy One revealed in our days. This is our great hope!

Rabbi Sutton's original essay contains twenty-one sections, four of which were selected for this collection. For those interested in obtaining the entire essay, or inquiring about other works, please contact Rabbi Sutton via his website (www.geulah.org) or through Targum Press.

RABBI YAAKOV ASHER SINCLAIR

Stargazing

Nearly four thousand years ago, the father of the Jewish people emerged from his tent and stood in a pristine desert, his eyes turned skyward. The constellations wheeled above him in their silent slow-motion dance. Avram could read the stars. He saw very clearly. He saw that he would be childless.

Then something took place which cannot be understood by the laws of nature. The Creator of the universe took him from where he stood. He lifted Avram beyond what the eye can see and the mind can grasp. He elevated him until Avram stood above the stars. Then, the Creator changed his name. He added just one letter to his name — Avram became Avraham. The whole cosmos changed. The Creator of the world rewrote the script of Creation. It was true that Avram would be childless, but Av-ra-ham would have progeny. With this action, God raised Avraham and his offspring, the Jewish people, above the stars.

The phrase "Mazal Tov!" is usually translated as "Congratulations!" or "Good Luck!" Neither are accurate translations.

The Hebrew word *mazal* means a constellation. The word itself is from the root meaning "to flow." When we say Mazal Tov, we are giving someone a blessing that their happiness should cause an influx — a flow — of good and blessing to the world. So why are the constellations called *mazalot*? What do they have to do with "flowing?"

The mystics teach us that nothing can exist in this universe without an infusion of spiritual energy from Above. The stars and the constellations are one level through which this energy flows. Astrology is not mere nonsense. It is indeed possible to intercept the transmissions that flow from the Creator through the celestial bodies. However, the Torah prohibits prognostication of all forms, including predictions based on the stars. If these predictions were nonsense, there would be little need to prohibit them. Rather, it *is* possible to ascertain the future by astrology — but the Creator doesn't want us to do this.

However, there's another more potent mistake that we might make when we gaze starward. At the dawn of history it was common knowledge that God created everything and that the stars and constellations were merely vassals obeying His will. As time went on, the idea took hold that, seeing as the stars were God's emissaries, they too were deserving of respect. This innocent mistake is the root of idol worship. It's a small step from giving honor to the servants of the King to thinking that the servants have independent power themselves. Judaism defines idol worship as the idea that anything can have a power that is independent of the Creator.

When we look at the stars, they seem full of light yet their light casts no shadow in our world. They shine very brightly, but in our world they illuminate nothing. The stars shine but they cannot illuminate our lives, they cannot guide us. All they can do is reveal that they are the conduit of the light, the reflection of the light of the Creator — the channel through which flows Divine energy from above.

Every nation and every individual is governed by a constellation. Every nation, that is, except one. Our sages teach that "the Jewish people have no *mazal*" (*Shabbos* 155a). This doesn't mean the Jewish people have no luck. (Although a superficial examination of our history might leave you thinking this!) It means that the destiny of the Jewish people is not superintended by any star. We are literally above the stars.

Given all this, it is difficult to understand why the month of Shevat, the constellation of Aquarius, is called the sign of the Jewish people. Didn't we say that the Jewish people are above the stars, that they have no constellation?

In Hebrew, the sign of Aquarius is called *dli. Dli* means a water pitcher or bucket. The root of the word means "to draw up." The job of the Jewish people is to draw up spirituality and cause it to flow into the world. A bucket has only one purpose — to hold the water. Its whole reason to be is to carry the water. The Jewish people are the water carriers. Our entire existence is to learn, to celebrate, and to transmit the holy waters of the Torah.

In Yiddish, the sign of Aquarius is known as *der Wasserman* — the Waterman. Man is the ultimate purpose of creation. God created Man as the being that would recognize his Creator. Purpose is always recognizable through form. For example: a spoon. The purpose of a spoon is to stir. For this reason its form is that it has a slender handle which can be grasped and a spatulate end which will move food around effectively in a pot. The form of a spoon is its shape. However, nothing can have a shape unless it has matter through which the shape can be expressed. A spoon without any metal is no more than an a bright idea. For things to exist physically, there must be a marriage of form and content, purpose and matter.

Just as Man is the essence of purpose, of form in the world, water is the essence of matter seeking a form, a shape. Water has no form. It flows and assumes the shape of whatever vessel in which it finds itself.

The job of the Jewish people is to be "Man" — to fulfill God's purpose, to be the creation that recognizes his Creator. The job of the Jewish people is to take this "waterworld," this world of myriad permutations, a world of matter which can so easily turn into materialism, and to reveal its purpose — to give it the shape of man.

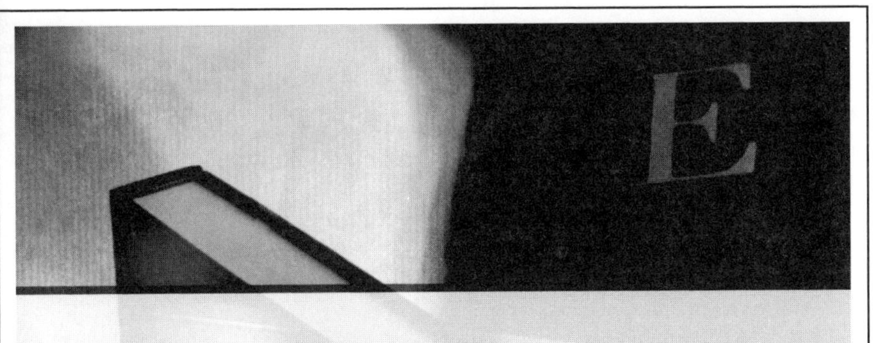

Psychology and Self-Help

REBBETZIN RUCHOMA SHAIN

When the Answer Is "No"

Many times we adults ask Hashem for different things that we feel are very important for us. We continue to pray to Him to answer all our prayers. However, we do not always receive the answer "yes," and we might feel discouraged when the answer is "no."

The following true-life experience illustrates that a little girl accepted whatever Hashem answered, even when the answer was "no," because she understood in her childish mind that Hashem surely knows what is best for her.

The little girl had a dolly that she cherished with all her heart. She kept her dolly close to her whenever she had the opportunity to be home with her.

One day as she was playing with her dolly it dropped from her hands and the face cracked open. She picked up her broken dolly and held it tightly, sobbing with all her heart.

Her older sister came over and suggested, "Why don't you ask Hashem to fix your dolly and make her like new?"

The little sister immediately started to pray to Hashem. "Please, Hashem, make my dolly new again." Over and over she repeated her prayer to Hashem, but to no avail. The dolly remained damaged.

After a while, her sister came over and said, "You see, Hashem did not answer you and your dolly still remains broken."

The little girl thought for a few minutes and then looked up at her big sister with her tear-filled eyes and answered, "Hashem did answer me but He said 'no.' "

We adults can learn a valuable lesson from this little girl, who understood in her childish mind that whatever Hashem answered — whether it is "yes" or "no" — it is His answer and we should accept it.

RABBI HADAR MARGOLIN

Bein' Happy

My uncle is a thinkin' type of guy. He and I could stay up a whole night discussing all kinds of things. We do it sometimes. Discussing anything. Shootin' the breeze about life.

So, once he told me that he was thinking about what being human is. What significant statement could every human being make about when he is alive. Everyone, regardless of belief or lifestyle. If we could come up with a common goal, we'd be better able to define what being human is all about.

So, after contemplating this for a while, he came up with one important statement. And that is: *I want to be happy.*

The goal is common to all people, religions, and cultures. This is basic humanity. This is as close as you can come to defining the ultimate goal in life, on the deepest and most human level.

I, myself, have investigated to some extent the topic of happiness, what brings it, and what you can do about it. I'd like to share it with you. Let me try to define some specific strategies.

1) Cultivate appreciation.

Learn how to appreciate the good things in your life. It's an art that can really be learned. When one learns to appreciate the good things, one's whole life pulsates with a different beat.

So just take a few seconds and think of all the things in your life that are good, maybe even write them down. Fill your heart with gratitude and thankfulness to God for granting them. See if it doesn't change your whole outlook! See if it doesn't make you feel like a million bucks, even without adding a cent to your bank account.

2) Make others happy.

Recently, I attended a wedding. A middle-aged man sat himself down near me, a casual acquaintance from years before. "You are involved in education," he said to me. "Can you tell me how to develop my personality? I'm not talking about my son," he hurriedly added, "I mean for myself. How do I work on character development?"

This situation required an answer that was short yet powerful. This is what I came up with: "Always think about other people. How can I help them? What can I do to make them feel good? How can I assist them to build their own self-esteem?"

That's all. It's wonderfully simple, almost deceptively so. Everyone can do it, and, by golly, everyone must do it. The most beautiful thing about this is that it works. It really does. It's effective. Empowering others will develop your own personality.

But it's really much more than that. You not only develop your personality, you also become happier. The joyful characteristics of living actually become a part of you. Since you are striving to bring happiness into other people's hearts, you have to become one who radiates happiness. There is simply no other way.

When you have a goal to make others happy, it will include building and strengthening your own inner happiness. You will be happier. That tremendous buoyant feeling will permeate you!

3) Put things in the proper perspective.

During the Gulf War in Israel, a mother was preparing supper for her kids, and part of the meal was french fries. Alas, the family was out of ketchup. Imagine such a calamity. French fries with absolutely no ketchup! The kids were complaining and whining, as kids sometimes do.

Mom tried to calm things, so she asked the kids: On a scale of 1 to 10, what score would they give the "tragedy" of not having ketchup with their french fries? Each kid had his own method for scoring, but the numbers for the three kids were 9, 8, and 10. Sounds pretty ominous.

So, to put things in proper perspective, Mom explained, "If a scud missile hits our living room that's a 10. How much did you say not having ketchup rates?" The subsequent answers were a lot more modest.

4) Give a compliment.

One of the strongest motivating factors we humans have is other people's opinion of us. Our actions are determined to a great degree by the reactions they elicit from family, friends, neighbors, and coworkers.

Social approval or disapproval really affects us deeply. We need others to acknowledge our presence, appreciate us, and compliment us. We need to know we are important in other people's eyes.

If it is important to us, it is also important to the other guy. Others want us to recognize their good qualities and to appreciate their successes. Oh, and of course, to tell them about it. To let them know we have noticed.

Only when they know that we know, only then is their success complete.

5) Create a friend.

Creating a friend involves a special tone of voice, an atmosphere of words and the way they are said.

Friendship is an issue people often deal with. Having a good friend is not a luxury; it is a basic human need. We all need someone to lend us a listening ear and an understanding heart. Someone with whom to share our dreams and experiences, our difficulties, dilemmas, and heartaches.

And so often, the thought crosses our mind: That person looks like he'd make a good friend potentially. How do I make it happen? How do I create a friendship between us? Do I have the guts to approach an unfamiliar face?

"How are you?" Very standard words, usually expressed politely and calmly in a courteous fashion. That's fine. Think, though, how you say the words to a dear friend you have just unexpectedly met and are really delighted to be talking to. It's a totally different ball game! The words get a special emphasis; the tone of voice is endearing and radiates camaraderie. The enthusiasm expressed in the tone of voice reflects the special situation.

Now go a step further. Imagine such a person would come to you and greet you with this radiating, endearing opening. What would your response be? The only response that could be given to the atmosphere created by the question would be correspondingly warm and special.

Let's get to the bottom line. You start. Learn to initiate an atmosphere of friendship, closeness, warmth, and camaraderie. You are not just open to accepting friends, you actually create them. You will open previously locked gates.

Wait, hold on. I have more to add. You, yourself, will change. You will be more outgoing, friendlier, and more open. You will learn to accommodate all kinds of different personalities, since everyone you meet has his own character.

Your exposure to experiences, outlooks, and varied approaches will increase tenfold. Let go of hesitation, uncertainty, and doubt! Go ahead and just do it. Overcome the obstacles and start greeting people. Create situations!

6) Keep smilin', brother.

Just the other day I met a friend of mine. He told me I had helped someone tremendously. That person was feeling quite depressed. He saw me walking around bubbling with joy, and I had given him a nice smile. That smile had lifted him out of his depression.

Since then I have been smiling at everybody! I wish I could lift the whole world out of depression!

RABBI AKIVA TATZ

Gaining a Monopoly on Simchah!

Is it a mitzvah to be happy? There is no commandment to be happy. On the other hand there are statements in the Torah that make it sound like an obligation.

For example, we have "*Ivdu es Hashem b'simchah.*" That sounds as if you have to serve Hashem through happiness, that you have to work on being happy, that it doesn't come naturally. If that is correct and it is an obligation, why is it not a commandment in the formal sense? What is the meaning of something that needs to be done that is not a commandment?

The *pasuk* says that Hashem delineated the curses that would befall the Jewish people, and the Torah lists a number of curses that are almost unspeakable in their holocaust brutality. After the Torah gets through around one hundred curses it gives what purports to be a reason: because you did not serve Hashem with happiness. Is it conceivable that we have been through the horrors and intense brutality of Jewish history because we did not work on being happy?

What does it mean "you did not serve Hashem with happiness"? How is it possible to be happy always? What about sitting on the floor and mourning? There are times when you cry. Rashi says that you don't have to cry when you mourn but you have to go through the motions of certain actions of sadness; laughter is certainly inappropriate.

What does it mean to be happy always? In case you think it is an accident, or a misprint, or an exaggeration, it is worth looking at a letter of the Chazon Ish in his collected letters. The Chazon Ish makes an almost incredible statement. He says that for someone who recognizes the lights of truth, *"ein eitzev b'olam"* — there is no sadness in the world!

He can say that the world is a happy place at times, but how can he say that there is no sadness in the world? Did the Chazon Ish forget about sitting on the floor in mourning? Did he forget his own personal tragedies? Did he forget the pain and suffering of the Jewish people on his shoulders throughout his life? How could he say that there is no sadness in the world?

Objectively, it's hard to find any happiness in the world. The *meforshim* say that there has not been one good day in Jewish history. There were forty years during the reign of Shlomo HaMelech when, kabbalistically speaking, the moon reached its peak. Forty years during which time there were no wars. The Jewish people were at peace — a glimmer of the messianic phase. The climax of the forty years was the dedication of the Beis HaMikdash that Shlomo HaMelech built. However the Gemara tells us that even at the moment of consecration, the same evening that they celebrated that transcendent moment, the Malach Gavriel came down and threw a staff into the Mediterranean. Around the staff grew the lands of Greece and Rome, which were the agencies of the destruction of the very Beis HaMikdash whose inception was being celebrated. At the very moment of the birth of the Beis HaMikdash, the energy of its destruction was founded.

How can a person say that there is no sadness in the world? And if it is a mitzvah to be happy, or some sort of obligation, how do you do that? How do you achieve happiness in a sad world? How do you achieve happiness when people are dying in agony or going through some immense psychological family trauma? Is there one Jewish family who doesn't know of someone at any moment of time who isn't going through some unspeakable agony? Does the Torah require that you should be so insensitive that you forget about it?

These questions arise because we have an immature Western notion of what happiness is. The correct understanding of happiness is self-evident. The correct definition of happiness, of real *simchah,* is that it is the response of the *neshamah* when it is doing what it should be doing. We cannot try to be happy. It's not something that you can do; it's something that happens. When you are doing what you should be doing, the response is *simchah.* The expression on the face is irrelevant. On the contrary, when the expression on the face is one of pain, then genuine *simchah* is generated.

The most extreme example is that you could be moving toward where you have to be, against such tremendous resistance that the pain could be agony, but the *neshamah* could be singing. When the achievement is taking place, and it's exactly what has to be achieved, that is the inner song of *simchah.*

Imagine a Martian who is taking a tour of the human race. He has a human guide who takes him to a gymnasium. The Martian puts his eye to the keyhole, and he sees a young man who picks up weights and stresses himself tremendously against the resistance. He sees the young man sweating and groaning with effort and pain. There is no question that the Martian would decide that somewhere outside his field of vision there is another human standing beside him with a machine gun, forcing this character to do this in a bizarre form of torture.

When the Martian steps into the room he will see that no one is forcing the young man. On the contrary, he is paying to do this, and loving every moment. He loves the pain, because he knows that the effort is building what he wants to build. He knows that any kind of achievement has to be done against the resistance that is set up. The pain of the work itself is the real pleasure.

When the *neshamah* is moving through life and you are on a path that you have to be on, the path is difficult and it's stormy. You take three steps forward; you are lashed by the wind and the rain and it's two steps backward. But you are on the road you have to be on and you are moving ahead. There is no greater happiness than that.

When you are going on a journey towards the correct destination, and you are exactly where you have to be, it is irrelevant that the journey is difficult.

If a person is sitting on the floor crying, is that *simchah*? The Hebrew word for sadness is *eitzev*. *Eitzev* doesn't mean the sadness of mourning; *eitzev* mean the depression of hopelessness. A person is sitting and weeping at the pain of the loss he has been through. The Rambam says that the mitzvah of mourning is the mitzvah of accompanying the *neshamah* on its journey. We think that mourning, *aveilus*, is a process of adjusting psychologically. There is no question that it is healthy. But it is more than that.

The intrinsic nature of the mitzvah is to accompany the *neshamah* on its journey. Relatives have to mourn because they are part of the same spark; they are sparks of the same original flame.

The Rambam says that in halachah, if you fail to mourn for someone for whom you have an obligation to mourn, it's a cruelty, because you could be carrying part of the load for the *neshamah*. It is going through a series of changes in the spiritual world, transitions that are extremely painful. Since you are part of the same larger *neshamah* you can bear part of that load; you can help the *neshamah* through the changes and transitions. When you observe the mitzvah of mourning correctly, you have the certainty of the knowledge that you are doing exactly what you have to be doing now. The *simchah* is that this moment is being used correctly and it couldn't be used for anything else.

When you chase *simchah*, it disappears. An absolute guaranteed formula not to be happy is to go out and try to be happy. It is a recipe for becoming morbidly depressed. The recipe for happiness is to go and do what you have to be doing.

What does "*Ivdu es Hashem b'simchah*" mean? It doesn't say "be happy"; it says "*ivdu*." If you "*ivdu*," you will be happy. You take care of the *ivdu*, and the *simchah* will take care of itself. If you work, if there is labor, if production is taking place, if progress is being made, there will be *simchah*; that's guaranteed.

How can the Chazon Ish say *ein eitzev b'olam*? He doesn't mean there is no sadness and no crying, he means there is no depression in the world. *Eitzev* means the hopelessness of an utterly despairing situation that is going nowhere. How can there ever be a moment like that? If you are sitting and weeping in mourning, this day has been perfect for you. This day, Hashem wanted you to sit on the floor and do what you did. In consequence, the *neshamah* has a serene feeling of having achieved what it was meant to achieve.

When you are moving along a road to a destination, what generates the *simchah*? The happiness that is felt in a journey is the anticipation of the destination. Many times the anticipation is much more pleasurable than the result itself. The process, the progress and the journey, derive from the anticipation of the end point. If you are going on a journey which is difficult, and it's hot and you are bothered and tired, but you are going to a long-anticipated destination, the journey is fine...unless you are on the wrong train. The pleasure that you feel in the journey is not the journey itself; it's the knowledge that the journey leads to an end point. The end point is the sum total of the labor and the effort that one has put in to get there.

Every journey to a destination is a small model of this world and the next world. Every experience in life, which can be readily grasped and apprehended tangibly, is an analogy for something that happens in the higher world. Every phenomenon, every emotion, every experience you go through, is a *mashal* for something real. Hashem gives it to you because He wants you to understand Him and His world. Because you are not there, He gives you a model that you can understand.

Hashem wants you to know that in the physical structure of the world He exists. You can't see Him but it's His emanating energy that gives it life. How can you relate to such a thing? You haven't got an organ or a faculty that can feel the *Shechinah* in the world. Hashem says, fine. Look at a human being. A piece of flesh, tangible, physical tissue and inside there is something that you can't see, but you can know about. You have no doubt that it is there. When you understand that's what a human being is, you can understand that the body of the world has its own *neshamah*.

The Nefesh HaChaim says that every detail of the human body gives you insight into a world. The body eats, the world eats. The mouth is the place of connection, eating and speaking. The world has its place of connection, which is where the *korbanos* are eaten. That's where Hashem's voice speaks. Every aspect of experience in the world is a microcosm of the transcendent.

Deveikus is the obligation to raise yourself to a level where you bond with Hashem, in that amazing, magical, mysterious, and mystical experience of being one with Hashem and not losing your individuality. Being one with Hashem is a clear revelation of who it is that you are, in greater relief than you understood it before. How can we begin to understand such a thing? Hashem says "get married!" Two people becoming one unit is much better than the sum of the parts. When you manage that, it is a clear revelation of who you are as an individual.

We talk about this world and the next, but we have an ear that has been battered. We hear *Shamayim* and *aretz* as being heaven and earth. It has nothing to do with heaven and earth. The word *aretz* in Hebrew, from *ratz*, means movement; a word that describes this world as "moving towards." The word *Shamayim* means all the end points that you could ever express as being where the journey ends. That is what the next world is.

The concept of this world and the next is a movement towards an end point — a process of building, moving, and developing — and the result is where you get to. Incidentally, the word *sham*, which means "there," is also the same word as *shem*, which means "name." A name is also an expression of total essence. That's the final "there" of all that you are and move towards being; that's your name.

Our concept of this world and the next is a movement towards and then the result. There is no harder labor in life than moving towards, and there is no greater ecstasy than the result. What is the ecstasy of the next world? The work that you put in to get there. That's all you are there. Our concept of *olam haba* is that you get stripped of all the raw materials, the body, the tools, it all gets taken away; what remains is the work you did on the raw materials. The next world is a relishing of the work you did to get you there, because that's all you are.

Life is a journey towards an end point and that is the mechanism of the happiness of life.

If the joy of the work is the anticipation of the end point and the end point is the experiencing of the work that was done to get you there, there must be one unique moment that is so joyful that it is inexpressible. That is the moment when the two meet. When the work ends and the result is first felt. When the sower and the reaper meet.

It is a moment of transition from the constraints of the pressure of what had to be done, to the complete lack of any. When someone dies we call it *niftar*, it means that a person is exempt from obligations.

When a person works very hard all year and it comes to the moment when the workplace is locked, or the final school bell has been rung, there are no more obligations for now — it's an exhilarating moment. What happened? There was no physical pleasure. You are still sitting there. One second before there was obligation and bondage, in that moment of transition from slavery to freedom the bow had been drawn and the arrow released. That is the exhilaration of being in a place where there is no other place to go. You've gone right there. The *ratz,* movement, has become *Shamayim*.

In Torah there are two experiences that illustrate this, an experience in Torah and an experience in mitzvos. The first is learning Torah for its own sake. It is an experience of end point, that's why it is so delicious. You are not learning this information to use it; you are relishing the *chachmah* itself.

The second experience in the world of mitzvos is Shabbos. Shabbos is work and work and work, crescendo, climax, and then there is no moving, just being. One of the connotations of Shabbos is to sit in one place and not move. If you are out of the city on Shabbos you can only move *daled amos*. There is no progression. Shabbos is an end point.

Why do we call the place where we learn Torah, a yeshivah? What does sitting have to do with learning? You can learn standing. In the old days they used to learn standing. Can you think of anything more peripheral than that you have to sit there? Surely we should call it Torah, learning, *chachmah*, something...but sitting? A place of sitting? The answer is that when you are learning Torah, it is a place where you can sit down because the Torah is moving. You have entered the dimension of end point while yet in this world.

That is the sitting of Shabbos.

Torah is an end point, and the name of a *talmid chacham* is Shabbat, because he is a person of end point. He is there.

This movement from journey to end point in Torah is called Torah. In mitzvos it is called Shabbos. In the universal human experience it's called a game. A game is an experience where you enter a zone where there is no other place to go. A game is something you do for its own sake. Games that are the most trivial are the most pleasurable. When people play a game they go round and round and up and down, for three and a half hours. It's a time out of time; it's a world that's been carved out, that bears no obligations. You are living in the end point. There is something which is its own justification, which is what the next world is.

The Hebrew world for a game, an amusement, is *sha-ashua. Sha* means to turn towards. So *sha-ashua* means turning towards the turning towards.

I will finish with a story. I have a friend who told me that one morning, during the holidays, he saw his children playing Monopoly. At the end of the week, on the Friday, when he was getting ready to go to shul, his children were still playing the same game. He said to them, "Look kids, you obviously don't know how to play Monopoly. You can't play the same game all week. Monopoly has an end. Someone wins the money, someone goes bankrupt, and eventually someone has a monopoly of the money and wins the game."

The children said, "No, Abba, you don't understand. When one of us goes bankrupt we get together and make a *gemach* and put him back in business."

RABBI MENACHEM NISSEL

A Spoonful of Simchah

Last year I received several e-mails from students expressing concern about how hard it was for them to deal with the calamity of the 23rd of Elul (also known as 9/11). It was particularly hard for students of Stern College, living just several blocks from Ground Zero. Some students described how they suffered from sleepless nights, migraine headaches, and other stress-related conditions. When I had the honor to give them a *shiur* last December at Stern College, they asked to please give them *chizuk* in the aftermath of the tragedy. What could I possibly say?

The day of the *shiur* I visited the Philadelphia Yeshiva. I had the incredible *zechus* to speak to one of the *gedolei hador*, HaRav Shmuel Kaminetsky, *shlit"a*. I asked him for guidance. What should my message be for my *talmidos*?

His response was passionate and unequivocal. He put on his big friendly smile and said, "Tell them to work on *simchah*!"

He quoted *Chovos HaLevovos*, "Let your face radiate joy and the pain be kept within." *Tefillah* is the forum for tears. The rest of the time we must be filled with happiness and smiles.

As I left the yeshivah, I noticed a *yeshivah bachur* running after my car. He called out, "Come back! The *rosh yeshivah* has something else to tell you!" Uh-oh! I thought, I'm probably going to get some *mussar*.

Rav Shmuel was glad to see that I had come back. He immediately raised his voice and exclaimed, "Please make sure that you stress my message — they must really, really be *b'simchah*!" He then added a suggestion. Every morning when saying "*Elokai Neshamah*" we should focus on the enormous privilege of having a *neshamah*, a *tzelem Elokim*! We have a *neshamah Elokim mima'al* inside of us! How can we walk around without a big smile on our faces?

It takes patience, dedication, and practice, but with a little bit of willpower we can start focusing on the myriad of miracles and the overflow of blessings in our lives. As my Rebbe says, we need the laughter of Rabbi Akiva to get us through the bitter birth pangs of Mashiach.

Rav Shlomo Wolbe, *shlit"a*, stresses that the key to *simchah* is to see ourselves as part of the big picture, since we are an integral contributor to the *klal*. Every Jew is a letter in the big *Sefer Torah* of *klal Yisrael*. One letter missing or even fragmented — and the whole *Sefer Torah* is rendered defective. We have to believe in our mission. We have to be excited about our humble yet crucial role in bringing the redemption. We have to make our *simchah* contagious, so that everyone around us wants to know and be part of our little secret to happiness.

B'ezras Hashem, when I meet my students again, I look forward to seeing big smiles on their faces. And if their smile is not there, they had better be careful, because a *gadol* may start shouting at them...

MALKA KAGANOFF

Achieving Peace of Mind

Chazal tell us that peace is the pinnacle of all blessings. We pray for world peace and hope for peace within our family structures. There is another level of peace that is of inestimable value — peace of mind. Those who are blessed with this inner peace live on an island of tranquility, no matter how unsettled their outward circumstances may be. David HaMelech states, "My soul is at rest" (*Tehillim* 23:3), even as he traverses the valley of the shadow of death. He fears not, for he knows that Hashem is with him (ibid. 4). We wish we could emulate David HaMelech and reach this level of inner calmness and absence of fear and worry. But how do we achieve this state of mind? How do we banish our disturbing thoughts and enjoy a better quality of life?

David HaMelech has given us the key. He declares to Hashem, "For You are with me." He lives with an awareness that

Hashem is at his side, guiding and protecting him. *Tehillim* is replete with verses that extol the virtues of *bitachon,* sincere trust in Hashem. *Bitachon* has been called *emunah* in action. *Emunah* is our faith in the existence of Hashem and His power; *bitachon* is our application of these abstract concepts to our daily lives.

Succinctly put, *bitachon* is our understanding that Hashem runs the world and is the prime cause of all. Nothing can happen to us that He does not decree. He is all good and always prepares what is appropriate for us. This knowledge fills us with a deep feeling of security, since we realize that everything that happens to us is engineered by our Almighty and All Good Father in Heaven. Our input is to turn to Hashem in prayer and ask Him to grant us our desires, if they are right for us.

In turn, we have an assurance that "One who trusts in Hashem will be surrounded with kindness" (*Tehillim* 32:10). In other words, *bitachon* is our best method of meriting Hashem's kindness. Our constant turning to Him strengthens our awareness of Hashem and our relationship with Him. One who learns how to access *bitachon* has no need to worry; he knows that he is in good hands.

The goal of this article is not only to discuss *bitachon* on a theoretical level but also to translate these lofty concepts into concrete steps applicable to daily life. Often, our initial reaction to a situation is not one of *bitachon* but one of worry, panic, or despair.

Let us present the "three-step plan."

Step 1: Face your thoughts.

Pay attention to your initial thought and analyze it. Is this a proper thought or not? Have you polluted your mindspace with an unproductive thought? Is this the thought of a person working on his or her *bitachon*?

Step 2: Fix your thoughts.

Decide what the proper thought should be. If we think rationally, we can usually discover the correct thought pattern and replace our initial reaction with a more productive thought. If we are unclear as to what the proper Torah reaction is, then we can turn to a mentor for guidance. Once we know what the proper reaction is, we can control our disturbing thoughts and replace them with proper thoughts.

Step 3: Feel your thoughts.

This final stage is to allow your emotional reaction to be shaped by your intellectual awareness of proper response. Repeat the new thought again and again until you actually believe it. It is difficult to implant these proper thoughts in our hearts, but if we persevere we can reach a point that we truly feel the new concept. When we succeed in internalizing this reaction, we will achieve the peace of mind that comes with a worldview of *bitachon*.

An example:

Tova is on vacation and loses her wallet, which contains her spending money. She might react initially in several ways, each of them contributing to her agitation (Step 1). She will be frustrated at the change of plans caused by the loss of this money. She may be hard on herself for her carelessness or depressed about her bad luck. None of these thoughts are conducive to peace of mind. She realizes that she needs to access *bitachon* mode and formulate a new attitude.

In Step 2 she reminds herself that Hashem rules the world, and He determined that this inconvenience happen. "I will not lose my peace of mind, but accept this situation since it was engineered by my Father in Heaven. I will focus on exploring how I can grow from this situation."

Tova will not feel true peace of mind unless she expands her thoughts to influence her feelings (Step 3). She repeats her conviction again and again until she feels this trust that Hashem is taking care of her during this difficulty.

Bitachon is particularly beneficial to counteract worry. One who is infused with *bitachon* does not worry. He realizes that all his worrying will not accomplish anything, whereas the energy spent worrying could have been spent productively by turning to Hashem in prayer and davening for the item we are concerned about.

Face your worry and replace it with a prayer. Whatever you worry about, pray about it instead.

- "I am so worried that my baby might be getting sick." Replace with "Hashem, please help my baby to stay well."
- "I am so worried about my son — he should have been home an hour ago." Replace with "Please protect my son."
- "I am worried that our finances are not stable." Replace with "Hashem, please stabilize our finances."
- "I am worried sick about the upcoming test (meeting, date, interview)." Replace with "Hashem, please grant me success in the upcoming test."

Shidduchim are an area that can be fraught with anxiety. How will I find the right one? How will I recognize that this is the right one? When will the phone ring for my daughter? In *shidduchim*, as well as in all match-ups, such as jobs, housing, seminaries, and yeshivos, one who is fortunate to trust in Hashem will be rewarded with a sense of calm and a lack of anxiety.

Disappointments are easier to accept if one is infused with *bitachon* that Hashem, in His goodness, has decreed that this is meant to be.

A major trip was cancelled due to rain. Disappointing, for sure, but if the would-be participants can react in *bitachon* mode, they will realize that although they thought this was the correct day for the trip, Hashem willed otherwise. They submit themselves to accept the changed plans by realizing that Hashem's will surpasses their own.

We will be filled with trust and acceptance if we see Hashem as the Prime Cause in all interactions and circumstances that life sends us.

The world of today can be an unsettling place. We used to assume that the streets were safe, and that mankind accepted a certain standard of human decency. Recent events prove that we cannot trust our fellow traveler — he may be a terrorist. But we can trust that Hashem runs the world and He can protect His people. Our best shield is the power of *tefillah* and the *bitachon* that accompanies it.

Bitachon does not mean that only what is nice will occur, but it does mean that what is right, as decreed by Above, will occur. May we all merit Hashem's protection and the peace of mind that comes with trust in Him.

RUTHIE PEARLMAN

How "Against the Wall" Came to Be Written

Sometimes I think that we are all in denial. All the time. About one thing or another.

We choose to ignore things about ourselves which are so patently obvious to others. I notice this in my work as a prenatal teacher and breastfeeding counselor. Particularly as my client base is mostly older, successful career couples having their first baby well into their thirties. These couples, with their self-indulgent, high-powered lives of which they are totally in control, expect that when they have their babies they will remain in control of their lives. The baby is only one small being after all; how much disruption can it possibly cause to two fully grown and responsible adults? It will fit seamlessly into their lives, and they will continue to go hiking in the Himalayas, take skiing holidays with Junior in the backpack, and meet with friends for elegant dinner parties, baby sleeping peacefully in his chair in the corner.

It comes as a dreadful shock to these couples when their schedules, far from remaining more or less the same only with an addition, change forever, and they find themselves out of control of events for the first time in their adult lives. Often these older parents suffer greatly as a result. A general dissatisfaction with parenthood and even postnatal depression is, in my experience, far greater in couples who have elected to postpone having their first child for reasons such as wanting to further their careers before settling down.

I, too, am guilty of denial. Last night I agreed to take my five-week-old granddaughter Tali with me to an adult get-together of prenatal teachers. It was a farewell party for one of my colleagues who was retiring. My daughter was being treated to a night out with her mother-in-law, and I thought I would allow my son-in-law a peaceful night's learning, instead of having to pace the living room with Tali in a sling. The baby, my daughter assured me, took a bottle of expressed milk beautifully; she had experimented only a few days ago.

I was in denial about how unpredictable new babies can be. I had forgotten my own, and how I would have been very wary of taking them to any adult gathering at which they were expected to reliably behave. Reliability and small babies don't go together.

I was also in denial about how tolerant my colleagues would be if the baby, as happened, misbehaved dreadfully. After all, we were all prenatal teachers, our business was birth and newborns; why would they object to a baby in their midst? But these women were long past their own birthing days. When you are mothering a newborn yourself, I find, you have the capability to tune out the chaos that a baby creates around you. You barely notice it. Not so these older women. They had come for an elegant, adult party, to sip wine, eat canapés, and chat, and they were not at all impressed by this harassed grandmother, trying to get Tali to take the bottle of expressed milk and failing utterly.

I could tell, as I struggled miserably with the howling infant, that my colleagues, although they smiled politely, wished me and Tali a zillion miles away, so that the party could progress in peace. I left early, feeling a pariah. I had been in denial of two elements; the unpredictability of the new baby, and the tolerance of adults gathered together for a social occasion.

When choosing to write a novel about the poignant and agonizing topic of Jewish teenagers at risk, I knew I would face denial from two quarters. Parents, for one. Parents who do not have a troubled teen of their own deny that it could ever happen to them or in their nice, tidy, *frum* little community. Teenagers going off the rails only happens in other communities, or in badly managed homes. Not in homes like theirs or those of their peers, where love and attention is lavished on their children; where televisions and other such deviant objects are strictly forbidden; and where words like "drugs" are never uttered. Sometimes even parents who do have a kid spinning out of control are in denial. Everything is fine. It isn't happening. I don't want to deal with it, because to deal with it is to admit it is real.

Teenagers themselves are in denial too. About their own mortality, and often about their own culpability for their actions. They will live forever, and never have to face the music. Or even if they don't live forever, that moment when it becomes relevant is so far off as to be of no real consequence. With all the kids I talked to when researching this book, I don't think I found any who had, even at their very lowest ebb, denied the existence of God. He was just too far away and remote an issue for them to face at the present moment; there were other, more pressing matters to deal with.

When I first sought to speak to teenagers and hear their stories, rather than just speak to those involved in their care and rehabilitation, I was told that the kids would not want to speak to me. However, as I am not the type who takes no for an answer, I persevered and found kids, lots of kids, who were not only willing, but eager to speak to me; kids who found pouring out their hearts and their innermost pain not only an immense relief and therapy, but also a huge privilege. They saw this book as a way of outreaching to others like themselves without having to actually go and do it. Some not only didn't mind having their real names appear, but insisted on it.

And you know what? Of all the kids I spoke to and listened to, at great length — kids who had literally been in the gutter just looking up at the stars but thinking they would never, ever reach them — of all of those kids, I never found one I could honestly say was a bad kid. Misguided, yes. Angry and rebellious, certainly. But bad, no. In all of them I found an endearing quality of vulnerability and defenselessness that made me want to try my utmost to make things better for them. And if writing this book does at least the tiniest bit towards that, it will have achieved its objective.

I called it "Against the Wall." A kid with his back against the wall is trapped, cornered, can go no further. By the same token the typical image of a sullen teen is one leaning against a wall, staring aggressively out at a world which has turned against him. The third meaning is to do with the Kosel, colloquially known as the Wall, our holiest site. To be "against the wall" could mean to turn your back on your beliefs.

I knew, when I began writing this book, that there would probably be people who would fervently wish I had never started, that I would leave this whole topic safely buried under the carpet where it is often hidden. But the more I work on this novel, and the more kids and rehabilitators I speak to, the more important the topic appears to me. At the risk of alienating a few, I intend throwing back that carpet and exposing everything underneath to the sunlight, and to your gaze. It is only then that we can begin the process of healing.

SHEINDEL WEINBACH

Oh, What a Riot – Here's Another Diet

These days, when I go to a *simchah,* or even meet someone on the street, the topic of conversation is not the latest birth — I'm beyond that age — nor is it, thank God, a recent ailment and what so-and-so did to recover. Friends will stop, do a double take, and hesitantly ask me, "You've lost a lot of weight, haven't you?" The hesitation? Because some weight losses are due to sickness, God forbid. And if it's due to a diet, well, they are hard put to believe it and are downright envious.

Okay, so I lost a lot of weight. "How did you do it?" they finally ask, after they are convinced that I feel better than ever. Sure, I feel better than when I had to lug an extra eighteen kilos (forty pounds) around, climb up stairs, haul myself up onto buses, struggle up Jerusalem hills, shlep *shuk* baskets (I am one of those last creatures still around using the plastic "Yad Eliezer" shopping baskets, if you know what I mean), and so on.

We must all have experienced those dreams where we are able to defy gravity and float around, getting from here to there effortlessly. I can't say that in real life it's quite like that now, but the new mobility sure feels good. And I certainly do get around faster without the huffing and puffing!

Okay, Sheindel, so how *did* you get rid of those extra kilos? (Is saying it in kilos more or less effective than pounds, which translates into 2.2 times the amount?)

Anyone who has successfully lost weight at any time, has probably done so before as well, and perhaps learned from past experience how to tackle it better the next time around, when she is good and ready. When is she good and ready?

It's all a question of motivation, we all agree, and timing, which translates into goal-setting. It has to do with ulterior, and not only exterior, motives. In my case, the trigger was a digital scale which came my way, and the boost – the month of Elul. There has to be some element of *l'sheim Shamayim* in a diet. At my age, you're not doing it for beauty, or for a *shidduch,* but rather for health and general feeling of well-being. And certainly, for that sense of personal accomplishment and getting that *yetzer hara* throttled at the gullet.

It was just before the first of Elul when the scale came into my possession. I stepped on it, and got the shock of my life. I converted kilos into pounds and got an even bigger shock, and quickly went back to kilos. It would be harder to lose kilos, but I made my decision, then and there, to shed a good many of them by Chanukah.

Chanukah has now come and gone, and I am eighteen kilos lighter, give or take one or two at any given moment. When I made the drastic decision, I had to have some plan of action. As all diet plans will tell you, a person has to have a certain strategy for those lean and hungry times, for that grumbling in the stomach that needs starch and sugar to assuage it. So what is going to plug up that hole?

I figured that I would need quantities sufficient to fool my mouth and body, so long as the consumption had hardly any calories. To begin with — that is, begin the day with — I drank coffee with saccharine. It filled, and the interesting bonus was that it left that strange aftertaste in my mouth, reminiscent of those early months of pregnancy when you don't have too much appetite. I used to chuckle at the idea, but realized that it was working.

Another trick, along the same lines, was to prepare a huge salad, which I never had time to do when I could substitute carbohydrate food, but my determination supplied the time. Here, the trick was to incorporate a small onion, which left the identical aftertaste in the mouth that lingered on and fulfilled the appetite for sweet things. And, you'd be surprised at how filling a huge salad is! Partially because by the time you finish eating it the initial hunger pangs are stilled. Your stomach is pretty full, and you can always wash it down with another coffee and saccharine. (Since I didn't want to be drinking too much coffee, I drank some other hot drinks, which were very satisfying: hot water with tomato paste or tomato juice; hot water with vanilla, milk, and saccharine; hot tea with milk; even hot water with some grapefruit or orange juice and saccharine.) Drinking helped a lot.

And another trick which most diets tell you — chew slowly. Busy people don't have time to do that, unless they have to plough through a salad!

You have to have a double list — foods that fill, and foods that fill needs. What do I mean? 1% or 2% cheese (or cottage cheese) fills. *Leben* (or low-fat yogurt) fills. Eat as much of these as you can and feel that they are contributing to the fight against osteoporosis. As for the other category, I used fruits to satisfy the need for something sweet. It takes time to peel an apple (my teeth are not what they used to be, and I need it sectioned) or a tangerine, but the sweetness is out of this world if you are sugar-deprived, as you will be. I didn't count my fruit calories because the satisfaction was worth it, and it provided necessary vitamins to boot.

Know thyself. I maintain that you have to create your own strategy and plan ahead for those lean hours. I would combine the two strategies of fill/fill needs and grate two apples coarsely, heap on cheese and some sprouts, and dig in. By the time I'd finished this meal or snack, I really wasn't hungry.

Another meal is to grate a carrot and a squash and boil them up into a soup. You can add string beans, cabbage, or other low calorie vegetables. A teaspoon of soup powder can go a long way in creating a dish that is temporarily satisfying, takes time to eat, and really has almost no calories. Two plates of this can constitute a good lunch after you've eaten my breakfast.

I began my day with a normal meal: two slices of any bread, preferably toast, to prolong the eating of it, cheese or some tuna, salad with onion, and a soft-boiled egg. The onion and saccharine left enough aftertaste to kill all extra appetite, and the wholesome food made me feel I had provided my body with enough nutrients to subsist on. The rest of the day would be a battle of fooling my stomach, a quiet conscience that I had enough vitamins, proteins, and minerals to survive a strict diet for the rest of the day.

So, that's it, in a nutshell — no, perish the word, in a *leben* cup. Know your own tendencies, prepare for the weak moments, have enough celery, apples, or oranges around, and weigh yourself every day to see if you've progressed... Good luck!

NECHAMA BERG

It's Here, Somewhere

The statement "It's here – somewhere" is probably uttered by anxious men and women in hundreds of different languages every day. The problem of misplacing things is a common one. I've combined the most likely reasons items get lost into four distinct categories. It is easier to come up with a solution to the problem when you know its cause.

The major reason for losing things is a disease I call "meantime-itis," from which millions suffer. It goes something like this: a woman is holding an object in her hand and she doesn't want to take the time, or doesn't have the time, to put it back in its "place." Therefore, she puts the item down wherever she happens to be standing, "just for the meantime." She has every intention of putting the item back, when she has the time. What usually happens is that she runs out of the house or gets involved in some project and forgets all about it.

Days pass by and suddenly there is a need for it. At this point, the woman looks in the drawer the item should be in and doesn't find it. The "meantime" location has been completely forgotten. Or, she remembers the "meantime" location but someone else — a husband or child — has stumbled across the item and put it somewhere else "in the meantime." Thus the item is tossed around and finally buried in a place no one would ever think to look. Sound familiar?

The cure for "meantime-itis" is to break the habit. Take the extra two minutes and put the item in its proper place. Whenever you are tempted to just put something down, repeat this slogan: "It pays to put things away." I'll tell you a story that happened to me which illustrates this point.

A few years ago, my refrigerator broke down and I called a repairman. He fixed the problem and gave me a receipt, which also served as a three-month warranty. If the fridge broke down again within the next three months it would be repaired free of charge.

Well, guess what? It broke down two months later. When the new repairman arrived he told me that the repair would be free only if I showed him the previous receipt. Because I am in the habit of saving all receipts in one folder, I knew exactly where it was stored. I was able to show him the receipt within literally twenty seconds of his request, thereby saving me money. If you don't like my slogan make up your own! Repeat it ten times a day until putting things back becomes automatic.

Another solution for meantime-itis is a catch-all drawer. A catch-all drawer is a drawer for all those miscellaneous items you have no time to put away. It is usually in a central location of the house, like the kitchen. When you are in a rush and can't put something back, make sure you put it in the catch-all drawer and nowhere else. Then, when you search for an item it can only be in one of two places: the usual location or the catch-all drawer.

Another possible cause of misplaced items is the "absent-minded professor" syndrome. It can strike anyone, but some people are more susceptible than others. It starts one morning when you are in the middle of cleaning the house and you get a long-distance phone call from an old friend with the news that she is flying in for a short trip and she can't wait to see you! Or, conversely, the school calls to inform you that your little Yankele is causing problems again in *cheder*. Can you come to the principal's office today at 4:30 for a short discussion? Your body is still surrounded by piles of laundry, but your mind is a hundred miles away.

You shift into automatic pilot and go through the motions of straightening up and cleaning the house but you aren't totally aware of your actions. This is the danger zone: because you aren't really concentrating on your actions you might accidentally put something in the wrong place. Later, after the excitement has died down and you come back to reality, you realize that something important is missing. One solution, when your routine is interrupted by such surprises, is to do something that doesn't require any concentration, such as washing dishes or hanging laundry. Or, simply sit down and think through all of your ideas and emotions. Take notes if you need to. Once you've thought through the whole thing, bring yourself back to earth and concentrate on each item you handle. Ask yourself, "Is this the proper place for it?"

A third possible reason for misplaced items is due to the "vagrancy problem." You've just brought home a new item. But where do you put it? Unsure of the perfect location, you put it down somewhere, anywhere, just to get it out of your hands so you can fix dinner and decide later what to do with it. After dinner you get sidetracked into another chore and uh-oh...the item is forgotten and lost for the time being. The solution, in this case, is simply to make a resolution that you won't bring something into the house without deciding exactly where it should go. If you can't think of the best place, remember the household maxim, "Store an item where it is used." If an item continues to wander around the house, consider finding a better location for it; perhaps the original place isn't the best one. Another possibility is to buy a duplicate. If your kitchen scissors keep turning up in the children's room then buy another pair for the that room.

Finally, the last major cause of misplaced items is unidentified borrowing on the part of your children. Without your knowledge an item is "borrowed" and never put back. By the time you realize the item is missing the borrower has promptly forgotten all about it. Some solutions: put the item behind locked cabinet doors; post a sign-up sheet with strict orders for each borrower to write his name down when taking an item; teach each child to ask permission before taking one of your things; or simply double up on that item. Give the children their very own whatever-it-is, so they don't have to borrow yours.

So pay attention to the four culprits of missing objects: meantime-itis, the absentminded professor syndrome, the vagrancy problem, and unidentified borrowing. From now on, instead of lamenting, "I know it's here—somewhere," you'll say with triumph, "I found it!"

RABBI ZEV LEFF

Remembering Miriam

There is a mitzvah in the Torah to remember what *HaKadosh baruch Hu* did to Miriam in order that we remember not to speak *lashon hara*.

A few years ago, the thought crossed my mind that this is absurd. It's paradoxical. The whole idea of *lashon hara* is the incorrect speaking and publicizing of other people's faults and *aveiros*. So how are we to remember not to speak in a derogatory fashion and not to berate other people, by speaking *lashon hara* about Miriam? It seems that every time we recall Miriam's sin, we are accepting *lashon hara* about her once again. Is it possible that the way we learn not to denigrate other people is to denigrate Miriam?

Basically, the Rambam says that Miriam didn't sin. There are many proofs for this, one or two of which I want to mention. Miriam didn't sin at all. She fell into *lashon hara* by accident and with good intentions. She saw that there was no *shalom bayis* (peace) in her brother's home; she became aware of this through a benign comment that happened to slip out of Tzipporah's (his wife's) mouth: When Eldad and Meidad became prophets, Tzipporah commented that she felt sorry for their wives, and Miriam questioned why. Tzipporah had innocently replied that her husband had separated from her when he became a prophet. Miriam was surprised, so she went to Aharon and told him there appeared to be something wrong in their brother's home. Her mistake was that she did not approach Moshe directly.

Of course, Moshe Rabbeinu had a very good reason for his behavior, because his prophecy was different from any other prophecy. His sister had good intentions, she had absolutely no reason to harm him, she had no malice towards him, and yet, with all that, she was still stricken with *tzara'as* (leprosy). Why?

I am reminded of a story that illustrates this. In Miami a woman was cleaning her home and she accidentally broke a bottle of bleach. As half of the bottle was still salvageable she poured it into an old Coke bottle. Someone came home, and seeing the Coke bottle, put it into the refrigerator, not realizing, of course, that it wasn't filled with old Coke, new Coke, or any kind of Coke, but with bleach! Her husband came home from a very tiring tennis match, reached into the refrigerator for something cold to drink, and when he put the bottle to his lips, he realized immediately that this was no Coke. It was not even Pepsi or Tempo! It was something else, and he didn't drink it.

Now, had he drunk it, his wife would have said, "I didn't mean to do anything wrong. I just wanted to save a few cents by keeping the bleach." Also, the person who put the bottle in the refrigerator didn't mean to do anything wrong. They all meant only for the good. Even the husband, obviously, would not have drunk it on purpose, but if he had, it would not have burned his insides any less, because whatever your intentions, when you drink poison, it poisons you.

Lashon hara is so devastating that if you fall into the trap of *lashon hara*, even unintentionally, the result is the same. That is precisely what we learn from Miriam. *Tzara'as* is the natural catastrophe that emanates from speaking *lashon hara*. It is a sickness. It is the result of the devastating effects of *lashon hara*.

One of the proofs of this is that every time the Jewish people sinned and Moshe Rabbeinu davened for them, he begged the *Ribbono shel Olam* to "forgive" them — but when Moshe davened for his sister he asked Hashem to "heal" her. Our Rabbis teach us that there was no need to forgive her; the problem was a sickness that required healing. Miriam merited to be the example of this for others to learn from for all generations to come.

The Midrash says that when Miriam was sent out of the camp for seven days, the *Ribbono shel Olam* did her a favor. The entire Jewish people stayed put because Miriam was outside the camp and they waited for her. In what merit did they wait for her? In the merit of her waiting for her baby brother Moshe many years earlier when he was put into the Nile River. She waited to see what would become of him. This enabled her to have him nursed by his own mother even though he grew up in Pharaoh's palace.

Sounds great, but again if you think about it for a second, it too sounds absurd. If I was Miriam I wouldn't want anybody to know about the fact that I had *tzara'as* and that I was spending seven days outside the camp being punished for a sin. I would much rather it be kept quiet and that the only people who knew were my two brothers and the *Ribbono shel Olam*. Suddenly, everyone in the camp was explaining that they weren't moving because they had to wait for Miriam — more *lashon hara*! If you were Miriam, wouldn't you feel the same? Maybe the Jewish people could just move on and the *Ribbono shel Olam* could arrange a helicopter to help you catch up next week! Wouldn't that be better? Instead, Miriam had a great reward: her sin was publicized to everybody.

What does the Midrash mean? It was clear to the Jewish people that Miriam had no malice towards Moshe Rabbeinu, but she fell into drinking that poison by accident. This was precisely how she could be the example for all generations to warn them not to speak *lashon hara*. There was no embarrassment to her; more, she wanted people to know. She had waited for her little brother, putting her life on the line, aware that the Egyptians would have killed her if they had known. This showed that the love for her brother was very great, and it was clear to everyone that what she had done now was totally unintentional. This proved the fact.

Why is lashon hara so devastating?

Chazal teach us that there are three sins for which a person receives punishment both in this world and in the next. These are the three sins for which one must give his life rather than commit them: immorality, murder, and idolatry. The Talmud Yerushalmi says *lashon hara* is equal in severity to all of them. Similarly, *talmud Torah* (learning Torah) is considered to be equal to all those mitzvos for which one is paid both in this world and the next. There must be a connection, therefore, between speaking *lashon hara* and learning Torah.

Basically, the Gemara says that a person was created to toil in this world. It asks if this refers to physical work, and replies that a person was put in this world to work with his mouth. The

Gemara then asks if this means plain talking or learning Torah. The truth is that each person was put in this world to realize his potential. Hashem could have put the *neshamah* straight into *olam haba* and given it its reward. However, a person is embarrassed, to a certain extent, to enjoy something given to him unearned. He wanted us to appreciate our gains through work.

Olam haba is a close, intimate relationship with *HaKadosh baruch Hu*, which is the greatest enjoyment a person can have. Therefore, we are put into a physical world and we're told to realize this potential for a relationship with Him through our own efforts. We are to make our *neshamah* the kind of *neshamah* which can have such a relationship. We elevate and make it Godlike by doing things in this physical world that separate us from the materialistic world and connect us to the spiritual world. This does not mean separating ourselves from this world, but utilizing this world in a way that does not drag us down into materialism.

The Gemara says that bringing out our *neshamos* through speech is our main goal. We daven and learn Torah with our mouths and we also communicate Torah to others. By communicating our experiences and our understanding of *HaKadosh baruch Hu*, we help others to complement and supplement their understanding and feelings for *ruchnios* (spirituality). No person can exist alone. We are all dependent on one another. This dependency rests partly on communication and that ability to speak, to bring out one's *neshamah* in *tefillah* and Torah. To communicate to others is the hallmark of man. This is what distinguishes man from the animal. An animal doesn't have a *neshamah*. There is nothing to bring out.

Speech, therefore, contains two basic ideas: The idea of expressing my *neshamah* through words, plus the ability to teach others to express themselves. The ability to communicate with others helps to strengthen one's spiritual life; a person who takes the gift of speech and abuses it, using it to denigrate others, is abusing both of these aspects of speech.

If speech is life, then the abuse of speech is death. How does a person become a living dead person, who has all of the biological signs of life, but is really not alive? That's *tzara'as*. *Tzara'as* is when a person's skin appears to be dead; he is basically a zombie. He's a living person inside a dead body. This is why a *metzorah* (a person with leprosy) has to mourn. Who is he mourning? Himself. He is dead for all practical purposes. That is why when he does *teshuvah* he becomes like a new person. He has to shave off all his hair like a newborn baby. The old person is gone and now he has another chance. Almost like the resurrection of the dead.

According to the Maharal, *lashon hara* destroys the person's essence as a human being. The Maharal explains that you have to give your life for the three sins of immorality, murder, and idol worship because each of those things destroys one aspect of a person's existence. Immorality emanates from the *nefesh*, the animalistic part of a person, the base desires. Murder devastates a person's body. You are taking someone else's physical life with your own body. Idol worship destroys your soul; it is a mental, intellectual thing. This destroys your *neshamah*. It is better to destroy your physical life, which is temporary, than your spiritual life which exists for eternity. *Lashon hara*, says the Maharal, destroys all three aspects of a person.

The Gemara mentions two *kaparas* for *lashon hara*. One is the *me'il* of the *kohen gadol* (the high priest's robe) which had bells and pomegranates on it. The incense was also a *kaparah*. The Gemara asks why we need two *kaparos* for *lashon hara*. It answers that one is for open, public *lashon hara* and one for private, whispered *lashon hara*. Why is it, then, that the incense, the *kaparah* "hushed" *lashon hara,* is taught to us through the encounter with *klal Yisrael,* who said openly that Moshe had killed the people of Korach? This wasn't secret, it was open. This means that apart from the *lashon hara* caused by your voice there is another hidden aspect of *lashon hara* that also requires a *kaparah*. That is the sickness that you've caused yourself. Even in the case where you caused no harm, like Miriam, the poison is still a poison, and you still need an antidote.

Talmud Torah is the opposite. There is *avodah,* there's *tefillah,* and there's *gemilus chasadim*. But *talmud Torah* is equal to all the rest in that it helps other people and also connects you to other people.

Transcribed from "Voices from Jerusalem" (Aish HaTorah) audio tape.

לעילוי נשמת
אמנו וסבתנו
האשה הגדולה והחשובה

מרת חנה גיטל צינר ע״ה

בת ר׳ אברהם ז״ל
נפטרה בכ״ב כסלו תשנ״א

ת.נ.צ.ב.ה.

לעילוי נשמת
אבי מורי, סבנו

ר׳ שמחה הלוי צינר ז״ל

בן ר׳ בנימין זאב הלוי צינר ז״ל
איש תם וישר
נפטר בה׳ אייר תשנ״ב
ת.נ.צ.ב.ה.

לעילוי נשמת
הילדה הטהורה, בתנו

אסתר חוה צינר ע״ה

בת ר׳ דניאל הלוי יבל״א
השיבה נשמתה לבוראה
בו׳ סיון תשמ״ג

ת.נ.צ.ב.ה.

לעילוי נשמת
אשתי, אמי וסבתנו
האשה החשובה והטהורה

מרת חיה לאה בראון ע״ה

בת ר׳ משה יעקב ז״ל
אשת ר׳ שמעון בראון יבל״א
החסד והבאת השלום בין איש לרעהו
היו נר לרגליה
נפטרה בג׳ כסלו תשס״ב
ת.נ.צ.ב.ה.

לעילוי נשמת

הרב נחמן בן מאיר בולמן, זצ״ל

In Loving Memory

of our beloved
teacher and spiritual guide

HaRav Nachman ben Meir Bulman זצ״ל

who taught us, among so many mitzvos, values, and life-outlooks, that the English language can become a supreme tool, especially in our generation, for genuine growth in the way of Torah.

ת.נ.צ.ב.ה.

In loving memory of our uncle and aunt

Rabbi Aaron and
Rebbetzin Chaya Paperman זצ״ל

They were totally dedicated to the
Torah way of life and showed us all
by their everyday actions what it means
to be servants of Hashem
and lovers of *klal Yisrael.*

Peshie Krivtsky
Sarah Shane
Jack and Gail Leib
Allen and Betty Ginsburg
Frank Shane
Ruth Shane
Yosef and Chana Leah Fleischman
Yaakov and Bayla Haber

In loving memory of

Sam and Violet Greenberg
David and Leona Greenberg
Shimshon and Anne Bergman
Norman Bergman
Hershel Bergman
Shirley Rabinowitz

Dedicated on behalf of
Baruch, Elise, Miriam and Shmuel Brodersen

לזכרון עולם בהיכל ה׳

לעילוי נשמת

Arnold [Aaron] Haltrecht

[1902–1974]

second son of Else and Davvid Haltrecht of Berlin, Tel Aviv, and Montreal.
From his children
Erik Haltrecht, Merle Haltrecht-Matte, Anna Haltrecht and families

לעילוי נשמת

Albert Haltrecht

[1904–1986]

son of Else and Davvid Haltrecht of Berlin, Montreal, and Toronto.

David Haltrecht, Edward Haltrecht, Earl Haltrecht and families

לזכר נשמת האשה היקרה

of my mother

Margot Haltrecht
Pniewsky Nemenoff ע״ה

[1907–1990]

only daughter of
Else and Davvid Haltrecht

Edgar Powers

לזכר נשמת האשה היקרה

of my mother

Margot Haltrecht

[1907–1990]

daughter of
Else and Davvid Haltrecht.

David P. Leonard

ת.נ.צ.ב.ה

Norma and Nathan Greenberg

and daughters
Nadia and Miriam

are honored to be part of the esteemed Haltrecht family and tradition.

לעילוי נשמת

S. Bernard Haltrecht

[1892–1962]

father of Muriel Haltrecht Gold Poole and family

לזכר ולעילוי נשמות

חיים יהודה בן דוב אריה

ואשתו

עטא בת שלמה הלוי

Shalom from Stanley and Sylvia Haltrecht

Montreal

Dedicated to the memory of

Haltrecht descendants

and their families who perished in the Holocaust

Marilyn Puterman Vasilkioti

ולעילוי נשמת

Nachum ben Zalman HaCohen

לעילוי נשמת

of my beloved father

דוד בן יעקוב הכהן ע"ה

whose generosity and kindness

and boundless love will never be forgotten.

His daughter Julie

לעילוי נשמת

נחא בת אלטר

לעילוי נשמות

חנה ביילא בת אליעזר

דוד בן אלי-הו

and in honor of
our dear parents

Dr. and Mrs. Howard Pielet
Dr. and Mrs. Joshua Riber

לזכר ולעילוי נשמות

זלמן זאב בן ראובן צבי
יוסף בן אורי בער
צבי בן ישראל זלמן
שלום בן ישראל זלמן
יעקב רדמסקי
אייזל בקר

טובה בת ישראל זלמן
חיה מלכה בת אברהם
חנה בת בערעל
בריינא בת בערעל
מנוחה בת אהרון יוסף
מני-ה בת דוד

לעילוי נשמות

פרידה אלקה בת יוסף
שמואל בן אברהם הלוי
שרה בת חנוך גרשון
שימשון בן יהודה הלוי

לעילוי נשמת

הי-ה בת יעקב מרדכי

In honor of my *kinder*

Tamar, Evan,
Rochel Laya
and Yosef Laivy
Pieczenik

A heartfelt Mazal Tov to

Michael, Debbie, Eric,
and Anna

on the occasion of Eric's bar mitzvah

Jonathan, Nicole, and family

In loving memory of our dear father

אברהם יהודה בן יצחק ז״ל

from his children
Avraham and Naomi Greenberg

Daniel and Liesbeth Harris
and their families

לעילוי נשמת

שמואל בן לוי ז״ל

לעילוי נשמות

לאה בת שאול
חנניה יום טוב ליפה בן אריה

לעילוי נשמות

גולדי בת פסח הכהן
פייגא לאה בת אדוורד

Dedicated to my wonderful cousins

Abe and Rosette Narkunski

Thank you for everything. May you enjoy good health and happiness until 120.

Nicole, Jonathan, and family

In honour of all our grandchildren

from

Lev and Faigy Lubliner

לעילוי נשמת

יסף בן משה

לעילוי נשמת

ראובן בן עמנואל

לעילוי נשמות

ליבא בת אלחנן צבי
חנה בת אלחנן צבי
לאה בת אלחנן צבי
לאה בת שאול
שלמה דוד בן אברהם אבא

לעילוי נשמות

זלמן בן מרדכי הלוי
בילא בת משה
טויבא בת זלמן הלוי
חנה בת זלמן הלוי
יעקב בן צבי
דבורה בת לבי
מירה פייגא בת יעקב

In appreciation of the dedicated team of volunteers of the Telshestone Library.
The books have enriched our lives and made reading a pleasure.

With tremendous thanks and appreciation for the Library's valuable contribution to the Monday morning Seniors' program.

Our heartfelt thanks for all the effort and long-term commitment given by the Library's dedicated team of volunteers. You have enriched the lives of the families in the Kiryah.

From grateful readers of the Library

The Telshestone English Library takes this opportunity to thank

Mr. Avraham Rosental,

Rosh HaMoatza Kiryat Ye'arim Telshestone, for his constant support of the Library.